The Christological Foundation
for Contemporary
Theological Education

The Christological Foundation for Contemporary Theological Education

Joseph D. Ban, editor

Mercer University Press

ISBN 0-86554-313-5

*The Christological Foundation
for Contemporary Theological Education*
© 1988 Mercer University Press,
Macon GA 31207

Library of Congress Cataloging-in-Publication Data
The Christological foundation for contemporary theological education.
Ban, Joseph D., editor.
     pp. 233   15 x 23 cm.   6 x 9″
     Includes indexes.
     ISBN 0-86554-313-5 (alk. paper)
     1. Jesus Christ—History of Doctrines.   2. Jesus Christ—Person and offices.
3. Theology—Study and teaching.   I. Ban, Joseph D.
BT198.C45   1988   88-13315
232′.09—dc19   CIP

Contents

This volume is dedicated to the memory of

John A. T. Robinson
a devoted scholar
and a devout Christian

Introduction

This volume examines Christology and its relationship to theological education as defined over the long expanse of the history of the Christian church. Christology is the deliberate study of the person, works, teachings, and the mission of Jesus of Nazareth, whom Christians confess to be the Christ of God. This confession means that the study of the person and work of God's Messiah is essentially a theological enterprise.

The chapters of this book examine the development of Christological formulations in order to understand better the Christological rationale for theological education. We continue to grow in our appreciation for the evangelical task of relating what we know of who Christ is and what he has done for our salvation. This active process necessarily involves every new generation of the faithful. Christology deserves to provide the foundation for all church education, especially the preparation of theological students for Christian ministry.

These chapters were originally presented as seminars held at the Divinity College, McMaster University, Hamilton, Ontario, Canada. The university's motto is unusual in that it is a quotation in Greek from the New Testament. The motto, from Colossians 1:17, was adapted shortly after the founding of McMaster University in 1887. The verse says that Christ "is before all things, and in him all things hold together." This verse is from a passage (vv. 15-20) that describes the place and function of Christ in the creation. This motto, along with the McMaster hymn, "Jesus, Wondrous Saviour," written by an early principal of the theological department, D.

A. McGregor (1847–1890), demonstrates the eminent position accorded the person of Christ in the original educational vision for McMaster University. This theological focus provided an appropriate capstone for Senator William McMaster's intention to afford "the best possible facilities for a thoroughly practical Christian course of education."

The Christology seminars at McMaster were supported by a Basic Issue Research grant from the Association of Theological Schools in the United States and Canada. The Basic Issues program of the A.T.S. sought to identify "primary order" issues in theological education. These fundamental issues were defined as the "assumptions that underlie and shape, structure and influence one's reflection" upon graduate theological education. The grant application from McMaster Divinity College stated as the goal of its inquiry the "explication of Christology as the basis of integration for theological education."

The several chapters in the volume discuss how Christology has been understood at various and significant periods in church history. The presentations make evident the many different understandings of the person and purpose of Christ. This historical study also provides evidence of the essential elements that are common to the Christological tradition. Jesus Christ was the saving Person and the liberating Son of the eternal Creator God. This volume thus focuses upon Christology as the vital foundation for contemporary theological education.

The publication of this volume has been made possible by a generous grant from the McMaster Divinity College. We are grateful for the support of the college and university and its friends and supporters who continue to encourage the faculty, students, and alumni in their growing knowledge of what it means to be in union with Christ in these times.

In the academic year during which the divinity faculty explored the subject of Christology, McMaster University was privileged to have as a distinguished visiting professor in the Department of Religious Studies the British cleric and New Testament scholar John A. T. Robinson. The Divinity Day lecture presented by him during the term of his visit constitutes his contribution to this volume. He was very interested in our series of seminars and took part in various discussions, with his flair for fresh insights and his devotion to the good news revealed in Scripture. This volume is dedicated to the memory of his contribution both to New Testament scholarship and to the life and mission of the Christian church.

Joseph D. Ban

Chapter One

Christological Foundations of Theological Education

Joseph D. Ban

Jesus Christ holds the central place in the commitments, confessions, and witness of the faithful. The average Christian shares with the theological student the struggle for a sense of what it means to be a follower of Christ in today's world. Whether it be the common call to be a good parent or the more specialized call to be a minister or missionary, the need for a decision represents Christ's inviting us to serve God and our neighbor. Christ does provide the basis for the continuing development of a personal identity as pilgrims who, in a broken world, seek the heavenly city. How the believing community understands the message and mission of Jesus determines the pattern for Christian behavior in everyday relations in the world. What Christians expect from themselves as well as others is patterned upon what they believe Christ expects of them.[1]

The centrality of Christ is especially true in the lives of church leaders, both ordained and lay. For example, the greater number of students who have undertaken divinity studies, past and present, have been moved by a keen personal call to a special role. The decision for a church-related vocation often arises from a personal relationship with Jesus Christ. Such a private, dynamic experience of Christ's inviting one into a career of ministry is part of our pietist tradition, especially among Protestants in North America.

Such an intimate sense of calling, whatever its particular form, has proven to be a powerful motivation for many. As such, the personal sense of vocation deserves respect as one of the many mysterious ways in which

---

[1]An earlier version of this chapter was published in *Ministerial Formation* 34, June 1986, a newsletter of the Programme on Theological Education of the World Council of Churches, Geneva, Switzerland. The chapter in its present form has undergone major revision.

divine love intrudes upon our individual and collective histories. We are also aware that such private experiences are prone to abuse. Many individuals have sought to maintain themselves in a profession to which they were not suited, no matter how convincing their original call may have been.

The call to ministry not only provides a vital link between the person and one's Savior and Lord but also shapes one's understanding of who Christ is and what Christ does. The nature of one's calling conditions how one walks the way of Christ. Our understanding of Christ thus determines how we view life.

It is therefore appropriate to address the question "How can Christology function as a foundational rationale for Christian education—more specifically, for graduate theological education?" We may find light shed upon this question as we consider some typical responses Christians have made at different times. This present volume examines Christology at specific periods in the history of the Western church.

In order to explore the theme of the Christological underpinnings of theological education, the various chapters in this volume explore Christological beliefs in an orderly manner. The sequence has been determined by the historical development of faith. Thus in chapter 2, Raymond Hobbs examines some of the essential formulations of the Old Testament. What role did these understandings play in the life of the early church as it dealt with experiencing the coming of the Messiah? In the following chapter Melvyn Hillmer spells out the various ways the writers of the four Gospels took hold of the early church's experience of the risen Lord and slowly developed a theological understanding of Jesus as Christ and Savior. Hillmer emphasizes the intention of the four Gospels to make plain the person of Jesus as the one in whom authentic and enduring life is to be found. In chapter 4, Patrick Gray describes some of the experience of the maturing church that, after the apostles, had the rigorous task of translating their faith into terms recognizable by a religious world informed by Hellenistic philosophy and conditioned by the mystery cults of the Mediterranean world. Later chapters in this volume similarly explore the historical context within which Christians were forced to relate their beliefs using the language and thought patterns and presuppositions of their generation while remaining loyal to the witness of the New Testament faith community.

Nearly forty years ago, the late H. Richard Niebuhr wrote *Christ and Culture,* a book that has long influenced Christological discussion. Considering evidence from Christian thought, H. Richard Niebuhr defined five types of responses that have been made, with some frequency, to the revelation of Christ as related to various cultural periods. One type of response has been a radical rejection of the world of human affairs and achievements. In the typical response that sets Christ against culture, Christians have been called to abandon the secular world. Such a view absolves Christians of responsible social involvement inasmuch as taking part in the affairs of the world appears to be futile and hopeless. In this view, Christ is seen as opposed to human culture. The Christian is urged to reject the world because it is basically evil.

As one reads Joanne McWilliam's probing analysis of the challenges confronted by Augustine, one may recognize the serious temptation such a negative view represented in his age. Though the good bishop of Hippo rejected his Manichaean legacy and broke away from such a tempting philosophy, many of his fellow Christians were not able to abandon such an alluring belief.

Niebuhr's second type was the opposite of the first. In this second view, there exists a fundamental agreement between the culture and the Christ who serves as its hero. In this category of the Christ of culture, Jesus is hailed as the Messiah affirming the existing social situation. The dominant institutions and the achievements of our culture are identified with Christ. No distinction is made between religion and the national culture and its patriotism. Robert Bellah has identified this intimate identification of Christ with the national way of life as "civil religion."[2] In such a view, our political and economic system is on the side of the angels, while the systems of our international opponents are inherently evil. In place of primary devotion to God in Christ, our society and its cultural formulations command our ultimate allegiance. This attitude is very much like the "Christendom" that Søren Kierkegaard attacked so vehemently.[3] Niebuhr includes Albrecht Ritschl in discussing this second type.

While the blasphemy of the German Christian movement during the Nazi era was plainly evident, it is often more difficult to recognize the naturalization of religion within our own culture. We so easily assume that Jesus is just like "one of us." As a comic-strip character answered the Christmastime question of an alien, "Was Jesus an American?" we are tempted to reply, "Well, practically so."

Niebuhr's third type of relationship found in our common history is that of Christ above culture. This is also called the synthetic type. God is at

---

[2]Robert N. Bellah, "Civil Religion in America," *Daedalus, Journal of the American Academy of Arts and Sciences* 96:1 (Winter 1967): 1-21. Cf. Jerald C. Brauer, Sidney E. Mead, and Robert N. Bellah, *Religion and the American Revolution* (Philadelphia: Fortress Press, 1976). See also Robert N. Bellah et al., *Habits of the Heart: Individualism and Commitment in American Life* (Berkeley: University of California Press, 1985).

[3]Søren Kierkegaard, *Attack upon Christendom,* trans. Walter Lowrie (Boston: Beacon Press, 1956).

work in human affairs through natural law. The body of principles derived from nature is one of the means God uses to fulfill the divine will. The Clement of Alexandria and Thomas Aquinas represent this view, which allows for Christ's saving work to be effective not through culture but through the sacramental ministries of the church. Thomas asserted that "whatever salvation means beyond creation it does not mean the destruction of the created."[4] Jean-Marc Laporte's discussion of Christology in the Middle Ages traces this development of the sacramental understanding of Christ's relation to culture.

The fourth of Niebuhr's types describes Christ and culture in paradox. This view may be found in the writings of Paul and in the Reformer Martin Luther. A duality in this position recognizes the authority both of Christ and of cultural values and norms. The Christian is subject to two distinct authorities who operate in two separate realms, both of whom must be obeyed. Niebuhr wrote, "In the *polarity* and *tension* of Christ and culture, life must be lived precariously and sinfully in the hope of a justification which lies beyond history."[5] In his chapter, Clark Pinnock spells out some of the difficulties that arose when Luther sought to use paradox as the means for formulating his Christological theory of the two natures.

This interpretive use of paradox emphasizes the conflict between the human person (i.e., "the sinner") and God as "Holy Other." Grace is afforded the sinful creature through the reconciling action of Jesus Christ. The distinction between this view and the first type, Christ opposed to culture, is that the dualist recognizes that all human endeavor, especially culture, has fallen under judgment. The only hope for humankind lies in the graciousness of God, who has sent Christ to make possible our salvation.

The fifth of Niebuhr's categories recognizes Christ to be the transformer of culture. This is also known as the conversionist view. Such an interpretation sees history as the record of human encounters in which God functions through the redeeming work of Christ. The holders of this perspective do not expect the end of this created world and its human culture. Rather, they are aware of the power of God to transform all things in order that the creation might correspond to the divine intention. The Christian, in this view, does not totally reject culture but believes that present social structures stand in need of conversion. Futhermore, God is already working to achieve such redemption. World history, in this understanding, be-

---

[4]H. Richard Niebuhr, *Christ and Culture* (New York: Harper & Bros., 1951) 143.
[5]Ibid.

comes the account of how God has acted mightily for human liberation and of how human beings have responded to such powerful intervention.[6] Niebuhr discusses the work of John Calvin as an example of the fifth type.

Reflection upon Niebuhr's five types of how Christians have related Christ to culture should throw light upon the variety of possible interpretations that we, as modern Christians, bring to such relationships. There are certain conclusions that result from such an analysis. It requires us to take seriously the cultural activities that shape us and within which we individually and collectively make our conscious and unconscious responses. We may have little choice in the cultural environment within which we reside and function and that most influences us. We do have, as persons and faith communities, the opportunity to decide how we shall respond to the values and demands of such a culture.[7]

All schooling, including theological education, takes place in human institutions. Divinity schools and theological seminaries are cultural expressions, cast in the languages and expectations of the civilizations present at their foundation and in their maturity. As creatures of culture, faculty and students in divinity reflect both the grandeur and the limitations of the nurturing culture, whatever its form at any particular time. The thesis of this chapter is that the alert faithful are responsible for correcting for the biases of culture. An awareness of both the Bible and the living religious tradition helps make such compensating balance possible. The New Testament, especially with its witness to Christ, discloses an authentic foundation for vital Christian ministry.

The recognition of our cultural indebtedness leads to the realization that all persons have been nurtured by, and normally have a need to be members of, human communities. By experience and faith, we testify to the equally urgent need to belong to that universal community of the kingdom of God as revealed by Jesus Christ. As Niebuhr expressed it, the world of human achievement and culture "exists within the world of grace."[8]

As we consider the nature of human community, we can grasp the paradoxical view of Christ and culture. Humans are always prone to play God by trying to impose unjust limitations upon other persons. This drive for domination over others represents an insatiable lust for power that inevitably corrupts and degrades human relationships. Whether Cain's murder

---

[6]Ibid., 194-95, 217-18.

[7]In these paragraphs, I acknowledge my indebtedness to my former teacher Albert Terrill Rasmussen. See his *Christian Social Ethics* (Englewood Cliffs NJ: Prentice-Hall, 1956) 147-48.

[8]Niebuhr, *Christ and Culture,* 225.

of his brother, Abel, or the brothers' sale of Joseph into slavery or modern industrial pollution of the natural environment, humans have demonstrated a propensity to harm their neighbors if there is something to be gained from it.

The incarnational theology of God's saving intervention in human affairs recognizes the reality of sin as a condition of human and therefore cultural relationships. Christological statements deal with the sinful condition of humans, the reconciling intention of God, and the liberating work of Christ's life, death, and resurrection. The various descriptions of who Christ was and what Christ's life and death accomplished for all humanity also point to the ways that created beings respond to the Creator God. God is not an absentee landlord or a benevolent despot. God's gracious love is made clear in the person, teachings, and actions of Jesus. God's initiative invites us to responsible involvement. Christian faith concerns as much the present and the everyday as it does the future and eternity.

It is appropriate at this point to anticipate some of the chapters that follow. I have mentioned the two chapters dealing with the Old and New Testaments. Raymond Hobbs describes what a rich heritage flowed into the maturing of religious thought that found rich expression in the age of Jesus. Melvyn Hillmer relates the various ways in which the important work of Jesus was interpreted in the four Gospels. The basic witnesses demonstrate a multiform testimony that is quite diverse yet possesses an essential and basic unity. This singularity of testimony speaks out about Jesus, the one who lived and died and was raised again into life. This work of Jesus was for our salvation and for the liberation of all humanity from the harsh consequences of sin and evil.

Patrick Gray traces the important connections between soteriology, or theological expressions regarding salvation, and Christology, or doctrinal formulations regarding the person and work of Jesus Christ. The Christian faith is founded upon an assertion regarding salvation. God has chosen to liberate humanity through the redeeming work of Jesus Christ. Whether stated in John's famous words, "God loved the world so much that he gave his only Son, that everyone who has faith in him may not die but have eternal life" (John 3:16 NEB), or in the apostle Paul's terms, "But now by Christ's death in his body of flesh and blood God has reconciled you to himself, so that he may present you before himself as dedicated men, without blemish and innocent in his sight" (Col. 1:22 NEB), the saving person is Jesus Christ.

Gray explores the historical connections between Christology and soteriology by examining the Arian and the Nestorian controversies. Soteriology played a central role in the earliest years of the Christian church.

Gray argues that, for both Arius and Athanasius, Christology was an imperative issue because it dealt with what people sensed it meant to be saved by God. As Gray describes it, for both the Alexandrian episcopal theology of Athanasius (the "good guys" in church history texts, today considered orthodox) and the defenders of Arius (the "bad guys" judged heretics by the church), "Christology is part of the struggle to do theology out of their experience of salvation." Gray issues an invitation for all who are engaged in contemporary theological education to be about the task of doing theology rather than just talking about it. This serious effort at integration would involve both the mentor and the novice in simultaneously thinking about and actually experiencing the saving connection with the living Christ. Gray's comments on theological education help us to focus the intent of this volume. In these chapters we seek to recover the dynamic encounter in which we recognize the liberating influence of Christ amid the demanding, vise-gripping events of our human condition.

Joanne McWilliam writes of a significant period and a towering personality in the life of the Christian church. Augustine's writings continue to influence our modern thinking, even among persons who no longer recognize the origin of such beliefs in his seminal ideas. McWilliam points out that Augustine's first Christological model grew out of his painful efforts to resolve a theological problem that was troubling him personally. As did his predecessors, Augustine closely held together his experiences of being saved and his thinking about the person of Christ his Savior. Augustine's struggle grew out of his earlier experiences of having associated with the Manichaeans, a sect that identified the material world as evil. In rejecting the Manichaean view of Christ, Augustine developed his own thinking about the person and saving work of Christ.

The earlier counsel of Patrick Gray is pertinent here. Just as Augustine was forced to do, so every theological student is challenged to fashion a coherent structure of meaning centered upon Christ as the active agent of our present and ongoing salvation. McWilliam describes Augustine's dynamic experience: "to feed interiorly on the Word of God, to be steadfastly subject to the one God, to cling in eternal contemplation to unchanging truth." Here certainly is a creative curriculum for theological studies that would integrate religious experience with intellective reflection.

Jean-Marc Laporte provides us with essential insights into Christology as articulated in the Middle Ages. In words that lend support to Gray's argument, this medieval scholar finds the examples of Aquinas and Bonaventure to be encouraging to modern followers of Christ. We are to be about the task of doing theology and of formulating our own understandings of who Christ was and what Christ has accomplished for our salvation. This book takes seriously Laporte's statement that "Christology and spirituality flourish together and languish separately."

Clark Pinnock examines the Christology of the Protestant Reformers. He contrasts the conservative reformation with the radical reformers. The Christology of Martin Luther and that of John Calvin are described and analyzed. These two represent what Pinnock has identified as the conservative reformation. The Christologies of the radical reformers Menno Simons, Michael Servetus, and Faustus Socinus are also studied. The consequences of such thought at first were minimal, but eventually it had an impact. Pinnock states that "the new experiments in Christology . . . sowed the seeds for widespread innovation in dogma that occurred three centuries later."

The four chapters by Iain Nicol, Russell Aldwinckle, Paul Dekar, and the late John A. T. Robinson bring us to the present. These chapters spell out how theologians have responded to the intellectual and experiential challenges posed by such cultural and historical developments as the Enlightenment, the evolutionary theory of Darwin, the holocaust resulting from the Nazi Reich, and the pluralism of the contemporary world.

Nicol evaluates the work of two intellectual greats, Friedrich Schleiermacher and Albrecht Ritschl. Thus we are drawn into the period anticipated by Pinnock's comment on innovations in dogma. In this volume we have sidestepped the long historical period collectively called the Enlightenment, a philosophical movement that spanned the seventeenth and eighteenth centuries. Nicol begins his chapter by dealing with some of the byproducts of the thought of the Enlightenment. The church fathers who had gathered at Chalcedon in 451 made use of the Greek philosophical terms *nature* and *substance* to describe the union of humanity and God in the person of Jesus Christ. This language suffered severe injury from the attacks of John Locke (1632–1704), David Hume (1711–1776), and Immanuel Kant (1724–1804). Nicol compares and contrasts the conclusions of Schleiermacher and Ritschl. Both theologians posit a continuity between the Jesus of Nazareth and the Christ experienced by the faithful today. In Nicol's words, "The Christ who acts in and through the Christian community is continuous with the Christ who once acted in history." While Schleiermacher's definition was revisionist, he did seek a firm connection between soteriology and Christology. God dwelt in Christ, according to Schleiermacher, through the God-consciousness of the redeeming person. Nicol discusses the merits and the difficulties of such a theological expression. Ritschl based his Christology upon the historical facts of Christ's loyalty and unwavering commitment to God's purpose. The allegiance of Christ to his historical vocation enabled him to found and head the kingdom of God on earth. The revolutionary aspect of Ritschl's thought as well as its continuity with traditional elements of Christological thinking are carefully analyzed by Nicol. The difficulties of such a position are also candidly evaluated.

As Nicol describes the responses of Christian theologians to the challenges of the Enlightenment, so Russell Aldwinckle examines the impact of Charles Darwin's theoretical description of evolution upon theological thinking. All theologians after Darwin have been forced to deal, in some measure, with the forceful way in which evolutionary motifs realigned intellectual images and cultural thought forms. Darwin's description of evolution had a significant influence upon how modern minds described the nature of being human. The theological doctrine of man needed to be harmonized with the doctrine of God. Aldwinckle deliberates upon the Christological implications of the new state of mind conditioned by the publication of Darwin's findings. A careful distinction is made between the thinking in matters theological of Charles Darwin and of those who followed after him, the Darwinists. This chapter deals fairly with the maturing of Darwin's own thought on the relationship between God and mortal creatures. The burden of Aldwinckle's exposition is to analyze how theologians have resolved the changed status of being human after the popularization of Darwin's views. Specifically, Aldwinckle describes the necessary adjustments in Christological formulations that resulted from a post-Darwinian anthropology. The second part of his chapter represents an examination of contemporary theological discussions regarding Christology. He also anticipates some of the emerging issues with which future thinkers must deal.

The concluding two chapters, by Paul R. Dekar and John A. T. Robinson, bring us directly onto the contemporary scene. Dekar's exposition stresses the interconnections between Christological formulations and present-day relationships of Christians and Jews. The gross tragedies resulting from the deliberate anti-semitic policies of Hitler and the Third Reich have seared the consciences of sensitive persons, especially Christians. This has resulted in a recognition that frequently Christians, in their enthusiastic expression of their beliefs, have caused injury to the persons and consciences of our fellow believers in the one God, the Jews. Dekar presents an analysis of the significant elements to be included in defining a Christology that is aware of and open to the Bible witness. The testimony of both Old and New Testaments expresses a preferential role for the progeny of Abraham. While the issues are similar to those discussed in the previous chapters, Dekar has challenged his Christian readers with a sharp awareness of the Jewish people as the elder brothers. We hear echoed the compassionate expressions of another Paul, in Romans 4. Dekar also causes us to reflect upon the appropriate responses to be made by those responsible for theological education in today's historical situation.

The closing chapter is by the late John A. T. Robinson. He summarizes the issues he had discussed at greater length in such writings as *The Human Face of God*. Robinson, in this chapter, spells out the imperative task of an apologist attempting to interpret a real truth to a contemporary audience. Which of its ancient trappings are essential to the very nature of that truth, and what is incidental, a product of the mental world appreciated by that distant audience? In some ways, Robinson is performing the same task undertaken by the other authors in this volume, recognizing how Christ's person and work were presented at particular times and under certain conditions. Robinson, like Dekar, is discussing Christology in our times and under the cultural conditions within which we presently live. Not suprisingly, in his lifetime Robinson often experienced outrage from those who assumed more than he was saying. As with arguments elsewhere in this volume, the reader must attend with great care to the precise meanings intended by the author before moving on to independent conclusions. Eventually each of us as thinkers and as persons wrestling with our own salvation will resolve, or have resolved for us, the question of how Christ has altered our relationship to God. Robinson, with the other contributors to this book, presents the questions that enable the significance of our study of Christology to emerge. For numerous generations, Jesus Christ is the way God has acted to intervene in order to bring health, redemption, and liberation to a sinful and alienated humanity.

This examination of Christology is a powerful reminder that we encounter Christ because of a company of witnesses (see Heb. 12:1). Throughout the history of the Christian church, such communal testimonies have been indebted to particular forms of cultural expression. Today we attempt to interpret this saving work of God in those terms of reference that will be most widely and easily understood by persons living in our own cultural period. We must undertake such an apologetic task in terms that do justice to the reality of God's redeeming activity in the life, death, and resurrection of Jesus Christ.

What does this discussion of Christology mean for the Christian educator? We need to be as aware as we can be of the particular Christology that informs our own educational approach. For if we understand Christ to be opposed to human achievement, we will provide an education that separates the Christian student from the sinful world. Some institutions actually have expressed this understanding by providing geographical distance between their school and urban settings. Others have designed a curriculum intended to insulate students from authors, novels, and points of view considered inimical to a desired Christian philosophy. Certain varieties of Christian day schools have been developed with the expressed intention of providing an alternative to the public-supported schools, which are considered to be secular and humanistic in orientation.

In the peculiar irony that marks much of human endeavor, some schools of modern Christian foundation have easily slipped from the type of Christ against culture into the second type, a school curriculum that espouses de facto a Christ of culture. Such a school starts out to provide a distance between the learner and what is considered to be a hostile, secular society. In time, it succumbs to the temptation of affirming the prevailing political and economic values as ordained of God. Certain Christian day schools as well as Christian colleges clearly espouse a conservative form of culture and patriotism. Especially in certain regions of the United States, an unexamined piety combined with a conservative social order have produced a supposedly Christian form of education that is essentially a replica of civil religion covered with a thin coating of religious zeal. What was considered reprehensible among German Christians is now deemed acceptable among "all-American" Christians.

The Thomistic theology that has long informed the theological formulations of the Roman Catholic church is an example of Niebuhr's third type. The thought of Aquinas has also influenced the organization and curricula of parochial and separate schools. Descriptions of natural law prevailed and influenced the studies of the natural and social sciences.[9] The chapter on the Middle Ages provides an informative discussion of a significant period in Christian history. The conclusions of the Second Vatican Council have partly modified this pattern of education. At the present time, considerations rising out of the liberation theologies are causing Catholic educators to reexamine their foundational presuppositions. Such theologies of liberation are themselves rooted primarily in the experiences of Latin American Christians forced to deal with the oppression occasioned by powerful oligarchies based upon ownership of land, wealth, and military power. Nevertheless, such educational efforts continue to emphasize both Christ's transcendence over human culture and achievements as well as the sacramental nature of the church, whereby God's gifts of salvation and counsel are made available to the repentant sinner.[10] But note the critical

---

[9]James Michael Lee, "To Basically Change Fundamental Theory and Practice," in *Modern Masters of Religious Education,* ed. Marlene Mayr (Birmingham AL: Religious Education Press, 1983) 254-323.

[10]Thomas H. Groome, *Christian Religious Education* (San Francisco: Harper & Row, 1980).

comments made by Dekar in chapter 10 regarding one particular liberation theologian.

The view of Christ and culture standing in paradox has also informed education both in the past and in the present. The paradoxical interpretation of Christ and culture incorporates the doctrine of two spheres, over one of which God is transcendent, and the other is governed under human authority. For centuries, theology reigned in the universities of Europe and the West as "Queen of the Sciences." Until the Enlightenment, at least, theologians enjoyed a certain preeminence. Even today, especially in higher education and in graduate faculties where a form of neo-scholasticism flourishes, theology dominates. Wherever a particular theology is considered to be the definitive interpretation, it is able to dictate how other disciplines are to be taught. For example, if theological presuppositions dictate that scientific evolution inadequately describes the process of creation, other explanations of creation must be used in the curriculum. Aldwinckle alludes to some of these problems in his chapter.

Niebuhr's fifth type of interpretation, in which Christ works to transform culture, also has consequences for Christian education. In this view, the conversionist envisions a redemptive role for Christ in the remaking of human institutions. Thus education has as one of if its primary functions the equipping of persons as agents for change. Christians are those who can see God through Christ at work redeeming history. Such Christians therefore seek to be engaged in the places where God is effectively bringing about justice, reconciliation, and peace. The transformational understanding of Christ in relation to culture provides an incentive for seeking ways and means for entering cooperatively into whatever redemptive activity God is already at work doing. Such education will need to be multidimensional. We will need to know the past in order to learn how prophets and apostles came to recognize the marks of God's saving actions. We will need to learn how to discern the signs of the future in order to be able to recognize the direction in which God is leading us. Such education will also provide us with the essential disciplines needed to understand the people and the conditions of the present time. Only in this way can we engage constructively with those who also are working, in their own way, to accomplish the agenda God has set before all the nations. For this reason, Christians need to be educated in in the humanities as well as in the arts, in social studies and the knowledge of the psychological, in the biological as well as physical sciences.

In the transformational model, God is recognized as active in the whole of history with the divine interest of liberating humanity from the limits imposed by evil and suffering. The consequent design for education provides for nurture and knowledge in every academic discipline that has as its chief goal the enhancement of the natural and social environments. The Gospel of John recognized God's love for the whole world (3:16). The apostle Paul sensed the travail of the physical universe as it also yearned for redemption (Rom. 8:22). Church education must have as the scope of its syllabi the entire domain of God's created universe. Only then can the faithful Christian effectively enter into the ministry of reconciliation to which God has called those who would be numbered among the members of Christ's body.

Let us now turn to a few examples of practical applications of such Christological understandings. What does this discussion suggest regarding graduate theological education? A focus upon the question of Christology indicates that theological education must provide the divinity student with an understanding of how to relate the Christian gospel to contemporary experience. This preparation involves the capacity to conduct a critical analysis of the issues arising out of the human situation, historical events, and social relationships. In order to accomplish this analysis with the necessary competence, the student needs to develop an understanding of the Bible sources and the long tradition of the church. Such an appreciation should be based upon an informed, critical examination of primary sources and interpretations. The theological student definitely deserves to gain experience in thinking dialectically in order to respect the truth residing in such apparent dichotomies as the faith claim that Jesus was "truly man and truly God."

The way in which many men and women have found that God has directed their lives into preparation for Christian ministry provides the occasion for a serious examination of Christology. As students struggle with a sense of being, they may ask, "What does it mean to be a Christian minister today?" The student's sense of calling suggests that a Christological awareness does provide the necessary foundation as he or she continues to develop a personal as well as professional identity in ministering in a broken world.

Christology is concerned with the theology of the person, works, teachings, and mission of the one whom history knows as Jesus. The Jew who grew up in Nazareth is the person whom we, in faith, confess to be the Christ. The several presentations in this book make evident the plurality of understandings of Christology. These discussions show clearly that the particular context for each Christological formulation influenced profoundly the content of the theological assertions made.

When we turn to the New Testament, we also find a plurality of views. For example, it is evident that, within the Synoptic Gospels, the Christ portrayed in Mark differs somewhat from that found in Luke and Matthew. The Synoptic descriptions do appear to have a more evident unity when the three are contrasted with the Fourth Gospel. In the Gospel of John the human element in the person and work of Jesus appears subordinated to the presence of the divine dimension. All four Gospels consistently emphasize one element. The inflection may vary, but Jesus definitely is portrayed as a historical, flesh-and-blood person. For the writer of the Fourth Gospel, the Lord was Jesus.

In Paul's letters the human person of Jesus is present, but the apostle's understanding is dominated by the saving work of Jesus Christ. Paul describes the work of Christ in various ways, including Christ as the agent of reconciliation, bringing justification before God to humanity (Rom. 3:24). For Paul, Christ mediated a new covenant, that of grace (5:8, 20). In the later parts of the New Testament, such as the Pastoral and general letters, the emphasis continues in the direction of Christ as "our glorified Lord" (James 2:1). The multiplicity of perspectives, however, must not obscure the essential unity and continuity of the New Testament understanding of the person and work of Jesus Christ. The Gospels and the Epistles—indeed, the whole of the New Testament—assume the humanity of Jesus and emphasize this particular person's essential mission. This historical human being, Jesus, born of Mary, was the Anointed One, the Christ of God. The power of the Eternal was present in this man's teaching and work, and the divine purpose was realized in him. Jesus was the essential saving, liberating Person.

Just as the experience of the church has provided for multiple perspectives on the person and work of Christ, so also we find that the forms for preparing leaders for Christian ministry have varied. The structures for training persons for ministerial leadership have reflected the context within which the church has carried out its task. How the church understood its mission at any time influenced the form of the theological curriculum. For example, the men trained in Geneva and Strasbourg under John Calvin or Martin Bucer displayed the profound influence of those Reformers upon the church's consciousness of the Word revealed in Scripture and grace as the essential factor in worship and faith.

The traditional pattern of theological education in North America displays a common characteristic, whatever the theological considerations there may have been at its creation. All such curricula appear to be derived from certain traditional academic fields. As a significant issue of *Theological Education* (Spring 1981) has demonstrated, the traditional pattern for studies of divinity has included four basic disciplines. Successive generations of curriculum planners have seen these to be essential. The four areas include studies in the Bible, with the necessary support of language skills; studies in church history and tradition; studies in theology in its various forms; and studies in the practice of the arts of ministering. While various modifications have attempted to maintain some balance between such polar tensions as action-reflection, theory-practice, academic-applied, and classroom-field experience, the pattern consistently has placed these four disciplines at the core of the theological curriculum.

How might an educational model that is based upon Christological foundations differ from this traditional pattern? In order to proceed further, it is helpful to deal with the question "What are the assumptions that underlie, shape, and influence our way of doing theological education?" Let us answer this query by examining a typical graduate theological faculty. Several strong influences are apparent. As with all church-related theological faculties, the denomination of churches for whom a school prepares pastors is an ever-present voice. Such influence comes in various forms such as direct official overtures from the juridical structures; less official but hardly less important communications from individual congregations and pastors; and, most informally of all, and possibly most important of all, the students preparing for ministry who choose to study with a particular faculty. The denominational influence upon curricular formation remains persistent.

Closer at hand, the modern university influences the shape and form of divinity studies. By the influence of the university I intend something fundamental and pervasive. The university "writ large" influences the way each member of a faculty of divinity individually perceives reality. Every one of us has struggled with the rigorous demands of an academic preparation, an obstacle course the sum of which experience allows many a theological school to announce that "every member of our faculty holds an earned doctorate." During those long years of academic preparation, academicians have learned how to identify, clarify, criticize, analyze, hypothesize, and theologize in myriad formulations and variation. During those disciplined years individuals have also specialized. Earned doctorates involve a high degree of specialization, assuring that each faculty person has proven expertise in one significant sector of knowledge. This high degree of specialization also guarantees that faculty members know little, if anything, about each other's area. Nor are faculty granted enough years either to familiarize themselves with the specializations of their colleagues or to discover, individually, how best to integrate these separate areas of specialization into a coherent whole.

The problem is common among the graduate theological seminaries in the Christian world. How difficult this must make it for the inexperienced student in a theological school. Many have become adjusted to it. It appears to be a fact of everyday experience in any university. Students have grown accustomed to having professors speak from deep within the echo chambers of their individual academic disciplines. So when these students matriculate into the divinity school, they are not astonished to find that here, too, each faculty member tends to view theological education from within the narrow frame of one's discipline. Yet this is most regrettable, especially, as Henri Nouwen says "at a time when young students are questioning the value of the complicated distinctions between academic disciplines and are trying to come to terms with what is central and unifying in their lives."[11]

This reality of disparate specializations is so commonplace that we tend to accept the situation as a necessary ingredient in academic life. How can we escape the stultifying influence of such invisible barriers to the integration of knowledge and experience? The pervasiveness of the problem was indicated in a letter from a concerned individual, who wrote, "I fear that, if you give historical or theological scholars free rein, they will deal with contemporary issues of Christology [in such a way as to] make the bridgework for dealing with theological education even more problematic." This same perception characterized several of the conversations held with academic heads at various theological schools, both Roman Catholic and Protestant, in Canada and the United States. For these reasons as well as others that are addressed in the current literature on the subject, we need to explore more intentionally our existing system for educating persons for Christian ministry.

In this approach to the renewal of theological curriculum, I make two assumptions. First, I assume that faith issues lie at the heart of theological education. Second, I assume that ministry is more than just another specialized profession among the various helping and healing professions. These two assumptions led to the question formulated in my conversation regarding the purpose of seminary studies with John Cobb, "What are we doing when we do theological education?" His terse answer was "Formation." This understanding means, for me, that the purpose of our teaching and our learning in graduate theological education is to enable growing persons to establish their Christian identity, using the fullest knowledge possible of how the church has formulated that identity at various times in the past. This way of stating the task of theological education moves us beyond an either/or situation such as that implied in the question "Is the

---

[11]Henri J. M. Nouwen, *Creative Ministry* (Garden City NY: Doubleday, Image Books, 1971) xvi.

role of the theological seminary to prepare leadership for the church of the future or is its primary obligation to hand down the traditions we have inherited?'' Such a polarization pits preparing leaders equipped for the future against a reconstruction of the patterns of the past and is neither necessary nor instructive. Rather, forming spiritual identity requires serious attention to the past, the present, and, as well, to the future.

Formation of Christian identity as the desired goal requires Christology as the basis of integration for the disciplines and practice of graduate theological education. How does the incarnational paradigm become a guiding principle toward a resolution of our major problems in theological education? My own conviction is that how we understand and interpret the person of Jesus Christ influences in great measure how we see the church, its ecclesiology, function, and mission, as well as how we perceive other critical theological issues, including evil and suffering, the dynamic relationship between God and humanity, and the question of eschatology. The relation between this conviction and the formation of identity of Christian pastors is clear and direct. As W. Marxsen wrote, ''For we can confess Jesus as Lord only when we understand what we mean and make it understandable for others.''[12] We need to pursue those questions that uncover the ways Christological assertions serve as presuppositions for theological education. What are the ways such affirmations regarding the place and work of Christ shape the particular form of our curriculum? We need to investigate the practical implications of alternative perspectives on Christology.

In the history of the church, Christology has informed the methods of educating theological students. For example, what does ministerial education look like when its primary emphasis is upon a soteriology of Christ? We can find theological programs emphasizing a theology of the blood of Christ in a number of the Bible schools in Canada and the United States. Again, Thomistic sacramental theology constituted an institutionalized Christology that made possible an ecclesiology founded upon soteriology in the medieval church.

A number of things can be said about the ministry of Jesus, all of which together provide insight into what is necessary to include in the curricular design of a theological program. It is apparent that Jesus held his own views of the nature of messiahship. While we may not know such views with the degree of precision desired by some modern scholars, we can make some assumptions. For instance, the Judaic view of Messiah encompassed noth-

---

[12]W. Marxsen, "Christology," in *Interpreter's Dictionary of the Bible,* Supp. Vol. (Nashville: Abingdon Press, 1976).

ing less than an event in which God would establish a perfect reign over the whole of creation, including all of its natural and historical structures. This insight is reinforced in all four of the Gospels. In Mark, Jesus announced, "The right time has come and the kingdom of God is near" (1:15). Luke related how Jesus assumed the aggravating burden and the promising hope of Isaiah's prophecy that the poor would hear good news, the captives would be liberated, the oppressed would be freed, and the blind would have their sight restored (4:18-21). Matthew shared the good news that Jesus was the promised Savior (4:16). The Gospel of John portrayed Jesus as the one sent to bring salvation to the world (e.g., 3:16-17). The context established by such good news determines the goals for the preparation of Christian ministers.

In a Christocentric curriculum the mission of the church establishes the context of teaching and learning. What is God's call to us in Jesus Christ? It is to be sensitive, at one and the same time, to the needs of the world and to the imperative of the gospel. Sensitivity to the issues that we face in the world today is essential to a Christologically based curriculum. Issues of war, justice, poverty, and native peoples' rights are among the national and global concerns of the day. We need to assist students now, while they are presently engaged in ministerial studies, to integrate their biblical, historical, theological, and practical studies with the urgent contemporary concerns of the day. As John Cobb has said, "Mission is *not* an add-on." It is my concern that an urgent sense of mission be inculcated in each of our students as we enable them to integrate their studies in divinity with an urgency about Christ's redemptive mission on earth.

A Christological foundation for theological education involves a perspective in ministry that imaginatively and creatively sees each discrete act of ministering as a partnership with ministries in all the world, joined to work toward peace, justice, and equity. A Christ-oriented ministry inspires hope in God's care for the whole of humanity. An authentic ministry in Christ looks beyond the borders of our province and nation for it understands God to be at work in all of creation. Such a ministry is confident that, in Christ, God has inaugurated a new order that brings authentic concord and dignity to all creatures as well as the natural realm (Col. 1:20).

Such a Christocentric curriculum would seek to avoid separating ministry and spirituality, as many present curricula appear to make possible. Such a Christ-oriented syllabus would encourage the maturing student to have the strength, confidence, and ability to live and deal with ambiguity, including the unavoidable ambiguities embedded in the statements that form the bedrock of our faith traditions.

What might a graduate theological curriculum look like, if we reformulated it on the basis of a Christological foundation? The proposed direction for a new synthesis makes at least one important assumption; namely, that one of the major strengths of the North American theological enterprise and of the curriculum by which it seeks to educate is the consistent effort toward integration. We have tried to overcome the polarities of action-reflection, academic-practical, classroom-congregation by continuing efforts at integration in our teaching and supportive programs. Thus we move into the future with extensive experience in attempting integration. We move forward from a position of proven strength.

It is demonstrable that most of the questions pastors confront daily are not oriented to some specific academic discipline. Why not, from the beginnning of their graduate theological education, have students working with professors and congregations to see how the acquired disciplines are actually integrated into effective ministry. Seminars could be initiated, planned, and implemented by faculty from various disciplines. A curriculum committee would have responsibility for reviewing the offerings for scope, asking, for example, whether we are teaching adequately the content that a theological curriculum ought to have?

What would one such seminar look like? During recent years, one seminar might have been dealing with the gospel and unemployment. It might have been planned by a team composed of a Bible professor, a theologian, and one faculty person from the practice of ministry. Together, they with their students would have investigated what the Bible teaches, what theologians have said, and what the practice of ministry involves when large numbers of our people are unemployed. Such integrative work would not necessarily take additional faculty. It would take more time for planning by both faculty and students. It would also limit the number of electives available. The trade-off would be experience in integration during the period when students are still pursuing their graduate theological studies. It would not leave major social concerns to be resolved until after the student has been graduated.

Other examples of new-style courses may be suggested. For instance, rather than present separate courses in biblical exegesis and preaching, why not offer an integrated course in which exegesis proceeds to preaching? Again, one of the major breakdowns in modern society is the dissolution of the traditional family. Consider the possibilities of an integrative course in which a biblical scholar, a historian-theologian, and a faculty person from the ministerial arts collaborate, along with students, in the discovery of appropriate Christian responses to this pressing concern. For clarity, I would suggest that we think of these courses as integrative courses rather than as interdisciplinary courses. The latter reintroduces the traditional fourfold pattern that is being called into serious question today. The integrative courses also assume that the planners will intentionally work from a Christocentric foundation as they analyze and synthesize.

This proposal for curriculum reformation develops out of a recognition that students normally do *not* come to a theological college to master a single discipline in order to go and practice that one discipline in a parish. A theological faculty has a mandate to help prepare pastors who are skilled both in the foundational disciplines and in the art of integrating knowledge and practice.

Christ remains the sure foundation of our faith. Christian education and especially graduate theological education deserve to be refashioned and reformed by critical reflection upon an incarnational theology. Conforming our instructional structures to the redemptive mission of Christ in and for the world would make our teaching and learning most relevant. For it is the person, the work, and the teachings of Jesus Christ that do "hold together" the educational enterprises of the Christian church.

Chapter Two

Christology and the Study of the Old Testament

T. Raymond Hobbs

Three centuries of modern critical study of the Old Testament, while moving in quite different directions, have grappled with matters essential to the relationship of the Christian faith to a collection of documents that, from a cultural and historical perspective, are alien. Until relatively recently, implicitly or explicitly, the issue of the relationship of the Christian faith (confessional) to the study of the Old Testament was never far from the surface in biblical studies.

Since the removal of Gerhard von Rad's masterful *Old Testament Theology* from its dominant position in the world Old Testament studies, the discipline of Old Testament theology has been searching for a method.[1] It needs to reconstruct the kind of synthesis of theological sensitivity and historical understanding that was a major part of the appeal of von Rad's work. In the last few decades several studies have been published that give evidence of vigorous intellectual activity, on the one hand, and a lack of consensus on purpose and method, on the other.

General introductory studies, such as those by Zimmerli, Westermann, Kaiser, and Martens, are valuable but are little more than probes in varied directions.[2] Two titles of a programmatic nature—*An Outline of Old*

---

[1]G. von Rad, *Old Testament Theology*, 2 vols., trans. D. G. M. Stalker (Edinburgh: Oliver & Boyd, 1962).

[2]W. Zimmerli, *Old Testament Theology in Outline*, trans. D. E. Green (Atlanta: John Knox Press, 1978); C. Westermann, *Theologie des Alten testaments,* Das Alte Testament Deutsch, 6 (Göttingen: Vandenhoeck & Ruprecht, 1980); W. C. Kaiser, *Toward an Old Testament Theology* (Grand Rapids: Zondervan, 1981); E. A. Martens, *God's Design: A Focus on Old Testament Theology* (Grand Rapids: Baker, 1981).

Testament Theology by Zimmerli and Kaiser's *Toward an Old Testament Theology*—illustrate this limited scope. In keeping with the current state of mind of the discipline, retrospective volumes have been published that hint at new directions.[3] Others have offered new approaches that try to do justice to the historical context of the faith of ancient Israel,[4] but these are to be seen more as histories of Old Testament faith rather than theologies of the Old Testament.

Some special themes have long been popular in Old Testament theology. One favorite topic is the covenant, which several recent studies have considered. They range from the historical and form-critical to the theological,[5] but none seems to have captured the imagination or attention of the scholars, and certainly none will resume the place once occupied by Eichrodt's important study of covenant in Old Testament theology.

Brevard Child's innovative "canonical critical" approach held some promise but on examination appears to be becoming more and more dogmatic, with less attention being given to the historical dimensions of Old Testament faith. The same can be said for the newer "literary" approaches to the text of the Old Testament, which show a great deal of ingenuity in detecting and interpreting textual patterns.[6] The contribution to the discipline of Old Testament theology however, remains minimal.

---

[3]See R. E. Clements, *Old Testament Theology: A Fresh Approach,* New Foundations Theological Library (Atlanta: John Knox Press, 1978); K. Haacker, ed., *Biblische Theologie heute: Einführung, Beispiele, Kontroversen,* Biblische-theologische Studien, 1 (Neukirchen: Neukirchener Verlag, 1977); G. F. Hasel, *Old Testament Theology: Basic Issues in the Current Debate,* rev. ed. (Grand Rapids: Eerdmans, 1975); H. Graf Reventlow, *Problems of Old Testament Theology in the Twentieth Century,* trans. J. Bowden, (London: SCM Press, 1985).

[4]See, for example, W. H. Schmidt, *The Faith of the Old Testament: A History,* trans. J. Sturdy (Philadelphia: Westminster Press, 1983).

[5]W. Vogels, *God's Universal Covenant: A Biblical Study* (Ottawa: Ottawa University Press, 1979), illustrates the form-critical approach. A theological orientation forms W. J. Dumbrell, *Covenant and Creation: A Theology of Old Testament Covenants* (Atlanta: Nelson, 1984); T. E. McComiskey, *The Covenants of Promise: A Theology of Old Testament Covenants* (Grand Rapids: Baker, 1985).

[6]B. S. Childs, *Old Testament Theology in a Canonical Context* (Philadelphia: Fortress Press, 1986). For literary approaches, see, for example, R. Alter, *The Art of Biblical Narrative* (New York: Basic Books, 1981); J. Licht, *Storytelling in the Bible* (Jerusalem: Magnes Press, 1979). A fine exposition of this approach to the Old Testament can be found in L. M. Eslinger, *Kingship of God in Crisis: A Close Reading of 1 Sam. 1.12,* Bible and Literature Series 10 (Sheffield: Almond Press, 1985). The work is detailed and persuasive, but the so-called theological conclusions (p. 428) are limited to a small paragraph of comment on the relationship of this study to an understanding of the ideological position of the rest of the Deuteronomistic history.

The new paths of historical understanding offered by those who seek to apply the tools of sociology does much to throw new light on old issues of the history of ancient Israel and Judah.[7] Some of the studies suffer from a poorly based methodology but nevertheless do hold out great promise.[8] Again, the issue of the contribution such studies make to the discipline of Old Testament theology is an important one. The conclusion of Gottwald's very important work *The Tribes of Yahweh* would indicate that Old Testament studies need to undergo a substantial shift in approach before the full relevance of his work for the theology of the Old Testament is made plain.[9] If, as Gottwald argues, the ideology (faith, theology) is the symbolic counterpart to social structure and is, in fact, generated from within the social matrix and not vice versa, then biblical theology is sorely in need of an overhaul. It seems that the rift between the community of faith, with its religious approach to the documents of the Bible, and the world of the historical scholar is widening. The likelihood of building a sturdy enough bridge between the two diminishes. In Gottwald's recent book *The Hebrew Bible,* the religious approach is seen as a minor option.

If Old Testament theology in general is at present stalled, this is equally as true of studies on the particular theme of the Messiah, a topic relevant to any attempt to deal with Old Testament and Christology. Studies from theologically conservative Old Testament scholars have concentrated on the theme of the promise, related incidentally to the covenant, and each attempt devotes considerable space to the notion of the Messiah.[10] However, the major fault of each of these studies is that the literature of the Old Testament is treated as undifferentiated. Prophetic texts are used at the same level as royal psalms and literary traditions of the monarchy. A synthesis is created and offered as the Old Testament teaching on the topic of messiahship. There is a difference between this approach and the older dogmatic approach of prooftexting, but not as sharp a difference as there perhaps should be. The purposes are essentially the same, namely, to dem-

---

[7]The literature is vast. For a convenient summary, see N. K. Gottwald, *The Hebrew Bible: A Socio-Literary Introduction* (Philadelphia: Fortress Press, 1985) and the bibliography on pp. 615-16.

[8]See the criticisms leveled at those who use too strict a model of "role theory," in T. R. Hobbs, "The Search for Prophetic Consciousness: Some comments on Method," *Biblical Theology Bulletin* 15 (1985).

[9]N. K. Gottwald, *The Tribes of Yahweh: A Sociology of the Religion of Liberated Israel, 1250–1050 B.C.* (Maryknoll, NY: Orbis Books, 1980) 667-709.

[10]See Dumbrell, *Covenant and Creation;* Martens, *God's Design;* and McComiskey, *Covenants of Promise.*

onstrate the growing expectation in the Old Testament of a coming ruler/ savior. Recent endeavors have added the obligatory "historical" survey. Other recent studies that deal with messianism and its related concept offer considerably less for the Old Testament theologian. Joseph Scharbert's *Der Messias im Alten Testament* was not widely circulated and is a historical survey of the word *messiah* and the practice of anointing in ancient Israel. A study such as Kearns's *Vorfragen zur Christologie* is again background material for a New Testament Christology and concentrated upon the term *son of man*. Henri Cazelles's book *Le Messie de la Bible: Christologie de l'Ancien Testament,* while it has a promising title, covers much the same ground as Scharbert's, with the added dimension of Israel's eschatological hope.[11] In passing, it is interesting to note that, in two recent programmatic essays on Old Testament theology, Clements's *Old Testament Theology: A Fresh Approach* and Brevard Childs's *Old Testament Theology in a Canonical Context,* the idea of the Messiah is given very little attention.[12]

Two matters of methodology need to be borne in mind when dealing with the Old Testament and Christology. The first is to avoid the "history of ideas" approach, which consciously or unconsciously, indulges in anachronism by pushing back into the past ideas that developed only later. Appropriation by a later age, or later group, of words and ideas from a distant past does not demonstrate that those words were intended to be interpreted in that way in their original form. Second, the nature of the literary context of words and phrases needs to be taken more seriously by students of the concept of messiah. This comment relates to the implied criticism of Martens and Dumbrell above. The fact that many "messianic" notions come from the circles associated with the royal court, capital city, and temple indicates that these notions are propagated by the cultural center of Israel.[13] They are designed to offer ideological support for that center. These statements and ideas should be understood differently from those on the

---

[11]J. Scharbert, *Der Messias im Alten Testament,* Skripten des Lehrstuhls für Theologie des Alten Testament, 7 (Munich: Institute for Biblical Exegesis, 1984); R. Kearns, *Vorfragen zur Chistologie, I: Morphologische und semasiologische Studie zur Vorgeschichte eines christologischen Hoheitstitel* (Tübingen: J. C. B. Mohr, 1978); H. Cazelles, *Le Messie de la Bible: Christologie de l'Ancien Testament,* Collection "Jesus et Jesus Christ," 7 (Paris: Desclée de Brouwer, 1978).

[12]In Clements, *Old Testament Theology,* the term is treated incidentally with the concept of promise. In Childs's work the concept is treated in just over one page (pp. 119-20).

[13]For a definition of this use of the term *centre,* see E. Shils, "Center and Periphery," in *The Constitution of Society* (Chicago: University of Chicago Press, 1982) 93-109.

same topic that emanate from the periphery of society—in the main, the prophetic circles, whose position is frequently antithetical to the center.[14] It cannot be assumed that groupings of persons with a common language either have adequate facility in that language or use the same words to convey the same meaning.[15]

In discussions of the messianic idea in the Old Testament, interpreters have concentrated on the so-called Davidic Tradition.[16] Martin Noth's and Gerhard von Rad's expositions of this tradition in their major works have recently provided even quite conservative scholars with a tool for fashioning a messianic ideal from the rough material of the Old Testament. But a few Old Testament scholars have inquired after the nature of a "tradition." Traditions do not have immaculate conception, nor are they nourished on emptiness. They become established, and are sometimes invented, to give a sense of continuity with the past. In Eric Hobsbawm's words, " 'Invented tradition' is taken to mean a set of practices, normally governed by overtly or tacitly accepted rules and of values and norms of behavior by repetition, which automatically implies continuity with the past. In fact, where possible, they normally attempt to establish continuity with a suitable historic past."[17] The modern world is replete with such traditions of greater or lesser importance.[18]

The so-called tradition of the Davidic line (using the term as is understood by Noth and von Rad) is of a different order from that of the Exodus-Sinai tradition. For one thing, it is a relative latecomer in the thought world of ancient Judah; for another, it has an obvious center of persons with a vested interest in its continuity. In its exposition within the Old Testament, it has incorporated other traditions from the past—the patriarchs and Sinai—to the point where all past history seems to be consummated in the per-

---

[14]See Hobbs, "Prophetic Consciousness," passim.

[15]On the social context of language, see P. P. Giglioli, ed., *Language and Social Context* (Harmondsworth: Penguin Books, 1972), (especially B. Bernstein's article "Social Class, Language, and Socialization," 157-79); T. F. Carney, *Content Analysis: A Technique for Systematic Inference from Communications* (Winnipeg: University of Manitoba Press: 1972) 77-110.

[16]See von Rad's classic statement of the tradition in *Old Testament Theology* 1: 306-54.

[17]E. Hobsbawm and T. Ranger, eds., *The Invention of Tradition* (Cambridge: Cambridge University Press, 1983) 1-2.

[18]See the recent musings of the Canadian "tradition" of multiculturalism by M. Alexander, "The Portable Mosaic," *Idler* 11 (Jan./Feb. 1987): 22-26.

petuation of the Davidic dynasty.[19] Contrary to many popular perceptions, the idea of a Davidic ruler as an eschatological figure does not play a prominent role in the statements about reconstruction in the late exilic and postexilic prophets. Greater concentration is placed upon the restoration of land, city, and temple. A Davidic ruler is rarely, if ever, seen. Traditionally interpreted "messianic" passages (i.e., the Old Testament passages that have played a role in the formulation of a Christian doctrine of the Messiah) have a much more immediate historical application. Postexilic prophets such as Haggai, Zechariah, and Malachi focus clearly on the restoration of the temple and the city of Jerusalem. Only incidentally is there any hint of a future messianic figure from the line of David in this period. To argue, as many have done, that the so-called messianic passages in the preexilic prophets are postexilic insertions is surely begging the question.[20] I am not arguing necessarily against the legitimacy of understanding the Old Testament as *praeparatio evangelium,* nor am I denying that the New Testament unashamedly interprets the Old Testament in a messianic way. I am suggesting that this is a later Christian *interpretation* of these passages, informed not by an appreciation of a sense of the historical moment of the passages but by a particular exegetical and interpretive method that developed at a much later time. The pattern is to move from (current) event to the text and, if necessary, to modify the text, rather than to begin with the text itself. It is a common one and can be seen in writers from around the first century such as Philo, the Gospel of Matthew, and the commentaries from Qumran.

One of the few studies to take these points seriously is that of Joachim Becker, *Messianic Expectations in the Old Testament,* whose careful survey of the evidence concludes, "The messiah is by no means a necessary concomitant of hopes for salvation. A distinction, however inadequate, must be made between the hopes of eschatology and those of eschatological messianism. Essential to messianism is the figure of a saviour, more

---

[19]See, for example, R. E. Clements, *Abraham and David: Genesis 15 and its Meaning for Israelite Tradition,* Studies in Biblical Theology, ser. 2, no. 5 (London: SCM Press, 1967); and J. D. Levenson, *Sinai and Zion: An Entry into the Jewish Bible* (Minneapolis: Winston Press, 1985).

[20]Texts like Isaiah 7 become an embarrassment only when they are interpreted in the context of a "messianic hope." If they are seen in their correct historical context, with an immediate historical application, then the awkwardness disappears. It is more likely that such statements, which incorporate royal ideology, would have been promulgated during the monarchy. See H. L. Ellison, *The Messianic Idea in the Old Testament* (London: Tyndale Press, 1960); and, from a different perspective, A. Benzen, *King and Messiah* (London: Lutterworth Press, 1955).

specifically a royal figure of Davidic lineage. *Until the second century B.C. one searches in vain for such a figure"* (italics mine).[21] To study Jewish messianic hope as background to the New Testament is therefore a matter not of Old Testament studies but of the investigation of "late" postexilic Judaism. Even there, one finds neither a unified picture nor a perfect blank shape into which New Testament Christology fits.

I

Historical investigation suggests that the traditional dogmatic approach to the biblical text, using it as a mine of propositional statements on dogma, should be discarded. Careful attention to the social matrix of the statements on kingship, messiahship, and related concepts suggests that the terms were intended for a purpose other than the development of a doctrine of the Messiah and ought not to be taken as material directly relevant to New Testament Christology. Older attempts to link the two, including some parts of the New Testament, were advanced with no sensitivity to the gulf between distant past and present. While there has been a strong case made recently to a return to a "precritical" exegesis,[22] I think this case is misguided. If traditional Christian interpretation of the so-called messianic passages in the Old Testament has to give way to an approach that is much more sensitive to the historical and social context of the passages, then one is faced with the question as to whether one can speak at all of the Old Testament with reference of Christology.

All is by no means lost, and I think it possible to understand the Old Testament as a precursor to a Trinitarian theology, even if the confident assertions of past (and some present) theological treatises are often cases of special pleading. This chapter suggests an alternative line of investigation, that of the way in which certain kinds of language are used in the Old Testament. The anthropomorphism of the Old Testament's speaking about God has long been recognized but, I believe, not properly interpreted. On the one hand, it has been regarded as a sign of primitive thought, recognized for what it was, but something that no modern writer would indulge in; on the other hand, it has been poorly understood because it has rarely been supported by a full understanding of the way the inhabitant of the biblical (Mediterranean) world viewed a person. Language itself needs to be seen in context—in the culture which gives it meaning. The biblical writ-

---

[21]J. Becker, *Messianic Expectations in the Old Testament,* trans. D. E. Green (Philadelphia: Fortress Press, 1980).

[22]W. Steinmetz, "The Superiority of Pre-critical Exegesis," *Theology Today* 37 (1980): 27-38.

ers, in common with others of their world, had a custom of using two powerful and similar language devices: metaphor and analogy.

Metaphor, according to Fernandez, has a strategic function, enabling us to understand and communicate our responses to new situations.[23] Metaphors are descriptive, and their use involves the borrowing of terms from different "domains of equivalence" and the application of those terms to other nouns or pronouns. Their use is strategic, in that the metaphor will enhance or detract from the character who is being described. "The man is an animal!" is a concise description of the character of the man under discussion. It could be refined by reference to particular animals if necessary. But not all animals will be understood the same way in different cultures. "The man is a snake!" has different meaning in Western society from the meaning in a snake-worshiping society. A metaphor helps us "leap beyond the essential privacy of the experiential process," to inform, to make known, but universal meanings cannot be inferred. "Yahweh is a man of war" is a metaphor designed to convey a new experience of God in the Old Testament. Isaiah's description of the nation of Judah as a sick body, "with wound bruises and putrefying sores," is a powerful strategic use of what was probably a common metaphor. Such groupings (bodies) of people have "heads," that is, leaders. The metaphor is a striking one when compared to the modern use of a mechanical metaphor to describe society that "breaks down."[24]

Analogy has a long and distinguished history within theology and philosophy,[25] but it is not our purpose to enter into a discussion on the validity of using analogous language for theology today. To all intents and purposes, such a discussion is irrelevant to a study of the use of such language in the Old Testament. At its simplest, analogy is the use of referents from one realm to convey meaning about another. Because there seems to be an unconscious use of language in this way, it is not fair to characterize this use of the "concrete" to describe the "abstract." There is a metaphoric and analogical way of speaking in the Old Testament that is quite perva-

---

[23]J. W. Fernandez, "Persuasions and Performances: Of the Beast in Every Body . . . and the Metaphors of Everyman," in *Myth, Symbol, and Culture*, ed. C. Geertz (New York: Norton, 1971) 39-60.

[24]The correlation between the way society is viewed and the way the members of that society view themselves has been investigated in M. Douglas, *Natural Symbols: Explorations in Cosmology* (Harmondsworth: Penguin Books, 1973).

[25]See B. Mondin, *The Principle of Analogy in Protestant and Catholic Theology*, 2d ed. (The Hague: M. Nijhoff, 1968).

sive and that appears most evident in didactic and poetic books such as Proverbs, the Prophets, and the Psalms, although it is not restricted to these.

Analogy in the language of the Old Testament is seen clearly when the Old Testament talks of God. Here the analogy of a human being, the so-called anthropomorphisms, predominates. Unlike a recent attempt to rehabilitate God-talk in modern vocabulary,[26] God is never likened to natural phenomena such as whirlwinds. He is in such phenomena, above them, controlling them. His breath is like the storm, but he is not the storm.

God is described instead in human terms, has human emotions, feels sorrow, becomes angry. He has ears, eyes, hands, feet, a mouth, a nose, and, of course, a face. The first activity of God in the Old Testament is a human one, opening his mouth and uttering words. But to say, then, only that the Old Testament indulges in anthropomorphism in this way, whether by use of metaphor or analogy, when talking of God, is a truism in need of a fuller explanation. If languages used in this way are such a common way of understanding God, an investigation into the Old Testament's understanding of human beings is in order. It is irrelevant at this stage to talk of the refinements of the principle of analogy in Greek philosophy or in Thomist theology. Such refinements as "analogy of being" are not part of the Old Testament mind.

An obvious feature about human beings when they are described in the Old Testament is that they are devoid of inner psychological characteristics. The literary style of stories is to concentrate on activity to the detriment of inner reflection.[27] The reader understands that Gehazi is greedy (2 Kings 5), not because the narrator tells us so, but because the story describes a greedy action. Mood is created by what characters do. Attitudes are described not by reference to internal psychological states of mind but more by physical gestures.

It does not follow that this nonpsychological human being of the Old Testament world did not feel emotions or possess psychological attitudes. It is simply that people are rarely described in such a way. There is the odd exception such as the verb *ka'as* (to be vexed, angry).Instead the concentration is on the outward manifestation of such attitudes. To be angry is to "flare" (presumably the nostrils). To be stubborn is to be "hard of heart" or "stiff-necked." To respect is to "lift the face." Conversely, to humiliate is to "lower the crown (of the head)." To react in anger and vengeance

---

[26] L. Gilkey, *Naming the Whirlwind: The Renewal of God-Language* (Minneapolis: Bobbs-Merrill, 1969).

[27]See Alter, *Art of Biblical Narrative,* 70, for the dominance of speech in biblical stories.

is to "stretch out the hand," and to humiliate enemies is to "put them under one's feet." To be attentive is to "give the heart" or "to bend the ear." To be depressed is to have one's *"nephesh* cast down." Indeed, what the Western world would regard as an inner attitude, namely "to be ashamed," is, in the biblical world a very public, visible thing.[28]

II

In his delightful and provocative book *Materialist Approaches to the Bible,* Michel Clevenot has noted that there is frequent reference in the Gospel of Mark to parts of the body when the activity of Jesus is being described. The hands are used to transform life situations (Mark 1:31, 41; 3:10; 5:23, 28, 41; 6:6; 7:33; 8:22, 23, 25; etc.). Furthermore, the feet convey the traveler, Jesus, on journeys that are not only geographical but strategic and symbolic (1:16; 2:23; 4:1; 6:7, 9; 10:32, 50). Finally, the eyes and ears "refer to what we have called the analytical code, which serves to identify the practices of the readings of different personages"[29] (2:5; 3:1; 4:4; 6:14, 38; 10:21; etc.). Clevenot's conclusion for Mark is that the activity of the hands symbolizes the economic practice of love; the feet, the political practice of hope; and the ears and eyes, the ideological practice of faith. In Mark's presentation these are messianic characteristics, demanded of the followers of the Messiah. For the reader the question "Do I have faith?" should be transformed into "What is my practice on these three levels?"

Clevenot has identified an important feature of the Gospel of Mark. But there is more to be said. First, the tendency to use this bodily language is not unique to Mark but common to the whole New Testament.[30] Second, it is also very common in the Old Testament (and, one must add, the intertestamental literature). In other words, Clevenot has detected not so much a Markan invention but Mark's following a common eastern Mediterranean practice of describing people.

The pattern has been examined thoroughly by Bernard de Geradon in a little-known article published some thirty years ago. Entitled "L'homme à l'image de Dieu: Approache nouvelle à la lumière de l'anthropologie du sens commun," the work was a thorough examination of the occurrences

---

[28]See especially J. Peristiany, ed., *Honour and Shame: The Values of Mediterranean Society* (Chicago: University of Chicago Press, 1966).

[29]M. Clevenot, *Materialist Approaches to the Bible,* trans. W. A. Nottingham (Maryknoll NY: Orbis Books, 1985).

[30]See the exposition of this point in B. J. Malina, *The New Testament World: Insights from Cultural Anthropology* (Atlanta: John Knox Press, 1981) 51-70.

in descriptions of human beings in the Old Testament of the words *eyes, ears, mouth, hands, feet,* and their related terms.[31] To these de Geradon added another part of the body: the heart. Some examples of the use of this vocabulary for humans follow.

In Ecclessiates 5:1-2, the reader is advised, "Guard your steps when you go to the house of God; to draw near to listen is better than to offer the sacrifice of fools; for they do not know that they are doing evil. Be not rash with your mouth, nor let your heart be hasty to utter a word before God." In Psalm 17:3-5, the psalmist speaks of God's knowledge of his past behavior and states, "If thou triest my heart . . . thou wilt find no wickedness in me; my mouth does not transgress. . . . . I have avoided the ways of the violent. My steps have held fast to thy paths, my feet have not slipped." In Proverbs 6:12-14, the description of the wicked person runs as follows: "A worthless person, a wicked man, goes about with crooked speech, winks with his eyes, scrapes with his feet, points with his finger, with perverted heart devises evil, continually sowing discord." The chapter continues with a list of the seven things in a person that the Lord hates: "haughty eyes, a lying tongue, and hands that shed innocent blood, a heart that devises wicked plans, feet that make haste to run to evil, a false witness who breathes out lies, and a man who sows discord among brothers" (vv. 16-19). In Isaiah's eschatological vision (Isa. 32:3-4), the following statement appears: "Then the eyes of those who see will not be closed, and the ears of those who hear will hearken. The mind [lit. heart] of the rash will have good judgment, and the tongue of the stammerers will speak readily and distinctly." De Geradon concludes, "Décidément, le schème anthropologique est un ressort irrécusable du langage hébraïque."[32]

A full listing of the use of such language would be a task too large for this chapter, but it is clear that the language is consistent and is used as a matter of course in descriptions of human beings. If an understanding of a human being is to be sought in the Old Testament, it is to be found in this descriptive language. The human being possesses a will (heart), expresses the will (mouth), has the ability to hear the expression of others (ears), and acts according to the will (hands and feet). The heart is also often accompanied by reference to the eye. These three pairs of physical parts—eyes/heart, mouth/ears, hand/feet—constitute a human being. A person who behaves incorrectly is one whose will, expression, and action are per-

---

[31]B. de Geradon, "L'homme à l'image de Dieu: Approche nouvelle a la lumière de l'anthropologie du sens commun," *Nouvelle revue theologique* 11 (1958): 681-95.

[32]Ibid., 687.

verted, as in Proverbs 6:16-19, or out of harmony, as in Isaiah 29:13. In the light of this understanding of the human being, we must view laws such as "eye for eye, tooth for tooth, hand for hand, foot for foot" (Exod. 21:24; Lev. 24-20; Deut. 19:21).[33]

As one might expect, with the Old Testament's tendency to use analogy when speaking to God, the same image of God is found in its pages. In contrast to the foreign idols, who "have mouths, but they speak not, they have eyes, but they see not, they have ears, but they hear not, nor is there any breath in their mouths" (Ps. 135:16-17), the God of Israel is active, has a mouth to utter his creative word, has eyes through which he sees the activity of his creation, and has ears to listen to the prayers of his subjects. History is created by his purposeful word (2 Sam 7:21), and in the words of the postexilic prophet, "The LORD's hand is not shortened, that it cannot save, or his ear dull, that it cannot hear" (Isa. 59:1). In fact, in the saving event par excellence in history of ancient Israel, the Exodus, God acts in perfect harmony with will. "I have seen [eye] the affliction of my people . . . and have heard [ear] their cry . . . I know [heart] their sufferings, and I have come down [feet] to deliver them" (Exod. 3:7-8).

III

By way of summary at this stage, the following can be stated. First, in general the descriptions of God found in the Old Testament focus on the activity of God. This generalization, however, is not to be taken as avoiding questions of character or personality. Rather, through such descriptions of action character is portrayed in the Old Testament. Second, the language used of God is the language used of human beings. The use of the human analogy is widespread. Being made "in the image" of God is, for a later writer, being endowed with the same physical-psychological characteristics as God. God gave humans "strength like his own, and made them in his image. . . . He made for them tongue and eyes; he gave them ears and a mind for thinking" (Sirach 17:3-6). Third, these physical-psychological features are often grouped into three consistent pairs. The eyes are the windows to the heart (the will), the ears and mouth are concerned

---

[33]See also the incident recorded in 2 Kings 4:32-37, in which the prophet Elisha lies atop a dead boy "mouth on mouth, eyes on eyes, hand on hand." The variants in the Greek tradition continue this pattern to the point of contortionism. The activity of the prophet cannot be rationalized as a "kiss of life," since more than the mouth is used. Nor is it proper to see this incident as some kind of magic, so. G. H. Jones, *1 and 2 Kings,* New Century Bible Commentary (London: Marshall Morgan & Scott, 1985) 2: 409-10. It is rather an identification of the prophet with the lifeless boy. See T. R. Hobbs, *2 Kings,* Word Biblical Commentary, 13 (Waco TX: Word Publishing, 1985).

with the expression of what is in the heart, and the hands and feet are concerned with acting on the decisions of the will. Any theological interpretation of God in the Old Testament must consider this presentation carefully.

But if God is so presented as having a will (eyes and heart), expressing his will (ears and mouth), and acting according to his will (hands and feet), then the understanding of God as having three aspects is already inherent in Old Testament talk about God. It would be a serious error to use the term *person* in this connection, since there is no Old Testament equivalent of this term as it is understood in later Trinitarian theology. The Hebrew term most closely related to the idea of person, *nephesh,* would never be used in the same way. The expressions about God are tied to his threefold activity—seeing (and understanding), speaking, and acting.

Also seen in the Old Testament is an identification of one physical activity of God, the use of the "hand of God" with the manifestations of power through the Spirit of God. Prophetic inspiration is described in straightforward terms of the Spirit of the Lord coming upon a prophet (1 Sam. 10:6, 10; Isa. 61:1-4; Mic. 3:8; Ezek. 11:5; etc.), or the "power of the Lord" coming upon a prophet (1 Kings 18:46; 2 Kings 3:15 var.; Ezek. 8:1; etc.). It is also the "finger of God," by which the heavens are made (Ps. 8:3).

This usage is no more a hypostatization of a third "Person" of the Godhead, than is the notion of the heart or mind of God a hypostatization of the First Person of the Godhead. In later theological language it is a mode of operation of the Godhead. It is the overt activity of God in creation, destruction, and general demonstrations of power. It is, however, inseparable from his heart and mind—that is, his will. Furthermore, it is also inseparable from the expression of his heart and mind through his Word. According to the ancient Israelite understanding of a human person, and because of the use of the analogy of a human person when speaking of God, it is inconceivable that the three would ever be separated.

It would be a mistake to argue for a Trinitarian doctrine of God in the Old Testament, as the doctrine came to be understood in later theology—not because the monotheism of the ancient Israelites would not allow for such an understanding, but rather because the language used of God in the Old Testament does not express such an understanding. Yet God is understood in a threefold way. In de Geradon's words, "ce triple plan d'activités offre en Dieu un caractère de profonde unité et de parfait harmonie."[34] But to use the terms *being, person,* and *essence* of this unity and harmony

---

[34]De Geradon, "L'homme à l'image de Dieu," 689.

would be anachronistic. To be sure, as de Geradon goes on to point out, the attributes of the heart adhere well to the person of the Father in the later doctrine of the Trinity; the attributes of the mouth (word, speech, utterance) lend themselves well to the later use of such terms of the Son (the Word of God); and the characteristics of the hand suit well the activity of the Spirit, both as later described and as depicted within the pages of the Old Testament. But this description is not the doctrine of the Trinity found in the Old Testament. These aspects, or modes, of operation of God are not always distinct, and there is some overlap. The creative power of God is seen as a manifestation of his Spirit (Ps. 104:30; Job 33.4) and also of his Word (Ps. 148:5; exp. 33:6); and the activity of God is accomplished, not always by his hand, but also by his Word (Isa. 55:11; Jer. 1:12).

IV

The search for a doctrine of the Messiah within pages of the Old Testament will prove fruitless and can yield results only by detaching the statements used to compile such a doctrine from their historical contexts.[35] However, the Old Testament uses language to describe a human being in terms of that being's activity. This activity is focused on three areas of the body—the eyes and heart, the mouth and ears, and the hands and feet. These pairs of physical features symbolize the will, the expression of the will, and the activity of the will. This language is also used, by analogy, of God. While such usage might tempt some to see in this terminology a hint at the threefold nature of God, such expressions are beyond the horizons of Old Testament thought.

The Second Person of the Trinity is absent from the Old Testament. That person can be found there only by the superimposition of alien schemes of interpretation on the text, such as allegory or typology, or by reading back into the historical progression of the faith of ancient Israel features that were not there at the time but were developed much later. The absence of the Son, however, is to be expected. It is quite consistent with the New Testament understanding of the former hiddenness of the mystery of God's will, now revealed in Christ (Eph. 3:6-9; Col. 1:24-27).

The intertestamental period, the latter part of which saw the flourishing of a ''messianic eschatology'' in which a Davidic figure was promi-

---

[35]The point is most forcibly made in S. E. Rosenberg, *The Christian Problem: A Jewish View* (Toronto: Deneau Publishers, 1986) 31-49. ''Not a single word in the Hebrew Bible, Jewish scholars aver, can be brought forth as proof that Jesus Christ was already pointed to, in Hebrew Scripture, long before his arrival in time'' (p. 34).

nent, did not see these ideas in direct connection with the "personhood" of God. That is, the messiah—be he king, priest, or prophet—is always an agent of God, and not a hypostatization of the Word or utterance of God. The Christology of the New Testament and the primitive church owes much more to the impact of the life, ministry, death, and resurrection of Jesus than it does to a "Christology" of the Old Testament.

Chapter Three

Jesus in the Four Gospels:
A Study in Christology

Melvyn R. Hillmer

The four Gospels of the New Testament are all concerned to present the gospel of Jesus Christ through accounts of his ministry, death, and resurrection. When they are read as four distinct writings, it is clear that there are differences and varieties of presentation and of theological outlook. The Gospels are too often read as harmonies, so that the diversity is obscured, and it is too readily assumed that all the Evangelists are saying the same thing. The peculiarities of each document ought to be allowed to stand, since this approach enables us to understand better the Christological insights and outlook of the various authors. What can we make of the fact, for example, that in Luke's Gospel Jesus is proclaimed by the angel at his birth to be "a Savior, who is Christ the Lord" (Luke 2:11), in John most of the Christological titles are given to him in the initial encounter with John the Baptist and the first disciples (John 1:29-51), while in Mark there is a theme of secrecy until halfway through, when Peter confesses him as the Christ (Mark 8:29)? These and many other features make it essential to look at the diversities of approach so that we can understand the intention and theological insights of the gospel writers.

This focus is important not only for the study of the Gospels but for the entire New Testament. It has in fact become customary in recent years to discuss the theology of individual writers, and for many years the attempt to write a New Testament theology was almost abandoned. Even books that bear titles suggesting that they are theologies of the New Testament often are not. The work of W. G. Kümmel, for example, approaches the task from the standpoint of a variety of theologies and is entitled *The Theology of the New Testament according to Its Major Witnesses: Jesus—*

Paul—John.[1] The more recent study of the theology of the New Testament by L. Goppelt comes closer than others to dealing with theological themes in a comprehensive and systematic fashion, with important suggestions for the study of theology.[2] Most interpreters approach the topics of New Testament theology on the basis not of an assumed unity but of diversity, with considerable hesitation to speak about the unity that may exist. The tendency is greatly heightened when the question of a biblical theology is raised, since the continuities between Old and New Testaments are even less evident.

Christological studies follow the same general tendency as most studies of New Testament theology. It is fruitful to examine the variety of ways in which the understanding of the person of Jesus, the presentation of his work, and the theological reflection on the whole event of his coming are expressed. Even a somewhat superficial examination of the Christological titles will reveal noticeable diversity in the manner in which writers refer to him.[3] The fondness of certain authors for selected titles and their absence in others leads to the inevitable conclusion of differences in emphasis at least, and perhaps more basic varieties of understanding. The diversity is to be seen not only in the use of titles but also in the total presentation of the portraits of Jesus.

There is, at the same time, a basic unity to the Gospels and throughout the New Testament, and this fact must not be overlooked. It is, after all, the same Jesus of Nazareth about whom the Gospels are concerned and upon whom the Christian church from the beginning has based its faith. When we ask questions about the kind of diversity that exists, we must ask also about the nature of unity and about the limits to diversity.

In this chapter I look briefly at some of the distinctive features of the four Gospels as far as Christology is concerned, studying the most important peculiarities in the various presentations of Jesus and his work. We see in them at once a diversity and a basic unity. The unity provides criteria for understanding the limits to diversity and the rejection by the church of certain Christological interpretations.

---

[1]W. G. Kümmel, *The Theology of the New Testament according to Its Major Witnesses: Jesus—Paul—John* (Nashville: Abingdon Press, 1973).

[2]L. Goppelt, in his *Theology of the New Testament,* vol. 1 (Grand Rapids: Eerdmans, 1981), has made a serious attempt at a theology of the New Testament, including its implications for systematic theology.

[3]Thorough studies of titles are to be found in F. Hahn, *The Titles of Jesus in Christology* (London: Lutterworth, 1969); and W. Kramer, *Christ, Lord, Son of God,* Studies in Biblical Theology, 50 (Naperville IL: Allenson, 1966).

It should come as no surprise that there is diversity in the presentation of Jesus in the four Gospels. The authors write out of their own backgrounds, from different localities, and to varied audiences. Form critics have made a major contribution to the study of the Gospels in establishing the fact that the stories about Jesus and the content of his teachings had an oral history during the period between his life and the time of the writing of the Gospels. Gospel materials were used in the churches for specific purposes in preaching, teaching, liturgy, and instruction within the congregations. The needs of individual churches, the form of traditional materials, and the purposes for which the books are written necessarily lead to considerable variety of presentation. Perhaps it should surprise us that the diversity is not greater.

The development of the techniques of approach to the text referred to as redaction criticism is also important. The emphasis here is on the contribution of the authors themselves as they use the materials of gospel tradition and give an order, shape, or interpretation in accord with their own intentions. The attempt is made to determine the theological motives of the writers and to see how this element has influenced the presentation. It should always be kept in mind that the Gospels are not biographies or histories but rather are appropriately called Gospels. Their purpose is not to preserve historical and biographical materials relating to Jesus of Nazareth but to proclaim the gospel. For this reason the focus of attention in all four Gospels is on the Passion story; the Crucifixion and Resurrection are theologically central to the proclamation of the gospel as the Christian message. Redaction critics are concerned with the way in which the various writers have, on grounds of theology and interpretation, approached their task from a distinctive standpoint and have carried it out in their own personal ways.

The importance of any study of New Testament Christology for theological education should be self-evident. It is clear, is it not, that our views of Christ are based on the New Testament? Unfortunately, the matter is not so simple and straightforward. Many students seem to have made up their minds regarding Christology before beginning their theological studies and are more concerned to defend traditional positions than to come to grips with the texts. The same is true regarding soteriology as well, as Patrick Gray argues in chapter 4. To a certain extent, students may be excused from the failure to distinguish between soteriology and Christology because the two are so closely interrelated, and definitions of Christology often include both the person and work of Christ, as Clark Pinnock notes in chapter 7.

One of the disturbing features of many discussions of Christology is how little attention is actually paid to the New Testament. There is much concern for Chalcedon, with attempts to defend it or criticize it, to talk about natures and persons, and to stress questions of ontology. This focus is evident in the essays of Pinnock and his review of the Reformers and also Nicol and his discussion of Schleiermacher and Ritschl, albeit from a very different standpoint.

It is necessary to look afresh at the theme of Christology as it is in the New Testament. In doing so, we must take full account of recent and contemporary scholarship as it relates to the person and work of Christ. We clearly are confronted with varieties of outlook and expression and should not naively expect identity throughout. To recognize diversity and to deal honestly with it leads to a richness of thought but does not lend itself to an easy construction of a single Christological model. This brief essay is an attempt to discuss some of the particular features of Christology in the four Gospels of the New Testament, not to provide a definitive doctrine but to indicate some starting points for theological debate. Whether for training of students for ministry or for theological formulations generally, the New Testament itself and New Testament scholarship form the basis of doctrinal development.

Christology of Mark

It is generally recognized that Mark is the first of the Gospels to be written and that his work has been used by Matthew and Luke along with other sources. In many respects the three Synoptic Gospels stand close to each other in that they all follow a basically similar approach to the story of Jesus and are clearly distinct from the Fourth Gospel. The peculiarities of John's Gospel have long been noticed,[4] and the theological motivations of the author are readily discernible. The recognition that the Synoptic Evangelists also have theological motives and that these are important in understanding the presentation of the person of Jesus and his ministry is more recent in New Testament scholarship. Discerning theological insights of the various writers and their individuals purposes is of great assistance in interpretation. It is essential to recognize also that each author writes for a particular situation as he addresses the needs of his own congregation.

All the Evangelists write from a post-Easter perspective. The Crucifixion and Resurrection have already happened, and the relation of the writers to the earthly Jesus is not simply that of historical memory, of re-

---

[4]Clement of Alexandria (c. A.D. 180) wrote that "John, observing that the bodily facts had been made clear in the [earlier] gospels . . . composed a spiritual gospel" (Eusebius, *Historia ecclesiastica* 6.4.7).

calling his sayings and deeds. They are people of faith, and their intention is to interpret the Christ who suffered and was crucified, who was raised from the dead and is now the present Lord. The Crucifixion and Resurrection are of such overwhelming significance from a theological standpoint that this event receives the central focus and is so decisive that all else is interpreted in light of it. At the same time, the gospel writers are concerned for the ministry of Jesus and insist on the identity of the earthly Jesus and the risen Lord; the same Jesus who was crucified is now risen. It follows that we look in the Gospels not for biographical details but for "the gospel," the proclamation of the Christian message that has its focus in the person of Jesus and especially in his crucifixion and resurrection.

Mark is probably the first to write in a new literary genre called Gospel. There were earlier collections of sayings of Jesus and of miracle stories, but it is not clear that these contained the passion narratives and the decisive emphasis on the person of Jesus as the center of faith. Attempts have been made to show that some collections of gospel material were actually Gospels, such as Q or the Signs Source of the Fourth Gospel, but Mark is at least the earliest extant Gospel.[5]

In Mark it is possible to determine certain theological motives and the Christological focus. The book begins with the words "the gospel of Jesus Christ, the Son of God" (Mark 1:1).[6] The statement is not a sentence and is more in the nature of a title. E. Schweizer observes that "Mark's objective is to proclaim Jesus as the Son of God."[7] Stated in its simplest form, this summary is true to Mark's purpose, as his use of the title *Son of God* shows. Mark does not often refer to Jesus as Son of God; he uses other titles a good deal more frequently. Those texts in which it does occur, however, are of special importance. In the account of the baptism of Jesus by John the Baptist, the voice from heaven declares, in words reflecting Psalms 2:7 and Isaiah 42:1, "You are my beloved Son; with you I am well pleased" (Mark 1:11). The affirmation appears in the transfiguration story, where the voice says from the cloud, "This is my beloved Son. Listen to him" (Mark 9:7).

---

[5]E.g., R. T. Fortna, *The Gospel of Signs* (Cambridge: Cambridge University Press, 1970).

[6]There is a textual problem, as some important early texts omit the words "Son of God." There is, however, strong attestation for their inclusion, notably B and D, and the title is of importance to Mark elsewhere.

[7]E. Schweizer, *The Good News according to Mark* (Richmond: John Knox Press, 1970) 12.

Certainly the most unexpected and surprising use of the title is in the proclamation of the centurion as he witnesses the crucifixion of Jesus. Mark writes, "When the centurion, who stood there in front of Jesus, heard his cry and saw how he died, he said, 'Surely this man was the son of God!'" (15:39). The words are unexpected because they are spoken not by disciples or followers of Jesus but by a Roman centurion. Nevertheless the title should not be deprived of its theological importance, because we encounter here one of the decisive emphases of Mark's Gospel. At the Crucifixion, and by virtue of Jesus' suffering path in life and death, he is to be recognized as the Son of God.

Central to Mark's presentation of the gospel is his view that the authentic role of the Messiah is that in which suffering is inevitable. This understanding of messiahship is so contrary to expectation that the disciples have great difficulty in recognizing or accepting it. Attention has been paid in recent years to the presentation of Jesus by Mark in the early chapters in terms of the traditions of the *theios aner* or "divine man," as found in the ancient writings known as aretalogies.[8] Contained in aretalogies are stories of extraordinary acts and performances by one who has divine power and is imbued with the authority of God. This "divine man" is not a deity but is superhuman, representing a combination of the divine and human. The similarities of Mark's Gospel to this literary genre are undeniable, as the narration of the acts of Jesus in the first half of the writing shows remarkable correspondence. T. J. Weeden observes, "Where one examines the Markan material prior to the Petrine confession, one is overwhelmed by the amount of material that is oriented to this particular Christological perspective."[9]

With the confession of Peter at Caesarea Philippi, the situation changes dramatically. Now with the raising of the question of Jesus' identity, the tendency to recognize him as Messiah on the basis of miracles and extraordinary acts is rejected. Peter's confession "You are the Messiah" (Mark 8:29) reflects an understanding of messiahship based on the acts of healing and exorcisms. In Jesus' words that follow immediately there is a correction to this identification in the change of title and the beginning now of an emphasis on suffering. The true understanding of the role of Jesus is to be found in his suffering and crucifixion and the refusal to accept this course as the work of Satan. In response to Peter's confession Jesus says, "The

---

[8]Cf. Helmut Koester, "One Jesus and Four Primitive Gospels," in *Trajectories through Early Christianity*, by J. M. Robinson and H. Koester (Philadelphia: Fortress Press, 1971) 187ff.

[9]T. J. Weeden, *Mark—Traditions in Conflict* (Philadelphia: Fortress Press, 1971) 53.

Son of Man must suffer'' (v. 31). This episode marks the turning point in Mark, and the focus henceforth is on the approaching inevitable suffering and crucifixion. It should be seen as a critique of the *theios aner* Christology, which is now replaced by a concept of suffering messiahship.[10] The change of title is due to the misunderstandings of the role of the Messiah. While the title *Son of Man* is filled with difficulties in interpretation, it is the one chosen by Jesus himself, and he seems not to have referred to himself as Messiah. For Mark, suffering is not inevitable because historical events determine it, but ''the Son of Man must suffer'' because God ordains it. Divine necessity leads Jesus to the cross.

A further brief examination of the titles used for Jesus in Mark's Gospel and particularly at Caesarea Philippi may be helpful in determining Mark's understanding of the identity of Jesus. Prior to this incident the question of identity has been raised repeatedly: the demons know he is the Holy One of God (Mark 1:24; cf. v. 34), the Son of God (3:11), and the Son of the Most High God (5:7), and it is remarkable that those of the demonic world recognize who he is but the disciples do not. The crowds wonder who he is that he teaches with authority (1:27), the scribes ask how he can forgive sins (2:7), the disciples question, ''Who is this? Even the wind and waves obey him!'' (4:41), and even Herod discovers that some people identify him as John the Baptist or Elijah or as a prophet (6:14-16). All such statements are designed to keep the question of identity before the people and at the same time to emphasize the failures of recognition.

At Caesarea Philippi it is Jesus who presses the question to the disciples, ''Who do people say I am?'' (Mark 8:27) and ''Who do you say I am?'' (v. 29). For the first time in Mark's Gospel, the disciples, with Peter as spokesman, acknowledge that Jesus is the Messiah. The dramatic turnaround in Jesus' identification is striking in his messianic declaration that ''the Son of Man must suffer'' (v. 31). There follows a series of Passion predictions and allusions to suffering (vv. 31-33; 9:31; 10:33-34), and the intention is to point to the true identity of Jesus as the suffering Son of Man. In reference to the betrayal by Judas, it is also as Son of Man that he is betrayed into the hands of sinners (14:21, 41). For Mark, Jesus is not to be understood as Messiah in traditional terms, not in accordance with the traditions of the ''divine man,'' the wonder-worker who would perform

---

[10]Koester notes that this interpretation is an answer to the problem of the ''Messianic Secret'' in Mark as posed by W. Wrede. ''The solution is obvious today: Mark's tradition, the stories of the divine man and Messiah Jesus, were subjected to the principle of the cross. In this way, the 'secret' revelation of Jesus in his miracles becomes intelligible'' (''One Jesus,'' 189 n. 105).

signs and wonders, but he is identified correctly only when seen as the Son of Man who must suffer and be crucified. "Jesus' role as a suffering servant was not only the central and most important element in his messiahship but was the role specifically ordained by God and the role by which he was finally accurately identified by man."[11]

The only instance in Mark where Jesus affirms the title *Messiah* is in the scene of the trial before the high priest. The form of the question of the high priest is interesting, "Are you the Messiah, the Son of the Blessed One?" (Mark 14:61). The question combines the notions of messiahship and sonship, a combination that is more typical of other Evangelists. Jesus' response in Mark is an unequivocal "I am," unlike the ambiguous forms of the statement in Matthew (26:63-64) and Luke (22:67-70). Yet again Jesus' own title for himself is different; "You will see the Son of Man sitting at the right hand of the Mighty One and coming with the clouds of heaven" (Mark 14:62). The Son of Man designation is the one accepted as the true identification of Jesus, particularly when combined with suffering and death.

At the heart of Markan Christology, therefore, we can conclude that there is, on the one hand, a rejection of the view of messiahship that saw Jesus as the divine man, the wonder-worker who was expected to perform signs. On the other hand, there is a declaration throughout that he is Son of God, whose suffering is inevitable. The Passion narrative, the story of the Crucifixion and Resurrection, is at the theological center of Mark's Gospel, as the road to the cross is the only way to authentic messiahship. The affirmation of such a Messiah is intended for the community in which Mark lives and for which he writes. To be a disciple is to accept also the way of suffering, not that of glory, self-exaltation, and superiority. It may well be that the church to which Mark belonged needed to be called to this hard but essential theology of suffering discipleship, the corollary of the identification of Jesus as the crucified Son of Man and Son of God.

John's Gospel

The Synoptic Gospels show considerable similarity in the general outline of the story of Jesus and in the forms of narrative and teachings. The Fourth Gospel, however, is different in many respects and stands in a tradition and line of theological development that is quite distinct. Whereas in the Synoptics the entire early ministry of Jesus is in Galilee and he goes to Jerusalem only at the end, in John he travels back and forth between Jerusalem and Galilee. The brief sayings are not found, and instead Jesus

---

[11]Weeden, *Mark,* 53.

speaks in long continuous discourses; the parables are totally lacking, and symbolic speech takes very different forms; and the theme of the kingdom of God, so central to Jesus' teaching in the Synoptics, is almost absent, while eternal life becomes the main doctrinal emphasis.

It is not certain whether or to what extent John knew the Synoptic tradition and, if so, how far he consciously attempted to present materials from a different perspective.[12] There is no clear evidence that the author of the Fourth Gospel has known or used any of the other written Gospels of the New Testament. Rather, he represents an independent approach. There is increasing agreement that this Gospel, along with the Johannine Epistles, has its origin in a particular Christian community or circle of believers that may not have been in the mainstream of the early church.[13]

The similarities existing among the three Synoptic Gospels and the distinctiveness of John have often obscured the fact that some features of the Fourth Gospel stand close to those of Mark. Similarities exist not so much in general outline and presentation of the life and teaching of Jesus as in common purpose and theological outlook, particularly in Christology. Like Mark, John intends above all else to proclaim the gospel in the person of Jesus of Nazareth and primarily in his crucifixion and resurrection. His statement of purpose makes this intention explicit. These things are written "that you may believe that Jesus is the Christ, the Son of God, and that believing you may have life in his name" (John 20:31). In the recognition of who Jesus is and through believing in him, life is to be found.

There are clear differences between John and Mark also, and one of the most obvious from the standpoint of Christology is in the application of titles to Jesus. In Mark there is considerable and intentional reserve in using the titles, as we have seen, and it is only with the confession of Peter that he is proclaimed as Messiah. In John there is no suggestion of secrecy or of delay in the use of the messianic titles. Rather, in the first chapter most of the titles, both those that are central and those of occasional use, are employed: he is designated Lamb of God (vv. 29, 35), Son of God (vv. 34, 49), Rabbi, or teacher (v. 38), Messiah (v. 41), King of Israel (v. 49), and Son of Man (v. 51). Previously, in the Prologue, the Incarnation has been affirmed as the divine Logos now become flesh and entered into human experience (vv. 1-18). There are other variations on the theme of sonship throughout the Gospel, but the only central title missing from this

---

[12]The arguments are reviewed in E. Haenchen, *John,* vol. 1 Hermeneia (Philadelphia: Fortress Press, 1984).

[13]E.g., R. Brown, *The Community of the Beloved Disciple* (New York: Paulist Press, 1979).

impressive list is that of Lord, which is found in the post resurrection setting in the confessional declaration of Thomas, "My Lord and my God!" (20:28). The writer is concerned to show that all these titles belong to Jesus, as the rest of the Gospel makes clear. Even before he begins his ministry, Jesus is recognized by John the Baptist ("Behold! The Lamb of God" 1:29) and by the disciples ("We have found the Messiah!" v. 41).

Important as the titles are to an understanding of Johannine Christology, other factors demand considerations as well. While there are clear differences between John and Mark, there are also features held in common—notably, a similar approach to a *theios aner* Christology. One of the sources standing behind the Fourth Gospel has been identified as a "Signs Source," probably a written document of some kind.[14] There is strong evidence that the emphasis on signs was in the form of an aretalogy with its focus on the divine man, comparable to that of traditions behind Mark. Like Mark, the writer of the Fourth Gospel presents the Christology of the divine man, but not uncritically. It is significant that in John the miracle stories are always referred to as signs, not just as miraculous acts of power. They are presented not as proof of the divine power of Jesus but as signs, as tokens of something quite different. E. Haenchen compares the use of the word *sign* with its occurrence in the story of Noah (Gen. 9:13-17), where the rainbow is likewise a "sign" that God will never again send such a deluge to destroy the earth and that he will remember his covenant with Noah.[15] Furthermore, Haenchen says, in commenting on the multiplication of the loaves and fish, "Anyone who experienced the miraculous feeding and then wanted to make Jesus king (6:15) did not really understand the sign precisely as sign (6:26). Otherwise they would have recognized that it pointed to the true salvific event, viz., that Jesus is the true bread from heaven."[16] The signs are to be seen, therefore, as pointers to who Jesus is and to the work of God now being accomplished in him. They are written, according to John's statement of purpose, to lead to faith in him as the Messiah, the Son of God.

Along with the use of the term *sign* in this positive sense by the Fourth Evangelist, there is also a rejection or critique of faith that is based on miracles, even as signs. To the official whose boy is healed at Cana, Jesus says, "Unless you see signs and wonders you will not believe" (John 4:48).

---

[14]Fortna argues that it is a Gospel; but even if it is a collection of miracle stories, it seems to have been a written document.

[15]Haenchen points out that the same word for sign is used in the LXX (*John* 95).

[16]Ibid.

This is the only reference to wonders in John, and it is understood in an unfavorable sense. One of the difficulties involved in the story is that, after this rather harsh statement and seeming refusal, Jesus did as the man requested and performed the miracle of healing. Raymond Brown's interpretation seems valid: "It was to lead him to a faith that would not be based on the wondrous aspect of the sign but on what the sign would tell him about Jesus. The man was led through the sign to faith in Jesus as the life-giver. . . . This fits in with the whole Johannine theology of signs."[17]

Central to the Christology of the Fourth Gospel is its emphasis on exaltation through suffering, on glorification through humiliation. Therefore any notion of glorification through the working of miracles in the *theios aner* tradition is rejected or placed in a very secondary position. The frequent occurrences of the verbs, usually in passive form, *to be lifted up* and *to be glorified* are theologically of primary significance. The lifting up of the Son of Man is understood in the double meaning of the verb as the physical lifting up in crucifixion and his lifting up in exaltation. This dying is, as in Mark, a matter of divine necessity. "Just as Moses lifted up the serpent in the wilderness, so must the Son of Man be lifted up" (John 3:14). Likewise when Jesus announces that, when he is lifted up from the earth, he will draw all men to himself, the Evangelist adds the comment "He said this signifying by what death he was about to die" (12:33). It may well be that the theme of the Suffering Servant stands behind the Johannine understanding, "Behold my servant shall prosper: he shall be lifted up and glorified exceedingly" (Isa. 52:13). In any case, the gospel writer intends to show that the lifting up of Jesus is both his death and his exaltation.

The glorification of Jesus is presented in the same kind of paradox: the hour of Jesus' humiliation and death is the hour of his glorification. Immediately after his words that the hour has come for the Son of Man to be glorified, he speaks of his death (John 12:23-24). Likewise in the prayer immediately prior to his Passion, he says, "The hour has come" and then speaks of glorification (17:1-5). The hour is at one and the same time the hour of crucifixion and the hour of glorification. Throughout the Fourth Gospel this paradox is true: the high point of exaltation is the humiliation of crucifixion, the glorification is in death. Crucifixion and resurrection should really be seen as a single event, and it is in this event as a totality that the exaltation is complete. It is recognized by the disciples, particu-

---

[17]R. Brown, *The Gospel according to John* (I-XII), Anchor Bible (Garden City NJ: Doubleday, 1966) 195. Brown also refers to the interesting parallel in Exod. 7:3-4, where God says to Moses, "Though I multiply my signs and wonders in the land of Egypt, Pharaoh will not listen to you" (p. 191).

larly in the words of the confession of Thomas, "My Lord and my God!" (20:18).

The theme of the revelation of the glory is to be seen in relation to the acts, words, and death of the earthly Jesus, yet how his life is to be understood has been sharply debated. E. Käsemann, as well as liberal theologians of an earlier period, have asserted that the Johannine Christ is presented as a divine figure walking about on earth, not really human and understood in quite Docetic terms.[18] For Käsemann the key statement is "We beheld his glory" (John 1:14). Others, like R. Bultmann, have taken the statement that "the Word became flesh" (v. 14) to mean that he really became a human being and this incarnation expressed in very realistic terms is crucial to an interpretation of the Christology of the Gospel. The difficulty lies, perhaps, in the whole question of the origin of Christ and the reality of the Incarnation. Unique to the Prologue of John is the hymnic presentation of the divine Logos (Word), closely associated with the personification of Wisdom in the Old Testament. This Logos has now entered into human history, has become flesh (*sarx*), and the language seems to reject any notion that he has not really become human. The reference to the revelation of his glory follows immediately after the assertion of his entrance into the human sphere, for it is in the realm of the historical that his glory is to be seen, especially in the Crucifixion and its humiliation.

The earthly life of Jesus in its entirety is understood also as the act of God. What he is, what he says, and what he does are consistently presented as originating with the Father. "God so loved the world that he gave his only Son" (John 3:16) is the affirmation that the whole of the gospel has its basis in the love of God. One of the most frequently recurring phrases relating to Johannine Christology is "the Father who sent me." For the Son to be sent by the Father means that he is here not on his own behalf but as representative of the Father. He does not speak his own words but those of the Father (4:34; 7:16; 8:26; 38, 40; 10:25, 37; 14:10, 24; 17:8), and he does not perform his own works but those of the Father (4:34; 5:17, 19, 30, 36; 8:28; 10:25, 37; 14:10, 17:4, 14). On this basis of the unity of words and actions of the Son with those of the Father, we understand what Jesus means when he says, "I and the Father are one" (10:30; 17:11, 21-22). The purposes and actions of Jesus are one with those of the Father, who is fully in charge, and there is no contradiction with the recognition that "the Father is greater than I" (14:28). As the one whom the Father has sent, Jesus does not seek his own glory but is completely devoted to

---

[18]E. Käsemann, *The Testament of Jesus* (London: SCM Press, 1968). Haenchen (*John*, 94) lists others who speak of the Christology of John in Docetic terms.

his Father. In humility he speaks the words of God and performs his acts, and in this is his honor and glory.

In concluding this brief summary of some of the distinctive features of Johannine Christology, I must mention the "I am" (*ego eimi*) sayings. It has been shown that these sayings in John belong mainly to a category described as "recognition formulas," in which the "I" is the predicate of the sentence.[19] The formulas provide answers to the question, "Who is the one whom we expect?" or "Where is the salvation, the light, the life that is to come?" In each instance the response is "It is I." The terminology that is used is drawn from the Old Testament and the language of the religious hopes and aspirations of the Jewish people. The claim is that the one who is expected to come and to fulfill their hopes is now present in the person of Jesus. The life, truth, bread, resurrection, and all that is part of the religious search are now come. Even those features that were traditional expectations of the future, such as the resurrection, are now present reality in the revelation of the one sent by the Father. It is noteworthy also that many of the kinds of images used in the Synoptic parables are now applied directly to the person of Jesus. The whole series of "I am" sayings and the use of the absolute "I am" formulation declare that Jesus and his words have divine quality, that the divine has become a historical and human reality in the earthly Jesus.

The Fourth Gospel has a profound and, in some senses, a unique Christological outlook. Jesus is above all Messiah, Son of Man, and Son of God, the one sent by the Father to accomplish his works. He is the divine Logos become flesh and entered into the realities of the human and the historical. He has revealed the Father and his glory, and his own glorification is not to be seen primarily in the miraculous acts as the divine man, for they are but pointers and signs to indicate that God's saving acts to give eternal life are now being performed. The glorification of Christ is to be seen rather in his humility and faithful performance of the works of God and the proclamation of his words. The glorification and exaltation are most clearly to be found in the paradoxical humiliation of the Crucifixion. The proper response is to recognize who he is, to believe in him as the Messiah, the Son of God, and in that belief to have life in his name. The Christology of John is directly related to soteriology, the giving of salvation and life as God's act of love.

---

[19]Brown, *Community of the Beloved Disciple*, 533-38, summarizes the arguments of R. Bultmann and E. Schweizer.

Matthew

It is now generally recognized that the Gospel of Matthew had its origins in a school situation at a time, probably in the 80s A.D., in which there was sharp conflict between the Christian congregation and the Jewish synagogue. This setting is to be understood as a school for teachers and church leaders, and in this context to a large extent the Gospel assumes the form of a manual for teaching and administration within the church. In this respect Matthew resembles some of the writings from the Qumran sect, notably the Manual of Discipline, which outlines the structure, order, and discipline of that community.[20] Furthermore, the form of interpretation of the Old Testament approaches that of the *pesher,* or commentary of a midrashic type from the same community. Here, more than in the other Gospels, the church and its order are explicitly in mind, so that the life and teaching of Jesus is presented in such a way as to provide direct instruction to the congregation addressed.

One of the significant features of Matthew is the manner in which he establishes the congregation's faith in Christ by references to the Scriptures of the Old Testament. In this Gospel more than in the others, the fulfillment of Scripture is the basis for understanding the identity of Jesus. Many of the messianic titles derive from Jewish writings about the Messiah, although by the time of writing they have become part of current Christian traditions. This is true of those that are clearly titles of majesty as well as those that characterize Jesus in terms of lowliness and meekness.

The presentation of the teachings of Jesus and his whole ministry as saving activity is to be seen in relation to the law of the Old Testament and to Moses the giver of the law. The division of the Gospel of Matthew into five sections of teaching and narrative is suggestive of the five books of Moses and also the fivefold division of the Psalms. Even more pointed is the way in which the first collection of teachings, the section known as the Sermon on the Mount, is presented. As Moses went up onto Mount Sinai to receive the law, so Jesus goes up onto the mount and utters his sayings (Matt. 5:1). The teachings themselves are presented under the motive of the fulfilling of the law (v. 17) and involve an interpretation of it. The Matthean Christology can be perceived as the setting of the messianic rank and authority of Jesus over against the teachings of the Pharisees and the scribes. The series of contrasts referred to as the antitheses (vv. 21-48) may be seen as the presentation of Jesus' messianic authority, for in each case the in-

---

[20]K. Stendahl, *The School of St. Matthew,* 2d ed. (Philadelphia: Fortress Press, 1968) 35.

terpretation represents an intensification of the Mosaic statement, taking it to its most radical intention. Some commentators have understood this contrast with Moses as Matthew's attempt to present Jesus through the contrasts with Moses as the giver of a new law, pointing to the Moses typology to establish the argument.[21] It is more accurate to say that the relationship to Moses is that of correspondence;[22] the law is not degraded but radicalized so that its proper meaning is brought out and is thereby fulfilled. It is important to note that the teaching of Jesus is the fulfilling of the law; he has the rank and dignity to interpret the law, an authority that can only be that of the Messiah.

Throughout his Gospel, Matthew understands Jesus as the Messiah, to whom belong the titles of majesty. A strong case can be made for regarding *Son of God* as the central Christological title.[23] At the outset in the birth narratives, it is made clear that Jesus is God's Son, conceived through the agency of the Holy Spirit. Matthew also introduces the confession of Jesus as Son of God at points where it is not present in Mark, notably at the episode at Caesarea Philippi. Matthew expands the simple confession of Peter, "You are the Messiah" as it is in Mark, to read "You are the Messiah, the Son of the Living God" (Matt. 16:16). In his dignity as Son of God, he is also the exalted Son of Man throughout his life and in eschatological expectation (26:63-64). Alongside these titles Matthew also has a number of titles of majesty drawn directly from Jewish life and thought. Jesus is the Son of David, the fulfillment of the prophetic promises for the establishment of a kingdom in Israel under the role of a future descendant of David. To Jesus as Son of David belong the acclamations of the crowd as he enters Jerusalem. Matthew alone of the Evangelists adds the title to the quotation of Psalms 118:25-26 with the words "Hosanna to the Son of David" (Matt. 21:9, 15). In similar fashion Matthew portrays Jesus more decisively than the other Gospels as King of Israel or King of the Jews.

Paradoxically, alongside the majestic characterization of Jesus, the Messiah, stands an emphasis upon his lowliness and humiliation. In his saving deeds he is the fulfillment of the prophecies of the Servant of God (note Matt. 8:17; 12:17-21). His miracles are not so much demonstrations

---

[21]E.g., G. D. Kilpatrick, *The Origins of the Gospel according to St. Matthew* (Oxford: Clarendon Press, 1946).

[22]G. Bornkamm, "End-Expectation and Church in Matthew," *Tradition and Interpretation in Matthew,* by G. Bornkamm, G. Barth, and H. Held (Philadelphia: Westminster Press, 1963) 35.

[23]As in J. D. Kingsbury, *Matthew: Structure, Christology, Kingdom* (Philadelphia: Fortress Press, 1978).

of his divinity and greatness as they are of his mercy; they are acts of kindness for the underprivileged and broken of humanity. The same is true of his teaching as he calls his followers to take his yoke upon them and learn from him, for he says, "I am gentle and lowly in heart" (11:29). The emphasis on lowliness is to be found also in the narrative of the triumphal entry into Jerusalem. Matthew alone quotes Zechariah 9:9, with its designation of the lowly king: "Behold, your king is coming to you, mounted humbly upon an ass, [and] upon a colt, the foal of an ass" (Matt. 21:5).[24] The humiliation is further stressed in the Passion narrative, where the Son of God, the kingly Messiah, suffers and dies in a voluntary act of obedience, and thus he fulfills all righteousness. The contrast is clear throughout Matthew that the exalted and majestic Messiah is gentle and humble, obedient and merciful.

A further and more difficult contrast in Matthew is that, over against this characterization of Jesus as gentle and kind, at least in his earthly life, is the severe note of judgment in his teaching. God refuses forgiveness to those who do not forgive others (Matt. 6:15; 18:35), and judgment is the principal function of the coming Son of Man. Vivid terms for judgment are used, such as "cast into outer darkness," "weeping and gnashing of teeth," and "punishment in eternal fire prepared for the devil and his angels" (note 25:30, 34, 36, 41, 46). As F. Beare notes, "The emphasis on Judgment is so pronounced as to cast a sombre pall over the picture of Jesus. . . . The terrors of the Day of Judgment hang perpetually over the heads of Matthew's readers."[25]

Matthew's presentation of the person of Jesus and his teaching have some correspondence also with rabbinic practices of contemporary Judaism. His teachings are often given in a form that is closely similar to that of the rabbis, and Matthew is clearly familiar with the methods of interpretation of the rabbis.[26] The frequent designation of Jesus as teacher or rabbi, especially by the Pharisees and by strangers (e.g., Matt. 8:2; 17:4; 20:33), indicates the importance of this feature of Matthean Christology. The sayings of Jesus are also given in forms of expression and in structures that recall rabbinic teachings.

---

[24]The introductory words are from Isa. 62:11, and it is remarkable, as Stendahl notes (*School of St. Matthew*, 119) that Matthew does not quote this text further, since especially the words "he is righteous and brings salvation, gentle and mounted upon an ass and a young colt" would constitute the very epitome of Matthew's Christology.

[25]F. W. Beare, *The Gospel according to Matthew* (San Francisco: Harper & Row, 1981) 43.

[26]Stendahl, *School of St. Matthew*, 119.

Going beyond this heightened recognition of Jesus as teacher or rabbi is his place as the teacher of wisdom. Close similarities to Jewish wisdom literature are to be seen in such passages as Matthew 6:25-34, with its instruction not to be anxious, partly because anxiety is fruitless but also because God, who is concerned for the birds and the flowers, cares even more for his children. The poetic forms and picturesque language as well as the universal care of God for his people are typical of wisdom teachings. Matthew goes beyond our understanding of Jesus as teacher of wisdom and even identifies him with personified Wisdom, or Sophia. Statements that originally were applied to Wisdom are now related directly to Jesus, such as "Wisdom is justified by her works" (11:19). In the words of Jesus' lament over Jerusalem, an original declaration made by Wisdom is now a statement of Jesus, and the material drawn from Q is altered to make the identification (23:37). Thus Jesus is understood to be not only a teacher of wisdom but is Wisdom incarnate.[27]

In conclusion we can say that Matthew presents Jesus in highly majestic terms, as Messiah with authority going beyond even that of the Mosaic law, as Son of God, and as Son of Man who comes in judgment. At the same time, he calls followers to him because he is gentle and humble in spirit, a servant of God who acts in mercy and love. In his suffering and death he is obedient to God, and in his humiliation as in his teaching he fulfills all righteousness.

Luke

In order to deal at all adequately with the Christology of Luke, it would be necessary to take into account the designation of Jesus in the Book of Acts as well as the Gospel of Luke. The issues in Acts are complicated by the fact that there are undoubtedly primitive sources behind the early chapters, making it difficult at points to be sure what should be regarded as the terms of the sources and what is Luke's own viewpoint. In addition the problem of the speakers confronts us throughout, raising the question as to how much, if any, the understanding is that of the speaker and how much it is Luke's theology, regardless of whose words they represent. Because of such questions and because our study is confined to the Gospels, attention here will focus entirely or at least primarily on the Gospel of Luke and the theology of the person of Christ reflected in it.

In contrast to Matthew, Luke writes for an audience that is predominantly Gentile Christian, and his narrative of the story of Jesus lacks the

---

[27]M. J. Suggs, *Wisdom, Christology, and Law in Matthew's Gospel* (Cambridge: Harvard University Press, 1970) 58, 63.

local Palestinian color and also lacks the direct citations of the Old Testament. More than the other Evangelists, Luke is a historian, shown obviously in the fact that he writes as a second volume of his work the Book of Acts, a history of the very early church. His historical interest is made clear in other features of his writing as well. He dates the life of Jesus in both Roman and Jewish history, in the time of Caesar Augustus when Quirinius was governor of Syria (Luke 2:1-2) and when Herod was King of Judea (1:5). His ministry begins in the fifteenth year of the rule of Tiberius Caesar, when Pontius Pilate was governor and when certain tetrarchs of various regions were in office (3:1). The historical concerns of Luke are important to his theological viewpoints, including his Christological outlook. Both history and geography relate to theology; dates and places play an important part in the interpretation of the life and ministry of Jesus.

While Luke is concerned to present the Christ event in a particular historical perspective, he is even more emphatic that the activity of Jesus is to be seen within an understanding of salvation history. The appearance of Jesus of Nazareth among humankind is seen as the carrying out of God's plan to bring salvation to human beings. The whole life and activity of Jesus is in accordance with a predetermined divine purpose: it is God's design (Luke 7:30), the Son of Man goes his way, as it had been determined (2:22), and the frequent use of "it is necessary"[28] all point to this sense of the fulfillment of a plan. Luke further interprets the events in accordance with the promises of the Old Testament in a thorough and decisive manner.[29]

In Luke's Gospel, Jesus stands at a particular place in this divine history of salvation, for he is at the center of time. Hans Conzelmann, in his influential book *The Theology of St. Luke,* summarizes Luke's understanding of history in three phases.

— The period of Israel, of the Law and the Prophets.

— The period of Jesus, which gives foretaste of future salvation.

— The period between the coming of Jesus and his Parousia, in other words, the period of the Church and of the Spirit. This is the last age.

We are not told that it will be short.[30]

---

[28]The term occurs many times in Luke (2:49; 4:43; 9:22; 13:33; 17:25; 19:5; 21:9; 24:7; 26, 44) as compared to once in Mark and once in Matthew. It is frequent in Acts also.

[29]J. Fitzmyer, *The Gospel according to Luke (I-IX),* Anchor Bible (Garden City NJ: Doubleday, 1981) 154.

[30]H. Conzelmann, *The Theology of St. Luke* (New York: Harper & Bros., 1960) 150. The title of the German original, *Die Mitte der Zeit,* is a more apt description of Conzelmann's focus and emphasis.

Luke's Christology and the whole understanding of the events of his ministry are set out within this emphasis on Christ as the center of time. The period of the law and the prophets was until John the Baptist (Luke 16:16), the forerunner who announces the imminent kingdom of God. He belongs to the old era; the new epoch begins with Jesus. This now is the decisive moment in the salvation history, the time when the kingdom of God was preached, the time when salvation in God's plan is actually achieved.

The ministry of Jesus is marked in Luke's Gospel by several clearly defined features. The Holy Spirit has a very important place in relation to his life, his preaching, and his acts. In the annunciation of the birth of Jesus to Mary, the announcing angel says to her, ''The Holy Spirit will come upon you, and power from the Most High will overshadow you. Therefore, the child to be born will be called holy—Son of God'' (Luke 1:35). At his baptism he sees the Holy Spirit descend upon him in bodily form as a dove, along with the heavenly voice he declares, ''You are my beloved son, with you I am well pleased'' (3:22). Following the temptation scene, the devil leaves Jesus for the time of his ministry, and he goes ''in the power of the Spirit into Galilee,'' where he begins his ministry (4:14). The first act in the Galilean ministry is to read in the synagogue at Nazareth from the book of the prophet Isaiah:

> The Spirit of the Lord is upon me, for he has anointed me to preach
> good news to the poor.
> He has sent me to proclaim release to the captives, and recovering
> of sight to the blind,
> to set at liberty those who are oppressed,
> to proclaim the acceptable year of the Lord.

(vv. 18-19)

With these and many other references Luke has placed emphasis upon the presence of the Holy Spirit throughout Jesus' life and ministry and presents Jesus as consciously aware of the influence of the Spirit on him. He does not act on his own but within the plan of God and the power of the Spirit.

The same quotation from Isaiah introduces in capsule form Luke's view of the ministry of Jesus. The bold assertion that follows the words of the prophet, ''Today this Scripture is fulfilled,'' is unmistakable: a new age is dawning in the ministry of Jesus, the kingdom of God is announced (Luke 4:43) and indeed is present (17:21). He is for Luke ''the kingdom-preacher par excellence,''[31] and his preaching is part of the divine plan: ''It is necessary

---

[31]Fitzmyer, *Gospel according to Luke*, 154.

for me to preach the kingdom of God, because for this I was sent'' (4:43). In Luke, as Conzelmann has noted, John the Baptist does not proclaim the kingdom, for this is the distinctive role of the Messiah, whose coming is decisively bound up with the arrival of the kingdom and its announcement.[32]

The quotation of Isaiah 61:1-2 presents a further understanding of the ministry of Jesus in Luke's Gospel—namely, that the concern for the poor, the captives, the blind, and the oppressed is a demonstration of the coming of the kingdom. The first disciples are called in Luke following the occurrence of some exorcisms and healings, and the call itself is accompanied by a miraculous catch of fish (Luke 5:1-11). The answer to the question posed by the disciples of John[33] as to whether Jesus is ''the One who is to come'' is given as a reference to his acts—''the blind receive sight, the lame walk, those who have leprosy are cured, the deaf hear, the dead are raised, and the good news is preached to the poor'' (7:22). In Luke's Gospel the signs and wonders are regarded as the evidence that he is ''the Coming One,'' in similar understanding to the words of Peter's sermon on the Day of Pentecost: ''Jesus of Nazareth, a man attested to you by God with mighty works and wonders and signs which God did through him in your midst'' (Acts 2:22). Jesus' messiahship is to be seen in the miraculous deeds; they are the demonstration that Scripture is being fulfilled and the evidence of the time of salvation now present in Christ.

For the most part, Luke's use of the central Christological titles *Messiah, Son of God,* and *Son of Man* does not differ markedly from the other Synoptic Gospels. There are, however, distinctive interpretations at certain points. The title *Messiah* is one of the frequently used titles and should be regarded as the most important. He is announced as Messiah at his birth (Luke 2:11), and he is confessed as the Lord's Messiah (v. 26) and as the Messiah of God (9:20; 23:35). As the Christ he is God's specially anointed agent to be the bearer of a new salvation to humankind, as is seen in his proclamation of the kingdom and his deeds, which are manifestations of its arrival. Consistent with Luke's presentation of the events of Jesus' life as divinely determined is his account of the Crucifixion. Early in the story of the ministry is the beginning of the journey to Jerusalem, the place of his death. For Luke this is the voluntary journey to the Crucifixion, and Jesus resolutely set out for Jerusalem (9:51). His death is also understood as the fulfillment of Scripture and as part of God's plan: ''Was it not nec-

---

[32]Conzelmann, *Theology of St. Luke,* 23.

[33]Note the contrast with John 1, where John the Baptist is the first to recognize and proclaim Jesus as the Messiah.

essary for the Christ to suffer these things and to enter into his glory?''
(24:26). Most emphatic is the expression of the necessity of the suffering
of Jesus as Messiah.

Luke also uses the title *Son of God* in a manner that virtually equates
it with *Messiah*. As Messiah he is king from the line of David, as is clear
in the birth story; even more, however, he is Son of God. When Jesus casts
out demons, they acknowledge that he is the Son of God, and Luke adds
the comment that ''they knew that he was the Messiah'' (Luke 4:41). The
divine sonship is emphasized also in the genealogy, as Luke traces the origin of Jesus through David to Adam, the son of God (3:38). As the Son
of God Jesus is conceived by the Holy Spirit, who empowers him for his
ministry; he knows the Father (10:22), renders to him complete obedience
(4:1-13), and is the bearer of the kingdom of God.

The title *Lord* is the most frequently used title for Jesus in Luke-Acts,
and it obviously has great importance for the author. It is generally reserved for postresurrection affirmations, but for Luke it can be applied to
Jesus even at his birth. In the sermon of Peter in the Book of Acts, it is
asserted that it was on the basis of the resurrection that ''God made him
both Lord and Messiah, this Jesus whom you crucified'' (Acts 2:36). In
his Gospel, however, Luke recognizes that, even at his birth, Jesus' messiahship and lordship may rightly be proclaimed; he is born ''a Saviour,
who is Christ the Lord'' (Luke 2:11). Unlike the other Gospels, Luke uses
this title with considerable frequency where the Evangelist himself is
speaking.[34] The fact that he also uses the same term for God indicates that
for Luke, Christ is now to be regarded in some sense as transcendent in
character, and the quality of lordship belonging to God is now extended to
Jesus, especially in his risen status.[35]

Finally, mention should be made of the ending of Luke's Gospel. Luke
is the only gospel writer to include a story of ascension (Luke 24:50-53).
His understanding is that, after the Crucifixion and Resurrection, Christ
entered into his glory through an ascension to the right hand of God. He is
therefore not present with the church, and instead it is the Holy Spirit who
now comes to be with the people of God. How different is the word of Christ
to his disciples, ''While I was still with you'' (24:44) from that in Matthew, ''I am with you always'' (Matt. 28:20).

---

[34]Luke 7:13, 19; 10:1, 39, 41; 11:39; 12:42; 13:15; 17:5, 6; 18:6; 19:8, 31, 34; 22:61,
24:3, 34.

[35]For a discussion of the difficulties involved in the background of the title, note Fitzmyer, *Gospel according to Luke*, 201.

Other Gospels:
Limits to Diversity

The varieties of Christological reflection are obvious even from this very brief analysis of the person and ministry of Jesus in the four canonical Gospels. The Evangelists write out a variety of backgrounds and present different interpretations in accordance with their own traditions and personal faith. In part also the diversity is due to their concerns for the needs of the congregations for which they write. Christian communities were different in character in various localities and times, with the result that accounts of the person and work of Christ were properly diverse in expression and emphasis as he was related to the life of specific congregations. The differences in theological formulation would be seen to be even more diverse if the study were broadened to include the pre-Pauline traditions, the letters of Paul and the deutero-Pauline epistles, as well as the Book of Hebrews, the General Epistles, and the Book of Revelation. The varieties of Christology are extensive and must not be overlooked. At the same time, however, there are features pointing to a basic unity as the early Christians recognized that, in the midst of diversity, it was necessary to set limits. These limits in Christology are clear especially in the struggles with Gnosticism in the second century.

The recognition of theological diversity within the New Testament and early Christian writing has not always had its rightful place in scholarship. In this regard Walter Bauer's book, published in English with the title *Orthodoxy and Heresy in Earliest Christianity*,[36] has had an impact on New Testament scholarship. Written originally in 1934, it did not appear in English until 1971, but his thesis is now taken seriously. Bauer's main purpose is to take issue with the long-dominant view that heresy in the first Christian centuries represented a later perversion of an original orthodoxy. Basing his study on an examination of Christianity in various parts of the Roman Empire, Bauer discovered that the lines between orthodoxy and heresy were not clearly drawn. Christian thought and practice in the first and second centuries took different forms in different areas. Since the criteria for orthodoxy were not determined, it is not legitimate to speak about heresy, even if some early theological formulations could be judged as heretical according to later standards. More recently James Dunn has attempted to define the diversity of New Testament viewpoints on a number of theological themes, including concepts of ministry, patterns of worship,

---

[36]W. Bauer, *Orthodoxy and Heresy in Earliest Christianity* (Philadelphia: Fortress Press, 1971).

the sacraments, the Spirit, Christian experience, and others.[37] He is also concerned to find the basic unity that holds the documents of the New Testament together. Dunn sets that unity almost exclusively in the person of Christ as the focus of the church's teaching and preaching, as well as its confessional formulas, its worship and ritual.

Attempts to write about New Testament theology in recent years have recognized the difficulties involved in the varieties of outlook and expression. As a result for several decades few books were written on the theology of the New Testament, and instead we have studies on the teaching of Jesus, the theology of John or Paul or Luke. The same characteristic is true in major studies on New Testament theology, with works divided into sections on Jesus, Paul, John, and so forth.[38] The problem of defining a New Testament theology is intensified by the fact that we are dealing with a collection of documents that represents only a small part of the thought and reflection of the early church. In addition there is no attempt to write a systematic study on a theological theme for the implications for the life of believers as the church worked out its place as a new community within the world. Attention must be paid to differences of time and place, to divergences and even contradictions; we must not force uniformity of thought where it does not exist, either in matters of Christology or in other themes of theology.

It is also important to recognize that there is a unity in the Gospels and a distinctiveness that sets them apart from other writings, sometimes called gospels, that were not included in the canon of the New Testament. There is first of all a unity of purpose, as each Evangelist is concerned to proclaim the gospel of Jesus Christ. The Gospels are not to be read as biographies or histories but as Gospels, a distinct and new genre of literature. The content of each focuses not on the life of Jesus but on his ministry of teaching and the performance of acts of healing. The climax of all four Gospels is the Passion narrative and above all the Crucifixion and Resurrection. Jesus is declared to be the Messiah, the Son of God, to whom belong all the Christological titles. Readers are called to recognize him and to confess him in these terms. This kerygmatic purpose, to declare the gospel of Jesus Christ, distinguishes the Gospels from other literary genres.

We find a unifying factor also in that the same person—Jesus of Nazareth, a historical man—is at the center of the formulations. This fact may

---

[37]J. D. G. Dunn, *Unity and Diversity in the New Testament* (Philadelphia: Westminster Press, 1977).

[38]Kümmel, *Theology of the New Testament*.

seem obvious, but it needs to be stated because of its importance. The reality of the historical Jesus as a human being, as the man from Nazareth who lived, suffered, died, was buried, and then was raised from the dead is at the heart of the gospel. The gospel writers all look back at the story of Jesus from the perspective of the post-Easter situation and interpret his life through the Crucifixion and Resurrection. Throughout they maintain the identity of the Jesus of earthly life and the risen, exalted Lord. This continuity has led to severe problems of interpretation, as Ernst Käsemann notes: "The heart of our problem lies here; the exalted Lord has almost entirely swallowed up the image of the earthly Lord and yet the community maintains the identity of the exalted Lord with the earthly."[39] Around that central focus the church could keep in tension a considerable diversity of viewpoints and accept the variety as part of the richness of its thought and message.

The central place of the historical Jesus distinguishes the four Gospels of the New Testament from other gospels that were written by early Christians. The typical Gnostic gospel was characterized by discourse or dialogue. The Gospel of Thomas, for example, one of the earliest Gnostic gospels, contains a collection of parables and other sayings of Jesus. In many respects the words of Jesus are close to the form in which they are found in the canonical Gospels. Lacking is any narrative of the ministry of Jesus, and totally absent is the Passion narrative; these are not of theological significance for the writer. The words of Jesus are introduced as "The secret sayings which the living Jesus spoke and which Didymos Judas Thomas wrote down," and they are understood as words of life. The Gospel of Truth, more decisively Gnostic in its emphasis, is likewise a reflection or meditation on the gospel, which is basically about the eternal Son, the Word who brings knowledge of the Father. In receiving this knowledge, including the knowledge of where the Gnostic comes from and where he is going, life is to be found. Again there is no focus on the words and deeds of the historical Jesus. These and other gospels not included in the canon of the New Testament are concerned with words of the "living Jesus" or the risen Lord, not of the earthly man of Nazareth. There may even be a rejection of the historical as a result of a theological outlook based on an emphasis exclusively on the presence of the eternal living one or the exalted Lord. In this respect such documents clearly are to be distinguished from the New Testament writings, which consider the reality of Jesus' earthly life to be of importance and especially his crucifixion. To

---

[39]E. Käsemann, "The Problem of the Historical Jesus," in *Essays on New Testament Themes* (London: SCM Press, 1964) 213.

reject the historical Jesus is to go beyond the limits of diversity as eventually accepted in the church.[40]

In other respects also the reality of the earthly Jesus was not shared by all Christians and came to be at the heart of the early church's struggle to define correct doctrine. The interpretation referred to as Docetism, from the Greek verb "to seem" or "to appear," was one of the earliest theological formulations to be rejected as heretical. While Docetism is expressed in a variety of terms, at its basis is the notion that Jesus was essentially divine and that, in his earthly life, his human form was only an appearance. He seemed to be human and to suffer, but this appearance was not reality. Lying behind such Docetic interpretation is the dualistic understanding in which the world of spirit and that of the physical are sharply distinguished. The world of spirit is the world above, the realm of the divine, and it is entirely good. The material world, on the other hand, is basically evil, and it is therefore impossible that the divine could become a real part of the physical. Hence it is necessary to reject a theology stating that the divine Christ became a real part of the physical and historical. His bodily form and especially his suffering and death could not have been real; they must be regarded as appearance only. This kind of interpretation was widespread in the early church and was typical of second-century Gnosticism. It must be kept in mind that the Gnostics were Christians, they were part of the church, representing a tendency from within, not an attack from outside. It seems likely, in fact, that in some places, notably Alexandria, Gnostics may well have been a majority for a time. In any case the struggle against the theology of Docetism involved Christians in an intense debate, with the result that the Docetic understanding was rejected.

In its broad outline Gnosticism represents in a radical sense the diversity within early Christianity. With regard to Christology the diversity was too great to be tolerated, and the church affirmed both the divinity and humanity of Christ. The criterion of the earthly Jesus is essential and marks one of the central distinctions between the New Testament writings, especially the Gospels, and those of the Gnostics. The Living One cannot be separated from the historical Jesus, including his life and his death. The insistence on the reality of the humanity of Jesus is clear in the assertion of the Fourth Gospel that "the Word became flesh" (John 1:14). The realistic term *sarx* (flesh) is used to emphasize the entrance of the divine Word

---

[40]Note the Gnostic gospels and other documents included in J. M. Robinson, ed., *The Nag Hammadi Library in English* (New York: Harper & Row, 1977). A helpful discussion of some other noncanonical gospels can be found in J. D. Crossan, *Four Other Gospels* (Minneapolis: Winston Press, 1985).

into the realm of the physical and historical, not in appearance only but in reality. At the death of Jesus, John says that, with the spear wound, "there came out water and blood" (19:34), again to stress the reality of the physical and of death.

The rejection of Docetism is direct and explicit in the First Epistle of John. Here the one who denies that Jesus is the Christ is called the liar or the Antichrist (1 John 2:22), for this is a denial of the Father and the Son. The criterion for the recognition of the Spirit of God is the same: "Every spirit that acknowledges that Jesus Christ has come in the flesh is from God, but every spirit that does not acknowledge Jesus is not from God. This is the spirit of the antichrist" (4:2-3). Ignatius, bishop of Antioch in the early part of the second century, carries on the same kind of polemic in his repeated insistence that Jesus was really born, really lived, really suffered, really died and was buried, and really rose again. Docetism represented a form of Christological interpretation that went beyond the limits of diversity to be tolerated as authentic Christian theology and hence was rejected. Of central importance to the Christian Gospel is the understanding of the person of Christ as one who has fully shared human experience with the limitations of the physical. He is the carpenter of Nazareth who through his ministry, crucifixion, and resurrection is recognized and confessed as the Messiah, the Son of God.

Implications

Recognition of the diversity and also the unity of gospel formulations has important implications both for New Testament interpretation and for contemporary Christian life and thought. As far as New Testament study is concerned, we must allow the diversity to stand and not assume that all writers are saying the same thing. They write out of different perspectives, and the variety of theological outlook is part of the richness of the Scriptures. We also affirm that, at the heart of the canonical Gospels and indeed the entire New Testament, there lies a basic unity in the person of Jesus Christ. In any Christian theology that personal unity is the central focus and must be the core of our theological formulations and our confession. Along with the varieties of thought and expression, the criterion of the historical Jesus who is the Christ, the Son of God, is essential. To lose sight of this center leads to a diversity too great to be tolerated as authentic Christian theology.

The very nature of this aspect of the New Testament ought to lead us to delight in the varieties of theological affirmation in the church of our time. In our varied situations and with our personal differences, we too can tolerate as broad a diversity of theological positions. Any attempt to reject those who hold to constructions other than our own and to force a unity on Christian doctrine does not take seriously the diversity within the New Testament itself. There are, however, limits to the diversity if theology is to be Christian thought; Christologically, we must stand with the Gospels of the New Testament. Their theology is focused on the gospel of Jesus Christ, on the Word become flesh, whose life and ministry demonstrate this messiahship. Most clearly in his crucifixion and resurrection, he is to be seen as the Messiah, the Son of God, and this assertion lies at the heart of our theology, our confession of faith, and our worship.

Chapter Four

Christology and Soteriology: Past Connections and Present Missed Connections

Patrick T. R. Gray

My own work is on the end of the age of the church fathers. In that work my fundamental question is "What happens somewhere between the fifth and the seventh centuries that brings the age of the fathers to an end?" One part of the answer has become clear. When the church came to the view that the great doctrines had been settled by councils such as Nicaea and Chalcedon, and by the great champions of orthodoxy such as Athanasius and Cyril of Alexandria, then its understanding of what it meant to do theology changed drastically. The church fathers of the earlier period had really done theology; that is, they had tried to articulate their religious self-understanding in a way that grew organically out of their own religious experience and out of their reflection upon Scripture. The age came to an end when theologians came to see their task as defending and systematizing the theology worked out by their predecessors. Only then was it possible to speak of "the orthodox faith" and to understand oneself as a good Christian theologian if one attempted to defend it.

My work is with those who end the age of the church fathers, but my heart is with the earlier fathers who were really doing theology. To my mind, the theological enterprise is genuine and healthy only when it grows organically out of experience. One has a real theology when one has reflected on one's life and found a way to articulate how in that life one has experienced the transformation we call salvation; one has a real Christian theology when that transformation was experienced in relation to Jesus Christ and when it is articulated in terms that adequately account for his role. In short, one has a real Christian theology when Christology (the doctrine about Christ) springs organically from soteriology (the doctrine about salvation).

In what follows, I shall begin by making some comments about the lack of such an organic connection in much contemporary theology, and then I shall attempt to show how, in some church fathers (and in the heretics who opposed them), there was such a great connection between Christology and soteriology. My point is to illustrate what it is that we have lost. I shall then offer some reflections on theological education, arguing that theological education should return to the patristic mode—enabling students to do theology, to articulate a Christology out of soteriology—rather than remain in the postpatristic mode that seeks only to teach and defend established doctrine.

Present Missed Connections

The modern malaise may be illustrated by the plight of students assigned an essay pertaining to some church fathers' soteriology and its relation to Christology (they might be students in any Protestant seminary in North America). Such students have difficulty even attempting to say anything about soteriology. They may often have a good deal to say about many aspects of the writer assigned, including some fairly perceptive things about his Christology—falling with glad cries on statements that sound orthodox from a modern conservative Protestant student's point of view—but precious little about soteriology, or any understanding of how it might have a connection with Christology.

This situation seems strange. Christianity, as a religion, exists on the basis of a soteriological claim: God has saved humanity through Jesus Christ. If Christianity was not founded on that claim, it is hard to imagine what other foundation it could properly be said to have. It is not, like the secular university, dedicated to the pursuit of objective truth. If it were, the Christological claims—statements about the being of Jesus—would be central; it would be Christianity's proper business to identify that reality, in the way that scholars investigate the reality of subatomic particles or the soundness of a historical interpretation. Early Christianity's undignified squabbles about Christology often suggest that "getting the doctrine right" was its central concern, but in fact the implicit issue beneath those squabbles was always the reality of the salvation that believers felt they had experienced in Christ Jesus.

How then do modern Christians happen to have such difficulty with saying anything about soteriology and with relating it to Christology? What is there about the modern situation that leads to this missed connection between doctrines that seemingly ought to have the most intimate connection?

When asked about soteriology, more-or-less conservative Protestants always end up owning to a soteriology of substitutionary atonement in some form or other. It almost always turns out that this is the view they have been taught and that they inherited from Calvin through the tradition. When asked about Christology, they claim in a rather vague way to be "Chalcedonian" (conservatives, sensing that Catholics and liberal Protestants are perhaps casting themselves adrift from the Council of Chalcedon, seem strangely anxious to defend it!), though further questioning reveals that their Christology is really more Nicene—that is, they like a good high Christology with a strong emphasis on the divinity of Christ; the niceties of Chalcedon, with its concern for balancing the human nature with the divine nature and for positing their union in one person and hypostasis, are all Greek to them. At any rate, what they have is a traditional Christology inherited from the fourth century and a traditional soteriology inherited from the sixteenth. This is not to say that a Calvinist soteriology is incompatible with a Nicene Christology. Indeed, for Calvin, Nicene Christology was in some sense presupposed. It is to say that modern Protestants maintain two separate traditional viewpoints (and can produce the soteriological viewpoint only when pressed), without any sense of a living connection between them. It is certainly not the living connection of the Nicene fathers, (Christ must be divine since he has saved me in such-and-such a way that I have experienced and that is the religious center of my being) or even of Calvin. Rather, one suspects there is another soteriological issue hidden in the underbrush behind the Christology they maintain: I cannot be saved unless I maintain the "right doctrine" of Christ. But let that pass. The crucial point is the absence of a living connection rooted in an experience of salvation.

Two questions arise for theological education. First, can a way be found of helping young Christians studying for the ministry to understand, believe, and formulate doctrines, not as traditional formulas demanding acquiescence (as if faith were something like the Red Queen's ability to believe five impossible things before breakfast!), but as forms giving expression to living experience in the way they did for the original formulators of those doctrines? To put it another way, can students be helped to *do theology,* rather than to learn someone else's theology? Is it not, in the end, more orthodox to do theology authentically than to repeat the formulas of others?

People have so much difficulty with soteriology for another reason, one that is symptomatic of a wider modern problem. When they turn to the great histories of doctrine or to the great studies of patristic Christology, they find no help in addressing the question of soteriology. The fact is that such histories deal with soteriology in appendixes or not at all, and they deal with Christology as if the point was to "get the doctrine correct" about Christ, quite apart from any living religious concern for salvation in Christ. In other words, modern historians have not generally understood or described the living connection and have abstracted Christology from its real situation in life. No wonder that people are unable to see the connection: the modern approach has tended almost universally to ignore it. This critique raises a further important pedagogical issue: can we move beyond the entirely artificial "history" that sees doctrines as disembodied forms arguing with each other and instead understand them as the expressions of living religious experience? In our teaching, can we go on to put our students in touch with this active doing of theology in the past, as a stimulus and guide to the doing of theology in the present?

Past Connections

So far only the "present missed connections" of the title have been identified. No doubt questions have been missed to which one cannot give very satisfactory answers. An attempt will be made at the end to offer some suggestions about where answers might lie. In the main body of this chapter we turn to the "past connections" between Christology and soteriology that exist in an authentic and natural way in the writings of some important patristic figures. We shall concentrate on two famous controversies, the Arian and the Nestorian, to illustrate the case.

First, though, note that some very recent work of historians *has* begun to point out the connections in much of early Christian literature. Elaine Pagels's popular *Gnostic Gospels* points to the connection, for instance, between the superhuman Gnostic redeemer and the Gnostic vision of escape from this world as redemption.[1] Suddenly the (to us) arid and endless cosmic genealogies of the Gnostics have a point and a dynamic thrust. They are not meant, primarily, to describe the structure of reality but to provide a roadmap of the limitations of life in the lower cosmos. Within the New Testament, too, the connections are appearing. Helmut Koester, in *Trajectories through Early Christian Literature,* has pointed to the connection, for example, between the Christology of Matthew (Jesus as the Wisdom of God) and his soteriology (Christians are saved by following the commandments of Jesus).[2] Other things besides Christology follow from the soteriological center. To use the example of Matthew again, the church is

---

[1]E. Pagels, *The Gnostic Gospels* (New York: Random House, 1981).

[2]H. Koester, "One Jesus and Four Primitive Gospels," in *Trajectories through Early Christianity,* by J. M. Robinson and H. Koester (Philadelphia: Fortress, 1971) 158-204.

to be a school ("Make disciples of all men, teaching them all that I have commended you") whose authority is expressed on the rabbinic model of the power of the keys. A similar case could be made for every writer in the New Testament.

The apostolic father Ignatius of Antioch seems to be maintaining a high Christology when he speaks of Jesus as "God and flesh." It turns out that the statement is soteriological, not Christological: the problem of evil is the problem of a cosmic schizophrenia of which the alienation of flesh from spirit is the most profound symptom; Jesus' transformation in his resurrection creates a new humanity in which God and flesh are reconciled and the great division overcome. Again other corollaries follow: because salvation brings unity, the authority of the bishop in the church must be absolute so that, through their common submission to him, there may be unity among Christians; because salvation at its fullest is the transformation of flesh into resurrected flesh at one with spirit, the martyr is the truest disciple of Jesus, and Ignatius actively seeks a martyr's death to become a "true disciple." These few examples must suffice to show how central was the place of soteriology in the earliest period of church's life. As Melvyn Hillmer shows in chapter 3, there is considerable diversity among the New Testament Christologies. It follows that there was an equal diversity of soteriologies too, if, as has been argued here, Christology corresponds to soteriology and, indeed, flows out of it.

When we come to the Arian controversy, we are at once reminded of the tendency of modern historians to miss the soteriological issue. This controversy has traditionally been viewed as a confrontation between the high Christology of Athanasius, who maintained that the Word of God was of the same order of being as God the Father, and the low Christology of Arius, who argued that, since the Word was "First-begotten," it could not have equality with the Father and must be a creature. They were both, in this view, concerned with the nature of God and the consequences that must follow. A recent landmark study by two American scholars, Robert Gregg and Dennis Groh, argues convincingly for a different view. The title of their book candidly states their case: *Early Arianism—A View of Salvation.*[3] In their view the controversy began, not with Arius, but with the thrust of what they call "Alexandrian episcopal theology" toward developing an "essential link between the Son and the Father." This thrust threatened not so much Arius's Christology as his soteriology. But this same Alexandrian episcopal theology is itself no exercise in abstract Christology, but a cor-

---

[3]R. Gregg and D. Groh, *Early Arianism—A View of Salvation* (Philadelphia: Fortress, 1981).

ollary of a radically different soteriological stance. The Arian controversy, then, while superficially a clash of Christologies, is at its core the clash of antithetical soteriological stances.

The connection between soteriology and Christology in the Alexandrian episcopal theology was stated succinctly by Bishop Alexander early in the controversy: "Only as natural offspring of the divine paternal essence could the Word, by assuming flesh, renew and deify humanity, securing it in imperishability."[4] This soteriology was expressed in nearly identical terms by Athanasius in his *On the Incarnation of the Word,* dating from his early ministry (before the Arian controversy began): "God became man, that man might become God." As he spelled it out, fallen human beings, by falling away from close fellowship with the Word, lost both that fellowship (which elevated human nature beyond its natural limitations) and their consequent immortality. The assumption of the Hellenistic world that made this soteriology seem workable was the assumption that the soul was able to be transformed into the likeness of whatever it knew—it could become more carnal if it paid attention to physical, fleshly things or more spiritual if it paid attention to divine things. Hence it could become "divine" and immortal if it paid attention to the Word, but only if the Word really were divine.

It is not difficult to see, though, that this process of divinization that constituted salvation for Athanasius was impossible if the Word was not really divine—that is, of the same essence ("consubstantial," as we have it in the Nicene Creed's usual translation) as the Father. To become one with the Son, as the Christian was held to do, was not divination and the basis of secure immortality if the Word of God was only a creature, however elevated. Athanasius gave a harsh caricature of what he took to be the implications of the Arians' view that the Word was a creature and therefore not the possessor of absolute being: "In thinking to be baptized into the name of one who exists not, they will receive nothing; and ranking themselves with a creature, from the creature they will have no help, and believing in one unlike and foreign to the Father in essence, to the Father they will not be joined, not having his Son by nature. . . . The wretched men henceforth remain destitute and stripped of the Godhead."[5] This passage illustrates, too, the central role played by sacraments in the orthodox view: divinization is communicated through baptism and Eucharist. One should note, as well, the emphasis on grace in this view. Salvation is accomplished by the Incarnation and merely received by the Christian.

---

[4]Ibid., 50.

[5]Ibid., 47.

Thanks to Gregg and Groh, we can compare the Athanasian position with the views of Arius with some precision. The Arians certainly believed that the Word and Son preexisted his incarnation—no one since the trial of Paul of Samosata had dared to think otherwise—but they did not believe that the Word was the essence of the Father. Why? Gregg and Groh put it simply: "Salvation for Arianism is effected by the Son's identity with the creatures."[6] It does not matter whether one speaks of the Son's preexistent being as Word or of his human existence in the Incarnation; still, as a creature he could not be unchangeable in principle. He had free moral choice and could have sinned. Now the Arians, whatever Athanasius said against them, had no desire to downgrade the Son or imply that he was in fact sinful. In fact, they held that he did not sin and so *moved* (on the model of Stoic ethical progress) from uncertainty to "apathy"—the incapacity to be changed by any external force—and so from changeability to unchangeability. The Word was therefore "Son," not by nature (the Arians abhorred Athanasius's biological reading of the Word), but by adoption, even as Christians become children of God by adoption. He can be called God and divine, but only in the sense that any perfected creature (for instance, the Stoic sage) led the "life of a God." Since the Arians held that all creatures, including the Word, are fundamentally the products of God's will, the fulfillment of creaturehood is expressed in obedience above all else. To the Arians, the Son's life, from his assistance in creation through to the supreme example of the cross, was a work of conforming "his life and work to the Creator's will."

All of this means that the Arians, "seeing redemption in a creature. . . . beheld the shape of their own redemption."[7] That is, in the ethical progress of the Word, and especially in his life as Jesus, he provided a model that was salvific, not only in what it taught humanity to do (i.e., obey God's will), but in the hope it offered on the basis of Jesus' triumph demonstrated on the cross and in the reward that followed in his resurrection. In this context, "grace" meant the adoption as children of God of those who followed Jesus' progress in wisdom, stature, and favor with God.

From a modern viewpoint Arianism may be thought to have a good deal to be said for it. It did full justice to the humanity of Jesus, so clearly asserted by the first and second centuries in the struggle with Gnosticism. It made better sense than Athanasius could of passages like Psalm 44, Proverbs 8:22, Acts 2:36, and Hebrews 1:4 and 3:1-2. Indeed, Arius had stud-

---

[6]Ibid., 8.

[7]Ibid., 26, 59.

ied under Lucian in Antioch and probably acquired from him an interest in the literal meaning of the text. At Alexandria before the crisis, his claim to fame was as a teacher of Wednesday and Friday Bible studies. In his own time his followers were by no means unaware of the potential attractiveness of the position to monks, for whom the struggle of the will to attain absolute obedience to God was very much at the heart of their desert asceticism. Gregg and Groh see evidence that the *Life of Antony*, published by the Arians' arch enemy, Athanasius, stresses underneath what may be Athanasius's editorial "corrections"—qualities like willingness, desire, and fixed purpose in Antony—which are precisely the qualities required for the obedience so dear to Arius and his followers.

Be that as it may, Gregg and Groh have made a convincing case for the view that soteriology is as much the central issue for the Arians as it is for Athanasius. If Athanasius required a Christology of absolute equality in essence with the Father so that the flesh of Jesus, and the rest of humanity united with it by grace, could be divinized, the Arians on their side required a Christology in which the Word and Son participated fully in creaturehood so that he could provide an example of the obedience to which all Christians were called and of the reward in resurrection that obedience would bring. For Athanasius, Jesus' sonship was unique; for Arius, sonship was the goal of Christian life for all believers. Modern critics of Athanasius's view have argued convincingly that the humanity of Jesus, while asserted, has no real function: it is the Word who renews human nature by his union with it and who grants it immortality, so that it may be said to be divinized. They have felt that Athanasius's nonliteral interpretation of texts led him far from their intended meaning. But let us not lose sight of the point that, whichever side of the controversy one speaks of, Christology is not a matter of abstract concern, a matter of getting the truth about the being of Jesus Christ set down correctly in writing. Christology is for them a living issue precisely because it is connected with real people's real sense of what salvation has meant to them. For the Alexandrian episcopal theology of Athanasius (which we, after the fact, usually call "orthodoxy") as for the school of Arius (which we, after the fact, call "heresy"), Christology is a function and an expression of one's whole experience of participating in the saving mysteries of Christ, illuminated by Scripture. For them Christology is by no means the functionless dogma of so many moderns. For them Christology and soteriology are not separate dogmas, inherited from different traditions and defended in the name of traditional orthodoxy. For both groups Christology is part of the struggle to do theology out of their experience of salvation.

If we look now at a later controversy, that between Cyril and Nestorius, a conflict that could be said to have had its outcome in the Council of

Chalcedon and the Second Council of Constantinople, we can see a similar conflict between experienced soteriologies at the heart of the controversy, however rarified the theological discussion may become. No one can deny that (1) Cyril and Nestorius were both unpleasant people and (2) political rivalry between the two great sees of Alexandria and Constantinople was involved in their quarrel, but these facts should not obscure the truth that the heart of the matter was really soteriology.

Both sides accepted the victory of Athanasius and the Nicene formulation of orthodoxy. The eternal Word and Son was consubstantial with the Father and incapable of defect or change. Both also recognized the defeat of Apollinarius. Jesus did, all now agreed, have a human soul as well as a human body. But in both cases what had been agreed upon was a formula in the realm of Christology—for, as always, it was easier to state things in terms of a formula about the being of Christ than in terms of his saving work. It is always easier to talk about something "out there" like theology; it is hard to talk about the felt experiences of religion. Athanasius's soteriology, or something related closely to it, carried on in Alexandria and was espoused by Cyril. Nestorius, trained in Antioch and operating as patriarch of Constantinople, did not share that soteriology at all. The stage was set for another confrontation, with Christology again as the front for the deeper soteriological issues.

Cyril, patriarch of Alexandria and successor in that post of his fiery uncle Theophilus, was a staunch conservative. He appears to have been educated in the monasteries of Egypt; with the monks, he was fanatically loyal to the memory of Athanasius and the decrees of Nicaea. The example of a monk's cell decorated with the complete text of the Nicene Creed as well as the more expected names of martyrs and saints, while it dates from a later century, illustrates the monks' fierce loyalty to formulas.[8] With it went a simple version of Athanasius's soteriology: Cyril, in his first letter to the monks of Egypt during the controversy, appeals to their belief that, if Christ was not God by nature, he could not overthrow death. The monks were won to his cause. As W. H. C. Frend puts it, "Real assurance of salvation could only come from the worship of one who was wholly God, and whose Eucharist guaranteed the partaker against the power of death, and the terrors of the underworld still thought of in terms of pagan legend."[9]

---

[8]W. H. C. Frend, *Rise of Monophysitism* (Cambridge: Cambridge University Press, 1972) 138.

[9]Ibid., 137.

Henry Chadwick has shown us how much Cyril shared with the Egyptian monks. Cyril's "fundamental objections to Antiochene doctrine," he argues, "lay rather in the repercussions of such thought upon the doctrine of the eucharist and the atonement."[10] Chadwick shows that both Cyril and Nestorius had a realistic view of the Eucharist—that is, that it involved the reception of Christ's real body and blood, not a symbolic remembrance of them. For Cyril, that realism is the basis of his view of salvation as appropriated by Christians. A favorite text of his is John 6:53-54, with its claim that, to have life, one must eat Christ's flesh and drink his blood. But how does one have life through partaking of the Eucharist? In his *Commentary on the Gospel of John,* Cyril spells out the connections, long before the controversy with Nestorius broke out.

> [Jesus Christ] is life by nature, inasmuch as he was begotten of a living Father. No less quickening is His holy body also, being in a manner gathered and ineffably united with the all-quickening Word. . . . And since the flesh of the Saviour hath become life-giving (as being united to that which is by nature Life, the Word from God) when we taste it, then have we life in ourselves; we too are united to it as it to the indwelling Word.[11]

In other words, believers partake of the real body and blood of Christ, but that body and blood are life-giving because they are united intimately and ineffably with the Word and Son of God, who is the giver of life himself. Since the gaining of immortal life and life "in Christ" thus depends on the intimate union of his flesh with the Word, it is no wonder that Cyril attacks Nestorius when he speaks of a separate human nature and a separate divine nature in Christ, seeming to divide them from each other and so to render impossible the life-giving union. For Cyril, Nestorius seems to destroy the possibility of salvation by making Jesus' human nature just an ordinary man: "We shall not account it as though it were the flesh of an ordinary man (for *how could the flesh of a man be life-giving of its own nature?*) but as having become of a truth the own flesh of Him, who for our sakes became and was called Son of Man."[12] Thus we see that soteriology is very clearly at the basis of Cyril's Christology (Christ's humanity and divinity must be united so that his flesh, partaken of in the Eucharist, can be life-giving). In this view Cyril was joined by the vast majority of

---

[10]Henry Chadwick, "Eucharist and Christology in the Nestorian Controversy," *Journal of Theological Studies,* n.s. 2 (1951): 153.

[11]Cyril of Alexandria, *Commentary on the Gospel of John,* vol. 1 (Oxford: Oxford University Press, 1874) 418.

[12]Cyril of Alexandria, *Third Letter of Nestorius,* in J. Stevenson, *Creeds, Councils, and Controversies* (London: S.P.C.K., 1966) 284.

the Egyptian church, both secular and monastic, as the course of events was to show. Cyril's view, again, is descended pretty directly from that of Athanasius.

For Nestorius the experience of salvation is quite different. For him salvation means, not the granting of divine life to humanity as a kind of self-transcendence or divinization as it was in Cyril, but rather its full humanization—to restore to humanity the image and likeness of God lost in the Fall, and with them immortal life. How does one regain these things? Speaking of Jesus' humanity, Nestorius says, "This is the likeness of God, to have neither purpose nor will of its own, but that of Him whose person and likeness it is."[13] As for the human Jesus, so for Christians: by imitation of him in perfect and lifelong obedience, Christians can recover the image and likeness of God that is the intended perfection of their humanity and so can receive the immortality that is its reward. Cyril, in seeming to let the humanity of Christ be absorbed into his divinity, was undermining the perfect human reality of Jesus, which was, for Nestorius, the basis of salvation. As a concluding note it may be remarked that, when Nestorius spoke of the Eucharist, he saw it as a way of participating in the perfect humanity of Jesus qua human (compared with Cyril's notion of participation in that humanity qua filled with the divine life).

Whatever side one sympathizes with in the controversies we have been looking at, it is clear that Christology arose out of soteriology, and theology was undertaken as an expression of a central experience of salvation in Christ Jesus. The connections whose absence may be lamented in our time were real and living connections then.

Making the Connections

One of many ironies of the present situation is the fact that the very Christology so many conservative Protestants espouse is that of Athanasius and Cyril, whose views triumphed over those of their opponents to a great extent. Yet those same conservative Protestants could not be further, generally speaking, from the experience of eucharistic participation in the life of the divine, or the experience of divinization, that led Athanasius and Cyril to express that Christology. They are by no means sacramental realists, for instance. They certainly do think of salvation as something they participate in by their willing obedience to the call of God in imitation of Jesus (precisely the soteriology of Arius and Nestorius). And they certainly expect to be humanized by their experience of salvation, not divin-

---

[13]Nestorius, *Bazaar of Heracleides* (New York: AMS, 1978) 1.1.62.

ized. These ironies point to disjunctions rather than connections at the heart of their theologies, a disturbing phenomenon.

These issues raise challenges to theological education. First could we find a way of helping students to formulate doctrine authentically as an expression of experience—that is, to do theology, rather than repeat the doctrines of the past? And then, could teachers of church history, and especially teachers of the history of doctrine, help students to see the past as a living expression of the religious experience of the Christian community and to be stimulated by the past to do theology in the present? I address the second question first.

Of course it *is* possible to begin teaching in this way, but it is difficult to do so. Part of the difficulty arises from the nature of so much writing in the field, with its strict and usual emphasis on particular doctrines like Christology simply qua doctrines. We have not been good at getting at the living experiences, the lifeblood, underneath the formulas. Also, as everyone who has tried teaching it knows, just getting students to understand the formulas is a daunting task, given the strangeness of the language and the historical distance between modern Christians and the patristic period. Nonetheless, it is possible to insist that the question *why* be asked of any formulation of doctrine. The clues are there, as Gregg and Groh have shown for Arianism and as Chadwick has shown for Cyril—and as has been shown here for Athanasius and Nestorius as well. As was remarked in passing, soteriology has always been difficult to talk about, and it has always been easier to focus on the more abstract and less threatening statements of Christology. One has to struggle for answers to the question *why* but one *can* find answers.

One further reflection follows from the last point made: If soteriology was hard for the fathers to talk about, so that they often preferred to talk about Christology, then one should not be surprised that the same is true of modern Christians. Even trying to think about why the fathers, so long ago, formulated the doctrines they did brings moderns close to the vital center of religious experience, and that is threatening. In marriage-preparation sessions, the really difficult issue to get candidates for marriage to talk together about is religion—what they really believe and feel. The teacher who would begin to make connections at that level must be gentle with his or her students' sensitivity as they approach the core of experience; gentleness is required, and firmness too—they cannot be let off the hook!

To go on to the first question, now, perhaps the best way to help students to *do* theology is to be doing theology oneself. The temptation to do indoctrination instead is very great, and it is not escaped if one stops teaching students to mouth the doctrines of the past but encourages them to imitate slavishly one's own theologizing! If one is genuinely doing theology, though, it is a kind of voyage of discovery upon which one wishes to invite others to embark. The excitement of the quest, if honestly expressed, with its attendant areas of doubt and uncertainty being admitted to quite openly, will carry others along. It is useful, perhaps, to begin with questions, not answers. The stimulus of being in the presence of a person who is actually engaged in thinking about a matter that somewhere touches one's own experience and one's own concern is almost certain to have the desired effect sooner or later of stimulating one to think.

Recent work in learning theory, such as that by James Fowler, suggests that there is another dimension to the problems we have been explaining, namely, the different modes of apprehending belief that are appropriate at different stages in life.[14] It is appropriate for late adolescents to have absorbed and laid claim to the positions of others as dogmatic truths. No wonder, then, that so many divinity students arrive with the remnants of the feeling that they are in a citadel of faith and must defend it against the attacks of an alien secular world—they could not have felt otherwise at the stage in life out of which they are coming. But given this feeling, or its remnants, it is no wonder if they often feel much safer clinging to the traditional doctrines traditionally expressed rather than adventuring forward into the frightening world of doing theology. This reaction is reinforced by the private nature of genuine religious experience referred to above.

And yet a reactionary entrenchment is decidedly not appropriate for people at their stage in religious life, for to reaffirm dogmatically the traditional formulas they have inherited and temporarily called their own, they must suppress the realities of their own individual experience, which inevitably must be at least somewhat different from anyone else's and which must therefore require an at least slightly different formulation. This is the learning crisis, as well as the personal faith crisis, that most divinity students face. Given their fairly general experience of humanization in salvation, for instance, can they go on forever with a Christology that fits better with, because it grew out of, an experience understood to be of divinization? Clearly the choices must be either suppression of experience or the reformulation of doctrine in a form that more authentically expresses experience. The task of helping students begin doing theology is thus necessary not just for a more authentic theology at a moment in the history of

---

[14]J. Fowler, *Stages of Faith* (San Francisco: Harper & Row, 1982).

the church when the disjunction between doctrines and experience seems particularly disturbing; it is necessary also for the authentic growth in faith of the students themselves. We may add that this inner need to resolve a disjunction is the teacher's best ally in the task described. While we all often resist change and growth, at least a part of us insists that we "make the connections" and "get our act together," responding positively to good teaching that helps the process begin.

It is only fair to take some account of the dangers involved in my proposal. The central danger has been pointed out by my colleagues: to begin with the experience is to open up the possibility of diversity in doctrine, since each will articulate the faith in a way different from every other person's articulation. The obvious corollary is that this approach ultimately invites the possibility of heresy. Hillmer's chapter 3 above on the New Testament is helpful in a preliminary way in that it shows that diversity has always been characteristic of Christianity. The notion of a monolithic apostolic set of doctrines is a creation of the late patristic period, not inherent in the materials themselves. I would go further and say that theology, to be alive and genuine in the sense maintained here, rather than an externally taught ideology, simply must allow for diversity. Perhaps, indeed, rather than attempting to reinforce students in an external "Christianity" that is not organically and internally theirs because it bears no real relation to their personal experience, we should be helping them to discover that they are not genuinely Christians. What good, after all, will they be able to do for their congregations?

Perhaps, too, there is something to be said for risking the possibility that some will be heretics. The Gospel of John appears to have been considered heretical by orthodox Christian writers up to the last few decades of the second century, yet it turned out to have permanent value for the church. Nestorius's teaching about the two natures of Christ was condemned by the Council of Ephesus but was exonerated by the Council of Chalcedon twenty years later. It might almost be said that vigorous champions of heresy are a necessary counterpoint to the vigorous and lively development of orthodoxy. At any rate, I would certainly say that, given fallen human nature, heresy always will accompany orthodoxy if theology is genuinely alive in the church, and there is no point regretting that fact, and no real faithfulness in opting instead for a merely ideological theology.

Finally, the function here envisaged for the teacher of theology is also the function that may be envisaged for the good minister. Like teachers, ministers are tempted to do indoctrination; like teachers, they probably ought instead to be helping and stimulating the people to whom they minister to grow in faith by making the connections for themselves.

I would like to close on a personal note. I sound as if theological education is where I began to see these issues, but that is not the case. It was in ministry that I discovered myself not indoctrinating (for I was going through my own redoing of theology and could not bring myself to assert dogmatically propositions I was in the process of reworking) but engaging with my people in a shared examination of our experience in faith and a shared attempt to find words for them. That experience has informed my teaching and my study. My conclusion is that, in teaching as in other kinds of ministry, connections must be made. We can learn from the past, not so much for its formulations (which are so often alien to us) as for what it attempted to do. But let us do it for ourselves, as they did.

Chapter Five

Augustine and Christology

Joanne McWilliam

Christians are followers of Christ; it seems obvious that Christology is or should be—at the heart of the theological curriculum. But is this only Christology taught systematically, dealing with the "two natures, one person" kind of question? Are the answers to this and other Christological questions worked out from ground zero in every generation? Is the knowledge of the thought of our Christian forebearers of no use to the Christian today? More particularly, can the teachings and examples of the past be helpful in ministry? Some would say no, that such knowledge is arcane or that Christology treated historically has now only antiquarian value. But others, including myself, think otherwise—that we can learn positively from the past, that, for example, the efforts made by Augustine of Hippo in his first years of Christian teaching can indeed be relevant to theological education today.

To all Christians who have the privilege of teaching and preaching their faith, there falls the obligation of presenting Christ in a manner that is appropriate to their hearers. That duty does not mean, of course, saying only what one's audience wants to hear, but rather involves teaching in a way that the material can be made the hearers' own. There is a mutuality involved. To present Christ appropriately demands considerable knowledge and several skills, but the words spoken ring hollow unless true to one's own understanding of Christ. Such presentation of Christ is not static; sometimes one facet of his saving work wants emphasizing, sometimes another. And as the teacher's understanding grows, the Christ figure taught and preached will become expanded and enriched.

Augustine was well aware of the need for the mutuality of conviction and receptivity, and he faced the questions it involved with a high degree of purposefulness. The changes in his own understanding of Christ are reflected in his teaching over the years, and although soon convinced that human acceptance of the word/Word is ultimately the work of God, Augustine used all his impressive rhetorical tools to aid that acceptance. Among those tools, simile was a favorite, and one of his most striking was the likening of the relationships of the Christian to Christ to Jacob's relations to his wives. This essay examines Augustine's estimation of those relationships, as well as the developments in his Christology in the years between his conversion and his ordination (C.E. 387-391).

Leah, Rachel, and Bilhah

In his treatise *Against Faustus,* Augustine gives us a not altogether consistent allegorical reading of Genesis 29 and 30, in which weak-eyed Leah represents those able to receive "the word of faith, the preaching of Christ crucified, which speaks also of his human nature insofar as it can easily be understood" (22.54-59).[1] Leah's children are those won to Christianity by this kerygma. Clear-eyed Rachel, on the other hand, ecstatically seeks the Word with God and thus contemplates divine truth. Leah is loved for the sake of her many children, but the children of Rachel—

---

[1]Subsequent references to Augustine's work are cited in the text using the following abbreviations:

BV	*De Beata Vita* (On the Happy Life)
CA	*Contra Academicos* (Against the Academics)
Conf.	*Confessiones* (The Confessions)
DA	*De Duabas Animis* (On Two Souls)
DeLA	*De Libero Arbitrio*
Ep.	*Epistula* (letter)
Fort.	*Contra Fortunatum Manichaeum* (Against Fortunatus)
Gen. Man.	*De Genesi contra Manichaeos* (On Genesis against the Manichaeans)
Imm. amn.	*De immortalitate animae* (On the Immortality of the Soul)
Mag.	*De Magistro* (The Teacher)
Mor.	*De moribus ecclesiae catholicae et Manichaeorum* (On the Morals of the Catholic Church and of the Manichaeans)
Ord.	*De Ordine* (On Order)
QA	*De quantitate animae* (On the greatness of the soul)
UC	*De Utilitati Credendi* (On the Usefulness of Believing)
VR	*De Vera Religione* (On True Religion)

In its entirety, this passage reads: "Nascantur autem eis facilius atque copiosius ex ille sermone fidei, quo praedicant Christum crucifixum, et quidquid humanitatis eius citius humana cogitatione percipitur, et infirmos etiam Liae oculos non pertubat. Rachel autem clara aspectu, mente excedit Deo, et videt in principio Verbum Deum apud Deum, et vult parere, et non potest; quia generationem eius quis ennarrabit? . . . Sicut elegit Rachel ex viro suo et ancilla suscipere liberos, quam sine filiis omnino remanere." The metaphor endured. Cf. Pope Gregory I, Letter 5 (in *Nicene and Post-Nicene Fathers of the Christian Church,* vol. 75), on Rachel.

loved best in herself—are few because her vision is virtually inexpressible. She must therefore resort to her servant Bilhah (human language, metaphorical or plain) to bring her offspring into the world—that is, to describe intelligibly the reciprocal presence of God and the soul.

That in the year 397 (when *Against Faustus* was written) Augustine applied the Leah/Rachel/Bilhah figure to himself is clear as he goes on in the treatise to identify Leah with the useful labors of the public servant, called from the pursuit of wisdom for the common good but anxious to return to the contemplation that Rachel personifies. This self-perception was not new. From the time of his conversion Augustine had seen himself called to "serve the church by writing" (*Conf.* 11.4.7), and that service to involve engaging in necessary controversy. Those controversies (and later his priestly and episcopal duties) kept him from the life of study and contemplation he had yearned for since leaving Cassiciacum.

None of the controversies was concerned directly with Christology, but as the years went on, he drew upon his growing understanding of Christ to put forward Christological models distinctively appropriate to the issues at stake, to confound and, if possible, convert his opponents. Rachel—the presence of the soul with God, the contemplation of the divine truth—is alluded to only obliquely and fleetingly in the controversial treatises, discussed more directly in writings destined for friends, and is described with any attempt at fullness only in *The Teacher,* written for his son, and in noncontroversial works such as *On the Trinity* and the *Tractates* on the Johannine Gospel and Epistles.

In the years from 387 to 391, the Leah/Rachel/Bilhah pattern took shape clearly. The Cassiciacum Christology, while accepting the authority of Christ and the church, reserved the most effective salvific role for the Second Person of the Trinity, the self-humbling and illuminating divine Word that is the source of all truth. In the writings of this second period, however, Augustine makes much more telling use of different facets of Christ's humanity. What begins in *On the Morals of the Catholic Church and of the Manichaeans* as a reluctant and awkward espousal of Leah—the presentation of Christ as man under the aegis of faith—becomes, in succeeding writings directed to his adversaries, progressively more skillful and elaborate. In these same years Augustine also worked out a scheme that presented the two functions of Christ as Son, both eternal and incarnate, as complementary both in creation and re-creation and in interior and exterior pedagogy. The first complementarity is most evident in *On Genesis against the Manichaeans;* the second, in *On True Religion* and *On the Usefulness of Believing.* The extension of the authoritative guide from the church to Christ, begun at the end of the Cassiciacum writings, is continued in the years 388-391 as the earlier skeletal figure is fleshed out.

The Christological Aspects
of the Early Anti-Manichaean Arguments

After Augustine left Cassiciacum, his intellectual energies were taken up largely by his writings against the Manichaeans, a concentration made inevitable by his past association with them. He had not only to distance himself publicly from that community but also to carry on much more extensively the work begun in *On Order:* the refutation of Manichaean teachings and the provision of alternative answers to the questions they raised. The list was formidable: the explanation of the origin of evil and its continuing association with the material world, the relation of the Jewish and Christian Scriptures, the nature of the human soul, and the existence of a free human will. It may seem surprising, given the centrality of Jesus in Manichaean theology, that Augustine did not in these years address this subject. It had not, however, been primarily dissatisfaction with their Christology that had caused him to break with the Manichaeans, and it was in coming to grips with the other problems that Augustine worked out an increasingly sophisticated notion of Christ.

The first writings after Cassiciacum were concerned with the human soul—its immortality and its potential greatness. *On the Immortality of the Soul,* written at Milan in spring of 387, contains no Christology as such, although the groundwork is laid there both for the description of the possible contemplation of the divine, which is the topic of the next treatise, and for the later *anima mediante* explanation of the union of the divine and human in Christ (*Imm. An.* 6.10, 11.18, 15.14). The same year saw four other treatises begun, one of which is lost, and three others (*on the Greatness of the Soul, On the Morals of the Catholic Church and of the Manichaeans, On Music*) that took two or more years to complete.[2] *On the Greatness of the Soul* contains a careful description of the soul's ascent to God through the ordered use of created goods, an ascent presented in terms of a contrast between all that is exterior, material, and human and all that is interior, spiritual, and divine. Contemplation, the seventh stage, is in fact not a stage of the ascent but its goal. As in the earlier treatises, divine wisdom brings the human soul to this stillness of possession. Augustine writes: "If we hold fast to the way God commands for us (and which we receive by conforming ourselves to it) we shall arrive, through the Power and Wisdom of God, at that supreme Cause, or supreme Authority, or supreme Principle of all things—whatever name best suits a Reality of such

---

[2]*De immortalitate animae, Disciplinarum* (lost), *De musica, De quantitate animae,* and *De moribus ecclesiae catholicae et Manichaeorum.*

grandeur. In knowing it, we shall indeed see that all else under the sun is vanity of vanities" (*QA* 33.76).

Augustine had cited this 1 Corinthians text (a favorite of the Manichaeans) before, in one case to his Manichaean patron, Romanianus (*CA* 2.1.1), but the chance to use it publicly against the Manichaeans and in so orthodox a context as that of contemplation must surely have afforded him a good deal of satisfaction. Christ's humanity is not spoken of in this treatise; Augustine's focus is exclusively on the work of the eternal Son in leading the soul to divine wisdom.

Augustine had been attracted to the Manichaeans by their claims of the reasonableness of their teachings, and his return to the church of his childhood had been marked by an explicit acceptance of its authority (*CA* 3.19.43). The last step in that return had been his conversion from sexual license to celibacy. *On the Morals of the Catholic Church and of the Manichaeans* was concerned with precisely those two topics—the authority of the Catholic church (particularly with regard to the Jewish and Christian Scriptures) and the sexual morality of the two groups. Augustine links them at the beginning of the treatise in terms of the attractions of Manichaeanism: "The Manichaeans have two tricks for catching the unwary. . . . One, that of finding fault with the Scriptures, . . . the other, that of making a show of chastity" (*Mor,* 1.1.2). It is only in deference to the Manichaeans' preference for reason, Augustine declares, that he begins the treatise with an appeal to it rather than to authority, and it does not take him long to dispose of the Manichaean claim to rationality. Reason, he argues, establishes that the human person ought to live so that his or her chief good (and that is, of course, the good of the soul [*Mor.* 1.5.7]) is attained. The principal good of the soul is that by which it is brought to perfection, and this means can be neither itself nor another human person, but must be God, "in following after whom we live good lives and in attaining whom we are not only good, but blessed" (*Mor.* 1.6.10). But how follow and attain a God who cannot be seen or comprehended? Only by heeding authority. "For although God is discerned not with the eyes, but with the mind, pray what mind is found capable even of trying to drink in [that] light? It is necessary, therefore, to take refuge in the precepts of those who probably were wise" (*Mor.* 1.7.11). Although the Manichaeans should thus be brought by reason to acknowledge the authority of the Catholic church, in which wisdom resides, they in fact refuse to do so (*Mor.* 1.18.33-34).

The necessity of authority to bring minds darkened with foolishness to wisdom had been part of the Cassiciacum writings (*CA* 3.15.34; *Ord.* 2.5.15), and *On the Morals of the Catholic Church and of the Manichaeans* sees a development of that theme as Augustine not only appeals to the authority of the church but as well expands his earlier Christological argument. In *Against the Academics* and *On Order,* Christ was described as the authoritative teacher and example of humility whose authority derived from the God, who, moved by compassion for the human condition, sent him (*CA* 3.19.42; *Ord.* 2.19.27). But in the Cassiciacum writings, the man Christ, despite his divine mission to bring the human race to wisdom, was not given the title *Wisdom* (although his work was equated with that of Wisdom); it was reserved there (as in *On the Magnitude of the Soul*) for the Second Person of the Trinity (*CA* 2.1.1; *QA* 33.70). It is in *On the Morals of the Catholic Church and of the Manichaeans* that Christ as man is for the first time called the Wisdom of God. The contexts in which this usage occurs are two: the acceptability of the Jewish Scriptures in the Christian dispensation and moral exhortation. In the first, Augustine uses the identity of the "Wisdom of God" in both Testaments to argue for the revelatory nature of the Jewish Scriptures. His method is that used at Cassiciacum: equation of function. The characteristics attributed to Christ in, for example, John 14:6 ("No one comes to the Father but by me") and to Wisdom in the Book of Wisdom 9:17 ("Who knows your mind unless you [God] give wisdom?") are the same, demonstrating the identity of the Wisdom to whom the two passages refer. Anyone who accepts true wisdom in one Testament cannot reasonably reject it in the other (*Mor.* 1.16.28).

To assert the continuity of the Testaments is to place creation and salvation within the same historical process, and to do so brings into sharp relief the question of evil. In the second book of the treatise, Augustine puts the Catholic position unequivocally: "When the Catholic church declares that God is the author of all natures and substances . . . [it] does not mean that God is the author of evil" (*Mor.* 2.2.3). Augustine's philosophical basis for this statement is his privative understanding of evil: God is the author of all things that have being, but not of that falling away from being and consequent disorder that evil is. Only the wholehearted love of God overcomes evil, and Augustine assigns a twofold role to Christ in that victory: human exemplar and divine illuminator. Divine wisdom established the authoritative Scriptures, which present Christ as the teacher by word and example of the love of God and the practice of virtue; he is thus the intermediate object of the human love of wisdom, moral strength, and truth (*Mor.* 1.13.22). But teaching and example are only the beginning; the contemplation of God requires divine help, and so, to complete the salvific circle, human minds prepared by the practice of virtue are illumined by wisdom. "We follow God by loving; we attain God by wonderful and spiritual contact and by being inwardly illumined and caught up by divine truth and holiness'' (*Mor.* 1.11.18). Rachel is alluded to here, but, precisely because Augustine considers the Manichaeans in need of fundamental conversion and far removed from the capacity to enjoy the vision she represents, the theme is not developed.

It is rather Leah—"the word of faith, the preaching of Christ crucified, which speaks also of his human nature insofar as it can be easily understood''—who is presented, but still in only a limited way. Augustine does not in this treatise either preach Christ crucified or do more than hint at him as example, but restricts his role to that of the teacher by moral exhortation. The Manichaeans rejected a great deal of the gospel narrative of Christ, accepting only the discourses (*Mor.* 1.7.11-12, 15.47, 18.34), and the motive for Augustine's narrow focus in this treatise may have been partly apologetic, a desire to meet them on their own ground. But he had more personal reasons as well, an inhibition arising from the character in 387 of his rejection of Docetism—although sincere, it was still only formal. He knew that the denial of Christ's full humanity was untenable within the Catholic church, but he had not yet been able to make the human body of Christ substantively part of his thinking and so could not use it in controversy effectively. Thus *On the Morals of the Catholic Church and of the Manichaeans* not only contains none of the arguments against Docetism that would have been pertinent in comparing Manichaean and Catholic exemplar Christologies but in fact contains no properly exemplar Christology. The morality urged is that presented in the human words rather than in the human actions of Christ.

A passage in a treatise of the previous year, *On the Magnitude of the Soul,* lends support to the statement that Augustine was not yet fully at ease with Christ's bodily humanity. Dealing with the question of the relation of faith and understanding, it brings together two facets of Leah—the acceptance in *faith* of the *humanity* of Christ. While *On the Morals of the Catholic Church and of the Manichaeans* consistently values authority above reason, seeing the former as a check on the aberrations of the intellectually immature of any age and most certainly appropriate for the Manichaeans, *On the Greatness of the Soul,* written to someone already a Christian, assesses their relative worth differently. Augustine explains to his friend Evodius that to follow authority is to take the short and easy way, a great boon for those who might otherwise go astray and for whom no other security is possible (QA 7.12), but not to be compared with the desire that impels reason to strive for truth. Using his frequent metaphor of the nourishing church (*CA* 2.5.13; *BV* passim; *Mor.* 1.10.17, 30.62-64; *QA* 33.76; *VR* 28.51), Augustine describes authority as the milk that babies need, that adults should be ashamed to drink, but that charity must make available to all who require it (*QA* 33.76).

Augustine did not generally see himself as a milk drinker, but in one particular he knew he was still. In the same passage he tells Evodius that, in the seventh and last stage of the soul's ascent to God (he is talking of contemplation in this life), one result of the vision of the Supreme Principle will be the intellectual realization of "the truths we are [now] commanded to believe" (QA 33.76). The two instances Augustine gives of the truths now accepted on authority that will then be known with certainty are the incarnation of the Word and the general resurrection of the body. With a docetic understanding of Christ in mind, he writes: "We shall despise those who scoff at the fact that a man was assumed by the almighty, eternal, changeless Son of God, to be the exemplar and beginning of our salvation, and that he was born of a virgin. . . . We shall consider those scoffers to be like children who think a man cannot be painted unless the painter adverts to another picture because they once saw it done that way" (*QA* 33.76).

The Christ the Manichaeans put forward as an example was not truly human and so, Augustine argues, they were urging that human behavior be modeled on that of a mere facsimile. Yet, even as he points out the ineffectiveness of a docetic example, the linking of the Incarnation and the Resurrection in this passage indicates that the positive status given the human body in Catholic teaching remained to this time an intellectual problem for him as well. On the other hand, the arguments that flow from his understanding of Christ as the divine power and wisdom have none of this constraint. His conviction of the identity in Christ of the eternal wisdom, which plays so prominent a part in the later Hebrew Scriptures, and the Johannine Word, whom the Manichaeans professed to revere, is the basis for his confident assertion that the Catholic church is correct in its reception of those earlier Scriptures, and he is able to urge this position wholeheartedly against that of the Manichaeans.

Creation

Augustine could be at ease with the bodily humanity of Christ only in the larger context of the goodness of the material world, and he begins his next treatise by trying to establish the case for that goodness. The Manichaean teaching of the evil of the material creation and their consequent refusal to attribute that creation to the Christian God are met by an integration of his theory of creation with his Trinitarian theology and by assigning the creative role to the Word. Thus in *On Genesis against the Manichaeans* (388-389), Augustine counters their literalist reading of the creation account, which leads them to an anthropomorphic and negative understanding of the Creator, with an interpretation of his own that includes an assertion of the instrumental role of the divine Son in creation (*Gen. Man.* 1.2.3-4). At the beginning of the treatise the Manichaeans are presented as posing one of theology's perennial pseudoriddles: "What did God do before the 'beginning' of creation?" The question gives Augustine a chance to reply that "in the beginning" has no temporal reference but means "in Christ because he is the Word who is with the Father," as evidenced by John 1:13 and 8.25. Creation is brought about by God through the Word, and creation is good; but because, unlike the Word, it is made, not begotten, it has not the goodness proper to divinity (*Gen. Man.* 1.3.6). This argument for the goodness of creation parallels that for the revelatory character of the Jewish Scriptures. In both cases, if the overall Manichaean theology is to be consistent with its professed belief in Christ, the Manichaeans must accept everything in which he plays a part, whether as wisdom or creative Word.

Augustine's understanding of the role of the Word in creation is that of Form: "The plan and form of God by which all created things are made is called the Son" (*Ep.* 12), he wrote Nebridius in 389, and this position will be explained in response to further questioning by his friend: "Whether that supreme Truth and Wisdom, the Form of all things, through whom all things are made . . . contains within itself the form of the human person in general or of each of us in particular?" Augustine, admitting the difficulty of the question, opts for a two-stage creation: "The form of the human person as such, but as well, in the succession of time, the forms of different men" (*Ep.* 14.4). In *On True Religion,* anxious not to appear to separate the work of the Trinity, he writes:

> Every creature, intellectual, animal, and corporeal, derives such existence as it has from that same creative Trinity, has its own form and is subject to the most perfect order. It is not as if the Father were understood to have made one part of creation, the Son another, and the Holy Spirit another, but the Father through the Son in the gift of the Holy Spirit together made all things and every particular thing. (*VR* 7.13)

The understanding of the Word as creative form arises out of a development in Augustine's understanding of the Trinity, found in this same treatise. It is interesting that here, where the focus is so much on Christ as moral preceptor and guide, Augustine's description of the Trinity also takes on that coloration. In *On True Religion,* in contrast with *On the Happy Life,* the description of the relation of the "First" and "Second Persons" (language Augustine does not use here) of the Christian Trinity is developed from the acknowledged power of the human mind to choose good or evil. Choice implies judgment, judgment a standard. Thus "the Measure of order lives in perpetual Truth. . . . The Son is rightly said to be from [that

Measure of order], other creatures through [the Son]. The Form precedes all beings, which complete the unity from which [that Form] is, so that everything else which exists, to the degree that it resembles that One, came into being through that Form'' (*VR* 43.81).

It is also early in this first of Augustine's many struggles with the Genesis creation account that the Manichaean association of the Creator with darkness (God must have dwelt in darkness before creating light) gives him once again an opportunity to hint of the Rachel unknown to the Manichaeans. It is they themselves, Augustine retorts, who dwell in darkness—the darkness of ignorance—because they understand only physical light. ''But we know another Light in which God dwells, from whence comes that Light of which we read in the gospel'' (*Gen. Man.* 1.3.6). That light does not serve the needs merely of the material world, as does the sun, but rather ''the pure hearts of those who believe in God and turn from the love of the visible and temporal to fashioning their lives on God's precepts'' (*Gen. Man.* 1.3.6). This identification of Christ with the divine light is developed elsewhere, but Christ as the principium of creation is immediately complemented in this treatise by a detailed exposition of the work of the Second Adam, as the creative role of the eternal Son is given a counterpart in the foundational salvific work of the incarnate Son, the New Man. Augustine is concerned to show not only the goodness of the original creation but the excellence of the re-creation, and he does so in a series of parallels between the six days of creation and the six ages of world history (*Gen. Man.* 1.25-43; cf. 2.8.10). In stressing the victory of the Second Adam, Augustine is countering the Manichaean linking of Christ with the primal man sent to rescue Adam and Eve, the man whose defeat ''involves the deity in a long drawn-out work of salvation.''[3] Augustine's Christ was victorious by taking ''the cloud of our flesh'' as a rebuke to human pride and in order to spread ''the munificent rain'' of the gospel, promising that anyone who drinks of him will have eternal life (*Gen. Man.* 2.5.6).

In 389, the Rachel-Bilhah partnership makes its most significant appearance of this period. *On the Greatness of the Soul* ends with a hint of works soon to be written (perhaps already sketched out). ''For this is the true religion, by which the soul joins itself in reconciliation to God, just as it severed itself from God by sin. . . . Nor will the Teacher who is above all desert those of us who seek him'' (*QA* 36.80-81). The term *teacher* is Bilhah serving Rachel, a metaphor drawn from the temporal and material world to express the inexpressible—the presence of God to the human mind

---

[3]H. Jones, *The Gnostic Religion*, 2d rev. ed. (Boston: Beacon Press, 1963) 217.

and soul. Referred to, but no more, in the treatises directed to the Mani-chaeans, the contemplative union of the human mind with the divine is given expanded expression in these years only in Augustine's colloquy with his son. *The Teacher* is the fruit of Augustine's identification of wisdom and the Johannine Word, and it expands the point sketched in earlier works that the plenitude of knowledge—indeed all true knowledge—is a divine, not a human, work.[4] We are brought to divinity only by divinity, to the contemplation of the one only by truth itself.

One facet of Augustine's Christology becomes evident in the well-known (and much commented on) context of his epistemology of interi-ority: the person who knows reality does so not through exterior signs or human language, part of the material world, for they are merely devices to recall sensible or intelligible realities already experienced, or to elicit be-lief in or to promote investigation of realities not personally experienced. It is rather the Teacher who, in an interior manner, presents the reality to be known to the mind and illumines the mind so that reality can be known (*Mag.* 11.38ff.). As another writing of this period puts it, the Son "forms the understanding" (*Ep.* 11.4). Adeodatus's closing words in *The Teacher,* "He alone teaches who, although he admonishes externally, dwells within" (*Mag.* 14.46),[5] harks back to the parallel works of the eternal and the in-carnate Son described in *On Genesis against the Manichaeans.*

The parallelism is spelled out in a letter of this same year (389) reply-ing to Nebridius's question whether the entire Trinity became incarnate, or only the Son. Augustine writes that it was fittingly only the Son, with whom "a certain learning and art . . . and also the understanding by which the [human] mind is formed in its thinking of things" are associated. The eternal function of the Son is given a correspondence in time because the Incarnation resulted in a certain instruction and example conveyed in Christ's life and teachings (cf. *Ep.* 11.4). This temporal activity is the pre-liminary work of salvation; the illuminative function of the Word is the fi-nal work. Leah must be embraced before Rachel.

Although Christ's flesh is described in 288 as a cloud, it is clear from *On True Religion* (written the same year for his friend Romanianus, still a Manichaean) that Augustine is beginning to resolve his difficulties with Christ's bodily humanity. He writes there: "In no way did [God] take more

---

[4]G. Madec, *DeMagistro,* 3d ed. (Paris: Desclée de Brouwer, 1976) 25, 29-30.

[5]" . . . eum docere solum, qui se intus habitare, cum foris loquerentur, admonuit." The interiority of the work of the Word, as contrasted with the exteriority of the Word in-carnate, is presented in several of the writings of this period. See *Gen. Man.* 1.3.6, *DeLA* 3.10.30 (although probably written three or four years later).

care for the welfare of the human race than when the very Wisdom of God—
the only Son, consubstantial with the Father and co-eternal—deigned to
take a man in his integrity, and 'the Word became flesh and dwelt among
us.' . . . And so the whole of his life on earth, through the man whom he
condescended to take, was an education in right living" (*VR* 16.30.32).
Making skillful use of the temptation narrative, Augustine expands this
theme of education. Christ is presented as an example in three ways, the
model adjusted each time to make a different point. Together the examples
provide a pattern that can convert the human person from entanglement with
lesser goods and fatalistic pessimism to the contemplation of the Divine
One. At the point of contemplation, the Word, the interior Light, takes over.

In establishing the context for his argument, Augustine confronts the
fact that, although the human soul (alone of all transient beings) has the
capacity first to transcend its impermanence and contemplate the divine
eternity (it is, in fact, made for this) and then, formed and prepared in and
by that contemplation, to merit eternal life, this capacity nevertheless more
often than not goes unfulfilled. Love of the material and ephemeral impedes
the necessary conversion to the spiritual and even deters belief in the existence of the spiritual reality that can be apprehended neither by the senses
nor by the imagination but only by the mind and the intelligence (*VR* 3.3).
Augustine understands this goal of contemplation of divine truth to have
been that of Plato as well, although equally unrealized in his day. He therefore demands rhetorically of the philosopher: "What if some great and divine man should persuade those able to grasp intellectually the truths of the
spiritual world to refuse to do so no longer, and those of lesser ability at
least to believe in those spiritual realities" (*VR* 3.3).

For this turning to happen, the answer comes, certain hitherto unheard
of conditions would have to obtain. "This man would have to be one whom
the very Power and Wisdom of God has exempted from the natural order
and illuminated from infancy not with human teaching, but with an interior
light." "Plato" continues: "[That Power and Wisdom of God] would have
adorned him with such grace, would have fortified him with such strength,
would have exalted him with such majesty, that, in despising all that the
wicked desire, in enduring all that they dread, in doing all that they marvel
at, he would, with surpassing love and authority, have converted the human race" (*VR* 3.3). Such a man has lived, Augustine declares; the process of conversion has its foundation in Christ (*VR* 3.4).

In *On the Morals of the Catholic Church and of the Manichaeans,* a
year or so earlier, Augustine first identified the Christ of the Christian
Scriptures as the wisdom of God. In the passage just quoted he has begun
to work out how this can be so; the attempt marks his earliest exposition

of the Christology of grace to which he returns throughout his life. Here, in *On True Religion,* he moves immediately from this presentation of the outstandingly graced and enlightened Christ, the awe-inspiring (and therefore authoritative) example of the right-ordered desire that marks the first stage of turning to God, to Christ's moral teachings as reflected in the exhortations and injunctions of the Synoptic Gospels: the condemnation of greed, lust, pride, anger, ambition, superstition, and curiosity. (*VR* 3.4). These teachings have already been accepted by many, he affirms; that acceptance is attested by the lives of those Christians who turn from the pursuit of temporal to eternal goods (*VR* 3.5). Morally purified, such a human soul is now enabled to know, love, and enjoy the Word, to perceive the eternal and spiritual Trinity in itself and in creation (*VR* 7.13). The contemplation of the Word corresponds to the seventh stage of the ascent described two years earlier in *On the Greatness of the Soul,* but there is a marked contrast between the two treatises: in the earlier writing the only reference to the incarnate Son is the difficulty of accepting the embodiment of God, but now Leah has led to Rachel.

Such a conversion presupposes a human freedom to reject evil, a freedom denied by Manichaean teaching, and therefore Augustine's second presentation of Christ as exemplar is directed at the error of determinism. His argument involves him in a dilemma: on the one hand, evil is not a substance, but a disorder, solely the work of the perverse human will.[6] Vice is the soul's own choice, and the moral difficulties that come from evil choice are its just punishment (*VR* 20.39).[7] On the other hand, human nature, despite a history of wrong choices, is not inherently vicious and has, in fact, a diginity of its own, shown by the Word's assumption of a man (*VR* 18.35). Augustine argues here that Christ's teaching by persuasion and warning is a reminder both that the human person is created with the power to choose freely and that the power of choice must be educated. To encourage its right use, Christ displayed a series of virtues to counter pervasive human weakness and vice, choosing, for instance, to be poor in order to rebuke greed and to be tortured to assuage the fear of pain. Manichaean fatalism in the face of sin has no validity; the man assumed by the wisdom of God has called us to liberty (*VR* 17.33).

---

[6]Emphasis on the freedom of the human will to choose good or evil and the location of evil solely in perverse human choice are constant themes in Augustine's writings of this period. See not only *On Free Will* but also *QA* 36.80; *Mor.* 2.7.10; *Gen. Man.* 2.29.43; *DA* 10.12.14; *Fort.* 18.20.

[7]For the converse, that the habit of virtue strengthens the soul, see *Gen. Man.* 2.29.27.

In his third depiction of Christ as example, Augustine moves from the model of Christian virtues and Christian freedom to that of Christian contemplation (*VR* 38.70). He begins by setting out the three categories of sins—sensuality, curiosity, and pride (following 1 John 2:16)—and shows that Christ's threefold temptation fits those categories. That these temptations had no power over him was due to his intimate relationship with God. "For whoever is fed interiorly by the Word of God does not seek pleasure in the wilderness [sensuality]. He who is to such a degree subject to God does not look for self-importance on a mountain [pride]. And whoever cleaves in eternal contemplation to the unchanging Truth is not cast down by the weakness of bodily vision [curiosity] in order to know temporal and inferior things" (*VR* 38.71).

To feed interiorly on the Word of God, to be steadfastly subject to the one God, to cling in eternal contemplation to unchanging truth—such practice affords such a protection against pursuing lesser goods. It will be recalled that Augustine began his treatise by describing such an intimate union with the divine as the human ideal unrealizable until the wounded and weakened soul is healed and strengthened (see *VR* 3.3). Christ's soul is thus presented as the human ideal, the soul that enjoys the state of Rachel, and Augustine is prompted to ask. "What prevents any human soul from remembering [and returning to] the initial beauty that it abandoned?" (*VR* 39.72). His answer is the same as that of Cassiciacum: it is a question of disorder, of a preoccupation with lesser goods. Yet, in its very choice of the inferior, the soul is affirming the existence of the superior ("the lowest beauty recalls the highest"). All are knit together in one harmonious pattern. This conclusion, in the context of Christ's strength derived from his contemplative intimacy with the divine, leads to the exhortation: "Return to yourself; truth is in the inner person. . . . Therefore, direct yourself there, from where the very light of reason is kindled from above. For where does all right reason lead, except to Truth?" (*VR* 39.72). Yet truth, Augustine goes on to say, is reached not by reason alone but by a certain disposition of mind, a right desire, a purified longing—the very characteristics displayed by the New Man (*VR* 39.72). At every stage of the ascent to God— the practicalities of moral living, the rejection of pessimistic fatalism and the strength derived from intimacy with God, the final contemplation of divine truth—the Christian will find that Christ has gone before.

On True Religion thus does speak of Christ's human nature "insofar as it can be easily understood" and in doing so presents Leah as the road to be followed to the goal of the much-desired Rachel. It remains for *On the Usefulness of Believing* (also written in 391) to stress another facet of Leah, the recognition of the authority of Christ, and the Catholic church and the consequent acceptance in faith of Christian teaching. The arguments that Augustine puts forward to his Manichaean friend Honoratus are the now-familiar ones. Just as the law is useful for those "who cannot be recalled from sin by reason," so authority serves those who cannot come to the knowledge of God through intellectual endeavor (*VC* 10.24). And even those who can do without the guidance of authority should respect it, lest they scandalize those who rely on it (*VC* 10.24). To recognize wise authority, even that of Christ, is not always easy, despite its intrinsic worth, and simple persons must be lured, as it were, by Christ's miracles (*VC* 14.32). When this initial influence is established it may be used to reform their lives, and moral reformation will in turn make the simple more amenable to reason. Augustine continues:

> Therefore, since as a man was to be imitated, and yet hope was not to be placed in a man, what could the divinity more indulgently and generously have done than that the very Wisdom of God, uncorrupted, eternal, and unchangeable, to whom we must cling, should have deigned to assume a man? This man not only did those things by which we might be invited to follow God, but he endured those things by which we might be deterred from that following. . . . In all other matters (which are too many to tell) he showed himself to be such that we understand the degree to which divine mercy can go and to which human weakness can be raised. (*VC* 15.33)

Faith is not credulity; the former is discriminating, the latter is not, and belief is praiseworthy only when the human mind yields to good authority (*VC* 9.22). Even the Manichaeans urge the authority of Christ (*VC* 14.31), but, Augustine argues (both recalling the Cassiciacum writings and anticipating a later Christological model, the "whole Christ"), the authority of Christ is found only in the Catholic church because its extension in space and time derives from Christ. "Therefore this man . . . bringing the medicine that would cure the utmost depravity, by his miracles recommended authority, by authority earned faith, by faith gathered the multitude, through the multitude he obtained continuity and by continuity he gave the religion strength" (*VC* 14.32).

Augustine is thus arguing in 391 the same point that he was in 387—the necessity of the Manichaean recognition of the authority of the Catholic church—but his argument is now supported by a much stronger Christology. The pedagogical work of the man Christ is presented as capable of bringing the Christian to the threshold of contemplation, and this work is manifestly an expansion of that of the Cassiciacum guide. Between sin and divine contemplation there is the intermediate state wherein the human person may tend to the one true God by moral conduct and Christian worship (see *VR* 10.19). In this context Augustine has developed the figure of the exemplary Christ, "the second Adam who did not sin" (*Gen. Man.* 2.8.10), and who both founds and validates the authority of the church in which this way may be followed and the human race recalled to the memory of the original goodness of its nature and its original vision of God. Augustine was prompted to emphasize these human roles of Christ by his perception of the necessity of affirming the real and positive role of the revelation offered in him. To affirm this salvific humanity was to argue against the Manichaeans' repudiation of the material world and for God's use of a historical man, with body and soul, who, by obedience to eternal law, offers the example of the soul made fit to be inhabited by the Teacher and led to the state of Rachel. In this manner the work of Christ the man yields to that of the Word. "Let us walk while we have the day, that is while we can use reason. Let us turn to God so that we may deserve to be illumined by his Word, the true Light" (*VR* 42.79).

Augustine's Christological sophistication grew in the years from 387 to 391. He was becoming aware as well of the classic Christological problems; the difficulty of reconciling the Incarnation and divine immutability (*Gen. Man.* 2.24.57), for example, and the extent of Christ's human knowledge (*Gen. Man.* 1.22.24; cf. 2.15.29). We see the beginning of an exactitude in Christological predication that would soon become one of Augustine's chief interpretative tools. In this period he was also devoting some attention to the relationship of the Word and the man assumed. In *On True Religion,* it will be recalled, the man is described as "honored by grace," "strengthened by firmness," "borne up by majesty"; the Word is said to direct and govern him. Later in the same treatise there is another series of descriptions of the close relationship: "inwardly fed," "subject to such a degree," and "cleaves to" (*VR* 3.3). But at this point Augustine was not prepared to go beyond these descriptive phrases.

Although better able to appreciate the reality and integrity of Christ's humanity, Augustine, like Jacob, was not yet completely reconciled to Leah. The subjects of faith as a means of knowledge and of Christ's humanity, "insofar as it can be easily understood" (i.e., as teacher and example), had been addressed, but the third component, "Christ crucified," had not yet been "understood" and integrated into Augustine's theology. This integration would require his intellectual development of the next five years.

Conclusion

Despite its (by later standards) unfinished character, the attractiveness of Augustine's triple-faceted model, ascending, gathering force, and culminating in Christ the enlightening Light, has made it one of the best loved of Christian theories of salvation. Although not the first or the last of its kind, it is generally seen as characteristically Augustinian, and by some as the heart and basis of his soteriology. But this conclusion overstates the case. It is better to observe only that it dominated his first five years as a Christian and remained an important motif in the years to come.

We can learn from following the development of the Christology Augustine taught in the years 387 to 391, and what we can learn is essential to good theological education. It requires intellectual discipline and honesty. Augustine worked hard at his understanding of Christ, and his presentations reflected the processes of his mind. When he did not intellectually grasp a teaching of the church about Christ, he said so openly. To understand Christ even partially is not a facile matter, and to teach Christ is not to parrot pious truths but to put forward with intellectual integrity the Figure one knows, and to do so in such a manner that that Figure can be appropriated by one's hearers. The essential character of such teaching has not changed beyond recognition in 1,600 years.

Chapter Six
Christology
in the Middle Ages

Jean-Marc Laporte

If we can believe the pattern emerging in the work of many authors of the last twenty years or so, our bruised and battered twentieth century is now seriously taking stock of itself.[1] This self-inventory is no mere jeremiad: it attempts to get at the roots of our discontent and to discern latent forces of renewal already at work in our midst. An older worldview, based on the quantitative presuppositions of Newtonian physics, has made it possible for us to harness the powers of nature in extraordinary ways, but at the same time it is eroding the intimate fabric of our lives, replacing quality with quantity.[2] Yet, little by little, a new worldview is emerging, one that gives pride of place to the intricate and inescapable interrelation of all things as theoretically formulated in various post-Einsteinian constructs of physical reality and that cares for the ecology of human action in the broadest sense of the word. To the extent that it is successful, such an integrally holistic approach will moderate our excessive reliance on the "quick fix" of technology and foster our appreciation of an ecologically motivated patience, without which there is no genuine and lasting quality of life.

In their quest for helpful models that will inspire us and guide us in our action, some of these authors look not only across to Eastern religions and

---

[1]A bibliography on this topic would include the following: F. Capra, *The Turning Point: Science, Society, and the Rising Culture* (New York: Simon & Schuster, 1982); Marilyn Ferguson, *The Aquarian Conspiracy: Personal and Social Transformation in the 1980s* (Los Angeles: Tarcher, 1980); as well as many works by Rollo May, Philip Slater, Theodore Roszak.

[2]See especially Morris Berman, *The Reenchantment of the World* (Ithaca: Cornell University Press, 1981).

their timeless wisdom but also back to an earlier Western tradition, more organic, more respectful of the fabric of reality. The latter means the Middle Ages in their earlier constructive phase, before strong centrifugal forces, finding theoretical justification in nominalism's compartmentalized view of reality, began to shape society according to what these authors term the older worldview.

To achieve an empathic and fruitful understanding of the Western Middle Ages, one cannot bypass Christology. Animating the endeavors of this period is a religious stance in which Jesus Christ is the beginning, center, and culmination of all reality, the one in whom the intricate dance of the universe finds its coherence. Medieval Christology is the theme of this chapter.

Of course the theme warrants much fuller treatment than I can give here. I select authors and topics especially pertinent to the objectives of this book. Among authors two stand out, Thomas Aquinas (1225–1274) and Bonaventure (1221–1274). In their similarities and differences they exemplify the best the Middle Ages has to offer to our own day. I begin, however, with the context and the methods of medieval Christology, spending more time on broader themes than on specific points of doctrine. Though extremely significant, the latter would lead us too far afield in a survey such as this.

The Shaping of Medieval Thought

The mind and heart of the theologian of any age is a crucible in which differing components come together to shape new understandings and new perspectives that give direction to a community caught in the tension between faith and vision. We will examine the components that enter into the shaping of medieval theology under the headings of tradition, experience, and challenge. These headings reflect my conviction, which I will state rather than justify at this point, that theologians who bring about creative advances in their discipline do so only to the extent that they are in touch with the Christian tradition as it is available to their age, with the personal experience of God present to and in their own hearts, and with the pastoral challenges that emanate from the context in which they live.[3]

---

[3]These three components reflect the dynamics of the fuller account of theological methodology to be found in Bernard Lonergan's *Method in Theology* (London: Darton, Longman & Todd, 1972). The first four of his functional specialities (research, interpretation, history, and dialectic) deal with the texts and documents of the past; the remaining four (foundations, doctrines, systematics, and communications) attempt to bring theology to bear on the cultural, political, and economic conjuncture of the day. Personal conversion, which

Tradition

The earlier Christian tradition was not fully accessible to medieval authors. Between the first flowering of Christendom, from Nicaea to the Barbarian invasions, and its rebirth in the West during the eleventh and twelfth centuries, there occurred a period of eclipse and dispersal, in the course of which the seeds of new life were nurtured in protective silence. Except for the text of the canonical Scriptures, the manuscripts available to us often were not available to medieval authors. What they all had access to, and what served as the basis for much of their teaching, were anthologies, or collections of "sentences" (opinions expressed and judgments proferred). Peter Lombard's *Book of Sentences* is the prime example of such anthologies. While the bread and butter of medieval professors of theology was the *sacra pagina,* at an earlier phase of their career most of them began their studies with Peter Lombard's nuggets of truth culled from the past, trying to organize them in coherent and systematic sets of questions and to resolve the contradictions that appeared between some of them. As was expected according to the academic practice of their university, the first major work of Aquinas and Bonaventure thus was a commentary on the sentences of the Lombard.

The lack of access to the *opera omnia* of key authors who had shaped their tradition was a limitation, but one of its by-products was highly positive. They could not, as we can, give full scope to the origins and development of the thought of the authors they studied as they attempted to resolve some of the contradictions they encountered in the texts they had at their disposal. But what they could do, and did do with a vengeance, was to scrutinize the texts they had at hand, using the grammatical, logical, and dialectical techniques of interpretation that were available to them.[4] These techniques helped them to set statements within their immediate context, to establish a range of meaning for those statements, and, when putting them in juxtaposition with apparently contradictory statements, to select meanings that did not lead to head-on conflict. Given the relative absence of techniques to deal with the genetic (diachronic) aspect of texts,

---

is an experienced reality, serves as the pivot that allows theologians to move from the first set to the second set of functional specialities, from appropriating what others have thought to speaking their own mind.

[4]The basic liberal arts training that served as the foundation of theological formation began with the classical trivium, the threefold way of grammar, dialectics (including logic), and rhetoric. The works of antiquity on which this trivium was based, above all those of Aristotle, were available relatively early, as well as commentaries by Boethius and Porphyry.

they concentrated on what today we would call the structural, or synchronic, aspect. They did so with a seriousness and sophistication leading to results that were remarkably insightful and respectful of the fuller reality of the authors they were studying.

Though critical of their predecessors, these medieval interpreters exercised their critical powers within a prevailing attitude that was welcoming, even reverent, toward the figures of the past. The presumption was that any text, especially of the earlier past that antedated the chaos out of which the Middle Ages had only recently emerged, had an authoritative status. Even crumbs were too precious simply to sweep aside. But the authority of these texts did not cramp the spontaneity of their interpreters, who would reject what was patently false and distorted—they had no trouble distinguishing orthodox from heretical teaching, including that of pagan philosophers whose works were gaining wider and wider circulation. In an initial moment they would seek ways of supporting, affirming, and integrating in a fuller pattern the elements of the tradition conveyed by texts of the past, allowing any element of truth to stand in the face of its contrasting truth. But then they would discreetly nuance questionable formulations, reinterpret them with great freedom, put a favorable construction upon them that often would go beyond their original intent.[5] That in the process they might sometimes distort the meaning that they really knew the author intended would not cause them scruples. Individualism had not yet become a significant factor in intellectual life. It was more important to release the truth embedded in a text that all might profit from it than to bring out what was distorted in it and set it aside.

This medieval attitude, unself-conscious and unstudied as it may have been, offers our age a contrasting model for the function of interpretation. The presupposition with which we ought to approach the many contrasting voices that we hear in our pluralistic world is a basic receptivity always on the alert for what can be affirmed, appreciated, and utilized in the human quest for truth.[6] One of the fruits of the ecumenical and world-religion dialogues of recent decades has been precisely to teach us how to allow our critical faculties to be tempered within the context of an underlying hospitality and reverence. Such dispositions are crucial in today's Christol-

---

[5]CF. M. D. Chenu, *Introduction à l'étude de Saint Thomas d'Aquin* (Paris: Vrin, 1954) 106-31.

[6]In the terms of Bernard Lonergan, this receptivity would involve extricating the truth from the counterposition in which it expressed, so as to allow it to be developed as a position. See the chapter on dialectic in his *Method in Theology*.

ogy, as we begin to articulate the significance of Jesus Christ in relation to religious perspectives in which he plays no part.

Experience

The medieval experience of God and of the world was marked by the freshness of new beginnings. This newness was both subjective and objective, residing not just in what was seen but also in the eyes seeing it; it was the newness of the child who in an innocent and self-effacing way is open to the new because of the freshness and simplicity within. The underside of these attractive qualities was what to us would come across as a relative lack of differentiation and self-appropriation. The barrier between childlikeness and naïveté is a very fragile one. Medieval experience, especially of the self and of God, was relatively unexamined. It did not readily come to explicit focus as it did in someone like Augustine, or does in our own introspective and analytical century. Though in many instances authentic and well-integrated, it remained for the most part tacit. In Jungian terms, medievals by and large had only begun upon the long path that leads to individuation. The ego and the self, the individual and the collective were at an early stage of differentiation. The price of progressing along the path of fuller maturity would be the turmoil and suffering of the following centuries, beginning with the anxious self-affirmation of the ego that occurs in the late Middle Ages and the Renaissance.[7]

Medieval experience in its religious dimensions was at times genuinely mystical, and it had a powerful impact on everyday life. The evangelical reform of religious life that emerged with the two mendicant orders of the thirteenth century, the Franciscans and the Dominicans, is an outstanding instance of this impact. A profound religious experience of God's call (witness especially the charisma of Saint Francis) was at the heart of this reform, which had immediate and lasting effects on the life of the church. Both Aquinas and Bonaventure give evidence (although with a certain reticence and self-effacement, especially on the part of Aquinas) of genuine religious, at times mystical, experience in accord with the charisma of their

---

[7]Cf. Rollo May, *The Meaning of Anxiety* (New York: Norton, 1977) ch. 6; "Anxiety Interpreted Culturally." Lonergan's contrast between two forms of genuineness applies here: "The genuineness of which we think when we speak of a simple and honest soul, is the happy fruit of a life in which illusion and pretense have had no place. But there is another genuineness that has to be won back through a self-scrutiny that expels illusion and pretense; and as this enterprise is difficult and its issue doubtful, we do not think of its successful outcome when we cast about for an obvious illustration of genuineness," (*Insight* [New York: Philosophical Library, 1956] 475). The first genuineness is like that of the Middle Ages; the second, akin to ours.

founders, Saints Francis and Dominic. To forget this factor when we examine their Christologies is to deprive ourselves of the depth dimension of their contribution to our own age.

This centrality of religious experience as animator and authenticator of theology in the Middle Ages can only encourage us to do our own theology, our own Christology, in close contact with our own religious experience. Unlike our forebears, we can make use of sophisticated tools of scrutiny and criticism generally available to our age, and we can call upon spiritual traditions that aim to develop the gift of discernment. But the complexity of the process involved ought not deter us from what ought to be as central to our endeavors as it was to those of our medieval predecessors. Christology and spirituality flourish together or languish separately.

Challenge

Though marked by a spirit of optimism and forward movement, the medieval period presented daunting challenges to those within it who wished to present the gospel message in a pertinent way. In the centuries prior to Bonaventure and Aquinas, secular society was under the tutelage of the church, which had served as a beacon of order and peace in the chaos of the Dark Ages, preserving cultural values of the past and serving as the matrix within which new ones could safely unfold. Now Western society was beginning to move into its turbulent period of puberty, to flex its muscles, discover its strengths, and act on its own. New towns, a new bourgeoisie, new guilds, and new patterns of trade and economic activity offered a sharp contrast to the feudal and ecclesiastical settlement of the earlier Middle Ages. The focus of thirteenth-century intellectual life was the university, still in great part under the supervision of the church, but beginning to have a life and a mind of its own. Scholars began to investigate philosophical questions in spite of the discomfort and disapproval of church authorities. A key instance of this was Siger de Brabant and his followers, whose radical Aristotelianism à la Averroes was condemned in 1277.

These challenges elicited a wide range of reaction, welcoming and suspicious, liberal and conservative. Bonaventure and Aquinas offer the contrast of two relatively balanced approaches. Their theologies are marked by a different style. Aquinas was perhaps more open to the newer currents, more interested in making use of the contributions of Aristotle, though the latter was seen to be a dangerous secular philosopher. Bonaventure was more in touch with the traditional religious values of which Augustine of Hippo was the vehicle par excellence.

The religious thought of their period, the thirteenth century, is possible only because of what is often called the twelfth-century renaissance. During that period, the treasures of the past were little by little coming to the light of day: not just collections of church-related authors and documents, but also the best authors of the Greco-Roman world were rediscovered, together with many insightful commentaries of recent Muslim authors.

As has been intimated, the recovery of the Aristotelian corpus, with its positive and negative aspects, was of crucial importance in this respect. In a first stage already complete before the time of Aquinas and Bonaventure, Aristotle's logical works became an essential part of the higher education of the day. They helped medievals hone to a very fine degree the skills of analysis, logical organization, and disputation, essential if they were to make their mark in the academic world of the day.[8] An early instance of these skills was Abelard's *Sic et Non,* a twelfth-century work that presented a series of apparent contradictions in the thought of the *auctoritates* of the past. He offered often dialectically brilliant resolutions that left many dissatisfied and suspicious. This pattern of disputation and resolution became a central feature of theology as it was both done and written in the subsequent centuries. It served to organize many works of theology, such as Aquinas's *Summa Theologiae.* The key dynamic at work was that of the disputed question. Authoritative views and logical arguments on both sides were presented, and the *magister* offered a determination or solution of the issue, responding to each authority and each argument, usually with the purpose of showing how the element of truth contained therein was included in his solution.

The second stage of this challenging recovery of the past occurs when the more properly philosophical works of Aristotle and of Muslim commentators such as Averroes and Avicenna came on the scene. The basic worldview that animated the thought of these authors in many respects opposed the worldview of Christian revelation. Nonetheless many categories and basic principles, extricated from an unacceptable worldview, offered a sound and insightful approach to the systematic organization of theological knowledge and, in some instances, offered a knowledge of the physical universe that called for integration in the wider body of knowledge that theology animated. There occurred, especially for Aquinas, a move from what Bernard Lonergan calls the world of common sense to the world of theory. Things begin to be seen in their relationship to one another, not just in their relation to us.[9] Bonaventure has a similar sapiential perspective but is less sanguine than his Dominican brother about the contribution of Aristotle to genuine wisdom.

---

[8]This process of logical refinement continued on in the later Middle Ages in ways that presage contemporary symbolic logic.

[9]See Lonergan, *Insight,* 291-92, and *Method in Theology,* 81-82.

The contemporary context is quite different, but a similar dynamic is at work in theology today, advertence to which will benefit our own Christological endeavors. The challenge of the Middle Ages was to use the newly available tools of Aristotle's metaphysics, purifying them, transforming them, but nonetheless using them to effect a radical breakthrough. Our challenge is to use the newly honed tools that come from reflection on the human reality in all its dimensions, tools that are not so much metaphysical as they are metapsychological and metasociological. Likewise, if we accept Lonergan's analysis, just as the medievals moved into the world of theory, we are moving into that of interiority.[10] In Christology, this shift means a doctrine that is open to the social, interpersonal, and intrapersonal dimensions of human and divine reality.[11]

Outcome

How can we describe what resulted when the recovery of a rich tradition, a new experience of the self and its constitutive relations, and a world in ferment came together in the minds and hearts of the theologians of the Middle Ages? In the first place, as apparent conflicts between authoritative sources in Scripture and tradition were resolved, there emerged clarity and cohesion within and between areas of theological thought, and pieces were knit together in ever-broader patterns, an achievement that will never be duplicated, given the impossibility for one person today to master the range of knowledge now available to us. This interwebbing of thought culminates in veritable cathedrals of thought, aptly known as *summae,* because they purport to sum up the entirety of theological knowledge in an organic way. Aquinas, who devoted his entire active life to theology, offers the clearest instance of this synthetic function. More than any other author of the Middle Ages, he integrates the world of human thought and endeavor that was being both rediscovered and created before his eyes, with the transcendent world of Christ proclaimed by the church as a fulfillment utterly beyond human resources. He brings the world of nature and the world of grace into ultimate coherence, the former bearing in its depths an

---

[10]See, for instance, his *Method in Theology,* 340-44, where he speaks of the intentionality analysis characteristic of this new phase.

[11]The exploration of this new field has only begun. I would mention William Thompson's *Jesus, Lord and Saviour* (New York: Paulist, 1980) as an instance of a contemporary Christology faithful to traditional perspectives yet open to the newer psychological dimensions. To some extent liberation Christologies, e.g., Jon Sobrino's *Christology at the Crossroads* (Maryknoll NY: Orbis, 1978), draw from the metasociological. A more systematic exploitation of these resources remains to be carried out.

orientation that only the latter can fulfill, and serving as the embodiment in which the latter is dynamically present in our midst.

In the second place, no matter how encompassing was its intent, this theology is creative, venturesome, and pluralistic. The era of closed scholastic systems and unrelenting ecclesiastical scrutiny is not yet at hand. One has only to delve into the theological output of the twelfth and thirteenth centuries to discover that no avenue was left unexplored. People felt free to make mistakes, and mistakes were made. Occasionally, in matters felt to be of greater moment, the church exercised a magisterial function. But more usually, debates among theologians served to sift out the wheat from the chaff. The climate was encouraging for the theological explorer, and many advances resulted, some exploited within the Middle Ages themselves,[12] and others left for later centuries.[13] Each thinker's contribution was toward a common good that transcended the individual. None hesitated to borrow from what others had written, enhance it, even transform it, and return to the public domain. The differences between such mature thinkers as Aquinas and Bonaventure epitomize, but do not exhaust, this organic pluralism of medieval theology.

The Shape of Medieval Christology

In spite of their differences, medieval Christologies bear a family resemblance, based in great part on the factors we have just surveyed. After considering their underlying similarities, we will consider the contrasting contribution of two great figures of the high Middle Ages, Aquinas and Bonaventure. Together they will give us a better sense of the medieval contribution to Christology than either one of them alone. Contemporaries who certainly knew and respected each other, even at times teaching side by side in Paris, they nonetheless allowed different emphases to shape their presentations of the doctrine of Jesus Christ.

---

[12]I am thinking of the fact that Bonaventure and Aquinas depend upon a host of earlier thinkers, Franciscan and Dominican. Especially significant for Bonaventure was Alexander of Hales, and for Aquinas Philip the Chancellor, whose breakthrough in the early thirteenth century played a significant role in Aquinas's doctrine of nature and grace.

We will concentrate on Aquinas and Bonaventure in this article. An excellent survey of a brader range of authors and themes can be found in "Christology," an entry by W. Principe in vol. 3 of *Dictionary of the Middle Ages* (New York: Scribner's, 1983).

[13]I am thinking particularly of Richard of Saint-Victor, a theologian of the Trinity active in the twelfth century, whose societal models for the Trinity are enjoying a rediscovery at the hands of twentieth-century thinkers such as Jürgen Moltmann and Heribert Mühlen.

Underlying Similarities

In first place, medieval authors by and large give a central place to the Scriptures as a source for Christology. This tendency may have been less true of late medieval theologians, who often tended to do theology at one or two removes from primary sources and who rightly incurred the opprobrium of Martin Luther, but in the thirteenth century the more sclerotic features of a school theology devoted to defending and illustrating the thought of an illustrious forebear had not yet emerged. Study of and commentary on Scripture was the main occupation of Thomas, Bonaventure, and their fellow masters in theology. They did not have access to the historical-critical method available to our century, had little sense of development in the understanding of Jesus Christ embedded in the very texts of the New Testament, but their grasp of logic and grammar enabled them to enter into the "literal" sense of Scripture with a rigor that offers some parallels to contemporary structural and logicical analysis of texts. At the same time, they are aware of various other senses of Scripture clustering around the literal.

Second, the settlement achieved by the first seven ecumenical councils in Christology was normative for medieval theologians. They did not question the affirmation that Jesus Christ is one divine person, God the Word, in two natures, divine and human. At first their knowledge of the conciliar texts was often restricted to the basic affirmations contained therein. From the mid-thirteenth century on, however, theologians had the advantage of a fuller knowledge of the conciliar texts themselves.[14] They shared a common set of foundational Christological truths, which, rather than exclude their differences on doctrine, made it possible for them to disagree intelligently and within the same universe of discourse. For instance, we find differences in understanding the notion of person, the notion of hypostatic union, and the relationship between the Incarnation and Redemption.

Third, they operated out of a similar basic understanding of the task of theology, formulated at the outset of the Middle Ages by Anlsem (1033–1109) in the classic terms of *fides quarens intellectum*. While reason and rational demonstration plays a role in theology for them, it never usurps the place of faith. The truths of the faith are not rationally demonstrated but are given in the sources of revelation, namely, Scripture and authentic

---

[14]Aquinas's stay in Rome in 1260–1261 enabled him to study a number of conciliar texts at first hand, and this was reflected in the differences between his earlier Christological work and that of the third part of the *Summa*. Cf. G. Lafont, *Structures et méthode dans la Somme Théologique de S. Thomas d'Aquin* (Paris: Desclée de Brouwer, 1960) 325.

church teachings. Theology seeks to understand these truths as far as possible, showing the reasonableness of each truth, its inner coherence with other truths.

Nonetheless in the eleventh and twelfth centuries, marked by the somewhat naive innocence of early-medieval theological endeavor, we find authors who appeared to be much more optimistic concerning human reason's range of potential achievement. Like children, they were engrossed in testing out new skills (in this case, skills of logical analysis and dialectical discrimination), pushing them to their outer limits. On the surface, it might seem that Anselm attempts to demonstrate with inescapable reasons how the Atonement could happen only the way it did; and Richard of Saint-Victor (1123–1173), how there had to be no more and no less than three persons in God. But such *rationes necessariae* were developed only within an implicit and all-pervasive context of faith and derived their cogency in large part from that context. Thinkers of those early centuries in many cases had not reached the mature self-appropriation that would have given them a better perspective on the limitations inherent to their own work. Little by little, critical discourse within the community of scholars, together with an occasional nudge from church authorities, led to a more modest and mature self-assessment of their own efforts at ratiocination. Bonaventure and Thomas in the thirteenth century thus each in his own way can acknowledge more explicitly the primacy of faith in theology. For them the role of reason is not to demonstrate the mysteries of the faith but to contemplate them and discover, if possible, their fittingness within the overall harmony of the universe that finds its center in God and to ward off arguments of reason attempting to disprove them.

Applied to Christology, this means that reason has absolutely no power to comprehend the inner mystery of Jesus Christ. Having acknowledged this mystery as revealed, it can go on to elaborate a view of reality that brings out its attractiveness and coherence. Theologians cannot pretend to demonstrate why God had to act in Christ as and when he did, but given the revelation of that action, they open themselves to the harmony and order and fittingness of that action as it stands revealed to them. Their theology is a wisdom that recognizes its own limits rather than an attempt to build a tower of Babel. In the realm of grace, human reason, just like human freedom, responds rather than initiates.

Fourth, just as authors did in the patristic period, medieval authors struggled with the paradoxical aspect of a mystery in which the human and the divine natures are conjoined in one person with detriment to neither nature. The tendency of the human mind, as evidenced in the struggles of the patristic period, is to affirm one nature at the expense of the other or to loosen their union in order to achieve what, by the standards of humanly devised philosophy, might appear to be greater clarity and coherence of thought.

Within the acceptable range of patristic thought, medieval Christology on the whole comes across in its speculative expositions of doctrine as having a greater affinity with Alexandria than with Antioch. This alignment could be, but need not be, a reproach: sharply distinct from uniformity, orthodoxy is quite capable of encompassing diverse tendencies. At the same time, by contemporary theological standards one might wonder, for instance, at the generally maximalist views of the knowledge available to the human Jesus espoused by medieval theologians, for whom the Cyrillic primacy of the divine nature is taken for granted. Other elements, however, present in the medieval religious culture served to balance their thought. The Franciscan tradition that shaped Bonaventure stressed the humility and poverty of the Incarnate One and treasured the devotion to the Nativity, retold in mystery plays and depicted in images and sculptures of the Christ child lying in the manger. In the Christology of his *Summa,* Aquinas gives extensive treatment to the mysteries of Christ's earthly life (3a.31-52), including those that pertained to the Dominican vocation of preaching the word (3a.42). In the course of subsequent centuries, this human dimension became somewhat neglected,[15] and there emerged a Christology that in many respects is abstract, remote, and disincarnate, a descending Christology that rightly calls for its complement in the ascending Christology that has emerged in the twentieth century.

Fifth, classical medieval Christologists, such as Thomas and Bonaventure, set their Christology against a similar cosmic backdrop. Both authors gave considerable room in their vision to the central Neoplatonic pattern of emanation and return. This pattern was already seminally present in the structures of John's Gospel, in which Jesus is portrayed as coming from the Father and returning to the Father, and it was carefully emended in the patristic period by the explicit addition of personal freedom and relationship at key points, in order to counteract the impersonal Gnostic doc-

---

[15]The absoluteness of this statement ought to be mitigated by the presence in the late Middle Ages of a devotion to the suffering Christ. There is something one-sided about stressing the passion and death to the detriment of the public ministry that gives them credibility and meaning, but nonetheless for the people of that period of painful social, economic, political, and cultural dislocation, the dislocated members of the suffering Christ, so graphically portrayed in the art of the day, were fraught with meaning. In later centuries, within the Roman Catholic tradition the development of the devotion to the Sacred Heart of Jesus kept the faithful in touch with one dimension in particular of the humanity of Jesus—his compassion and vulnerability.

trine seen as sharply contrary to a religion based on the personal covenant of God and humankind. What in the Gnostic scheme of things had been an emanation becomes a free act of creation. What had been an ineluctable return fostered by contemplative activity is seen as taking place only because of God's free bestowal of grace, centering in Jesus Christ, and a free response of human beings enlivened by the Spirit. Freed from necessitarian and impersonal overtones, the Neoplatonic scheme became a powerful image available to the Christian thinker seeking to craft an all-pervasive view of reality.

This image was introduced to the Middle Ages in large part through Pseudo-Dionysius. In it, God is the one from whom all creation flows and to whom all creation returns. In that return, humankind, created in the image of God and destined to fulfill that image in the perfect likeness of face-to-face intimacy, plays a special role, and within humankind the perfect human being, Jesus Christ, is to be singled out as indispensable source, center, and culmination of creation's return to God.

Characteristic Accents
of Thomas and Bonaventure

Both Aquinas and Bonaventure attempt to be faithful to the tradition they received, which included Scripture, the decisions of the ecumenical councils, and the work of the Western church's mentor par excellence, Augustine of Hippo. At the same time they are open to the new ideas coming to them from the pagan philosopher Aristotle and his commentators, ideas such as act and potency, the predicamental categories, the four causes, and the unmoved mover. Those ideas needed to be purified, at times to be rejected when they contradicted revealed truth, but they offered precious support to the efforts of reason to articulate the truths of the faith intelligibly.

Among his peers Aquinas was remarkably open to this Aristotelian input and he was led to develop more explicitly the principles and structures of a theology that allowed created reality its inner consistency and human reason its native scope. While conscious of the negative effects of original sin on the powers of reason, he still formulated a clear distinction between the realm in which reason could function effectively on its own and that in which reason utterly depends on the truths of revelation. In that sense he paves the way for later differentiations of human knowledge into theology and philosophy, philosophy and science.

Bonaventure was more suspicious of Aristotle's pagan propensities, more open to the Augustinian and earlier medieval worldview, in which the realities of this world were seen above all in their transparency to the mystery of God. Though he makes use of many of the same basic Aristotelian categories as does Aquinas, they are somewhat more subsidiary to the articulation of his thought. Indeed he tended to develop and articulate the basic principles of his thought more out of direct reflection on Christian revelation.[16] In that sense he is more akin to earlier medieval thinkers who were less keen on differentiating the powers of faith from those of revelation; for him the only philosophy is Christian philosophy. The explicit categories of his thought give more importance to the reality of personal freedom, especially that of God, whereas Aquinas's Christian personalism is present to his thought in a more deeply embedded way, underpinning all his theological endeavors,[17] while on the surface one might find in them, as did more conservative theologians of the 1270s, affinity with the necessitarianism of the Averroist Siger de Brabant and his followers.

Aquinas formulates two ways of ordering thought, one in which truths are discovered in their original setting (*ordo inventionis*) and one in which they are expounded scientifically (*ordo disciplinae*). For Aquinas the latter is the proper pedagogical order, the one he follows in his masterwork, the *Summa Theologiae*. His Christology is more scientific in the sense that it professedly begins with the most basic principles (as does, for instance, his doctrine of the Trinity) and works its way to the conclusions that bring that science to its fullness. He begins with the basic truth of the hypostatic union, and in systematic steps moves from that truth to various conclusions that concern the modalities of the Incarnation, of the human life of Jesus, of the Resurrection, of his atoning work, and so forth.

These two ways of ordering thought recur in contemporary theology, specifically in contemporary Christology. The *ordo inventionis* is deployed in a more fully genetic fashion: one approaches a doctrine "from below," retracing the steps by which one's predecessors passed from their first rudimentary understandings on the basis of primordial experience to ever more penetrating insights expressed with rigor and sophistication. Having come to the end of that process, one has grasped the fundamental principles as currently operative in an area of thought and is ready for what in contemporary terms would

---

[16]Cf. C. Tresmontant, *La métaphysique du Christianisme et la crise du 13° siécle* (Paris: Seuil, 1964), especially: "Bonaventure is less concerned than Saint Thomas with a lengthy and properly rational demonstration of the fundamental theses of Christian metaphysics. As a theologian and as a pastor, Bonaventure is often content with formulating the metaphysical exigencies of Christian theology, and to note, in the name of the metaphysical principles implied in Catholic theology, how certain philosophical doctrines are incompatible with Christianity. . . . [Bonaventure's question is] What metaphysics is implied in and by Christianity?" (p. 384; my translation).

[17]For this analysis, see J. B. Metz, *Christliche Anthropozentrik* (Munich: Kösel, 1962). The term *personalism* that I use here is linked with his term *anthropocentric* and is not without affinities with the usage of the Scottish philosopher John Macmurray.

be termed "Christology from above," and in Aquinas's terms, Christology exposed according to the *ordo disciplinae*.

Thomas's Christology has its own internal coherence, but it is also part of an articulated doctrinal ensemble that reaches its most mature expression in the *Summa Theologiae*. Though the organization of Thomas's *Summa* is open to considerable debate,[18] it is clear that Christology enters into a doctrinal context that is already firmly established. Thomas has already dealt with the mystery of God and of the creation that freely flows from God's goodness, and he has also dealt with creation's return to God through the free, graced acts of human beings. In the third part of the *Summa*, he invites the student of theology to reflect on the specific way that God in his providence has chosen for humankind to return to God, Jesus Christ who is God made man. The fact and modalities of the Incarnation are hidden in the mystery of God, and using his clear distinction between what is accessible to reason and what pertains to revelation, he refuses to sever the link between the fact of the Incarnation and the fact of Adam's sin, which appears to emerge de facto in scriptural revelation. Likewise, while he argues for the special appropriateness of the incarnation of the Son rather than of the Father or of the Spirit, he is adamant that, in principle, any of the persons could have been incarnate.[19] Had revelation offered clearer principles in these questions, we could have been more forthright in our affirmations about them. As it is, our most fitting stance is marked by a certain agnosticism.

Bonaventure's Christology is less easy to typify in the same way. He became master general of the Franciscans at an early stage of his theological career, and we do not have a work of his that compares in scope and maturity to the *Summa*. Nonetheless he has left an important and impressive body of work, most recently presented to us by Zachary Hayes.[20]

His perspective on reality is more explicitly hieratic, spiritual, affective, and, as we saw, more in touch with the traditional medieval emphasis for which all being is, in its depth, transparency to God. In many particulars—above all, those that pertain to defined doctrine—his Christology does not differ from that of Aquinas. However, in his contemplation of reality as a whole, to be known only through revelation, Bonaventure,

---

[18]See Lafont *Structures et méthode*, 15-34, where he outlines the attempts of Chenu, Hayen, and Person. On pp. 469-94, he offers his own conclusions.

[19]Ibid., 146-56; *Summa theologiae* 3.3.

[20]Zachary Hayes, *The Hidden Center: Spirituality and Speculative Christology in St. Bonaventure* (New York: Paulist Press, 1981).

moved by the boldness of love, is somewhat less cautious than Aquinas and formulates for us a clear vision, according to which Jesus Christ and only Jesus Christ is at the center of reality.

The Christocentrism is essentially linked to the notion of mediation, which in Hayes's interpretation of Bonaventure plays an explicit architectonic role that it does not have in the thought of Aquinas. The notion of the Second Person as the *persona media,* the middle or mediating Person within the Trinity, arose in the Trinitarian speculation of Richard of Saint-Victor. Bonaventure applies it to the hypostatic union, to the mediation between God and humankind that culminates in the Redemption, and it allows him to present Jesus Christ as the ultimate *coincidentia oppositorum.*[21]

Bonaventurean Christology is thus fundamentally not so much from above or from below as it is from the center. The Word is at the center of the Trinity, the *persona media;* the incarnate Word is at the center of the entire universe, of the process by which that universe descends from God and by which it then ascends to God. Less bent than Aquinas on distinguishing what pertains to the order of a nature that has consistency in and of itself, from what pertains to the order of revealed mystery, Bonaventure explores the contours of a vision of reality that integrates nature and grace, creation and God, around the central reality of Christ. He is more venturesome, more willing to use revealed data as a stepping-stone for further speculation. The results he achieves are remarkably akin to positions taken by Karl Rahner in the twentieth century. We find in him affinities to Rahner's theology of the Word as symbol, a movement in the direction of Rahner's position according to which the proper Trinitarian subject for an incarnation is the Second rather than the First or Third Person, and a similar struggle to bring together the gratuity of the Incarnation with the fact that it is central to God's purposes and not an afterthought.[22] This affinity of Rahner to Bonaventure is remarkable, since Rahner seems to have used Aquinas as a backdrop and starting point for his scholarly career, as evidenced by his thesis published as *Geist in Welt.*[23]

Thus Aquinas and Bonaventure present to us two helpful models for doing Christology today. In the first, sobriety, discretion, clear distinc-

---

[21]See ibid., 61-63, 87-90.

[22]Ibid., 55-60, 187-91.

[23]Interestingly enough, Bernard Lonergan began his work on Aquinas's epistemology as well, as evidenced by his early "Verbum" articles (now published as *Verbum: Word and Idea in Aquinas* [Notre Dame: University of Notre Dame Press, 1967]) and by *Insight.* The Christology Lonergan develops is more akin to that of Aquinas than to that of Bonaventure.

tions, and the scientist's unwillingness to go beyond the evidence are dominant; in the second, there come to the fore daring, spontaneity, and a passionate search for the mystery in which the entire universe finds its integration. But what is dominant in the one is also present in the other. Bonaventure and Aquinas are complementary, not contradictory. They are an example of the complementarity that needs to correct our twentieth-century tendency to build compartments, to isolate ourselves into schools of thought that have lost the secret of communication with each other. Dialogue, not opposition, is the hallmark of their work, and should be of ours.

Their success, not as individuals who have made it on their own against considerable odds, the typical model of success in our own world, but as colleagues within a universe of discourse that, though capable of sharp criticism, was ever hospitable toward the expression of newer facets of the truth, will never be duplicated. Yet in their footsteps we can open ourselves to the many resources our own culture makes available to us as we continue to explore the significance of Jesus Christ and seek to express in an open-minded and dialogical way whatever understandings are given to us.

Implications for Christology Today

What lessons can we derive from our medieval forebears as we carry theological reflection on Jesus Christ forward in our own day? Can they help us develop a Christology that will have an impact on our world in search of a coherence that continues to elude it?

Open-mindedness as an attitude permeated all the functions of theology in the Middle Ages. Medievals were open-minded toward all elements of the tradition that were available to them. They were quite able to criticize what was deviant or less appropriate, but their first instinct was always to discover, even to rescue, the elements of truth that were present in the multifarious strands of that tradition and to transpose them in newer language. While they were not sophisticated in matters of inner experience in the same way we might be today, it is clear that they allowed their own experience of God, of Jesus Christ, of grace, and of the church to permeate and to enliven their theology. Again they were, by and large, open to the reality of the world that was being transformed before their eyes and to the newer resources of thought, especially philosophical thought, available to them. In varying degrees they were willing to meet their challenge of modernity head-on. In sum, osmotic membranes rather than barriers were the order of the day.

The result was a theology that was remarkably diverse and pluralistic, but set within common parameters and animated by a common vision. Because of this communality, differences could and did become a fruitful source of dialogue rather than a frustrating impasse.

Openness today has to be much more sophisticated and complex than in the Middle Ages. We have struggled and are still struggling through the issues set by the Enlightenment; we have at our disposal tools of interpretation that enable us to be more discriminating than our medieval predecessors were in studying texts of the past. There is available to us a substantial and broadly based literature on the discernment of psychological and spiritual experience. The world developing before us offers an incredibly wide range of avenues and challenges for our theological thought. The Third World prompts us to develop a Christology of liberation; and the First, a Christology that also affirms and fosters the inner coherence of human persons and of the world in which they live. The metaphysical language of Aristotle can be supplemented today by various metahuman languages: as a stepping-stone for entry into the realm of mystery, we can call on a theoretical account of persons-in-relation rather than merely one that deals with physical reality. World religions deeply challenge the formulation of our faith in Jesus Christ. New dimensions of the one we believe in will emerge as we plumb the depths of insight and experience brought to us by those religions that were so remote in the Middle Ages and are so close today.[24]

We are called upon to do in our century what Aquinas and Bonaventure did in theirs, but we will not do it in the same way. Christology will become a more integrally collaborative endeavor. The Middle Ages offers us tools that will usefully supplement the ones we have available to us. The historical- and redaction-critical approaches to texts developed in the last hundred years are especially appropriate for the development of a Christology from below; the more rigorously grammatical approach to texts that was used in the Middle Ages, enhanced by contemporary structural and relational insights, will help us to move Christology forward and to expound less inadequately its mysteries in the from-above mode.

Do we have anything like the sense of settled parameters that enabled our medieval ancestors in the faith to face confidently the theological pluralism of their day? This is a particularly sensitive point. Each Christian denomination may have formulated parameters for itself, though one might

---

[24]One might question whether world religions were all that remote in the Middle Ages. After all, theologians like Aquinas were engaged in the defense of Christian truth against Islam, and the Crusader was an ideal of that period. Yet Islam to the people of that time was something on the edge of Christendom, a last remaining bastion to be brought to the faith without further ado. Only in the centuries following the Middle Ages did the extent and variety of cultural development that lay beyond Christendom become a part of the popular consciousness as it is today.

question how effective they are in channeling Christological discourse. The balance between pluralism and unity is delicate, just as liable to be disrupted by heavy-handed use of authority as by doctrinal nonchalance. If the Middle Ages can teach us anything, it is the reasonableness of counting on the fundamental soundness of the theological endeavor done in a context defined by mutual openness and mutual correction. The contributions of individual medieval theologians were uneven in their pertinence and penetration. Some were rejected and are now forgotten. But all contributions entered into an arena of lively discourse, open yet critical, that served to shape and solidify more profound understanding. Significant, even irrevocable, steps were taken in the unfolding of Christian thought; some theologians stood out by their ability to give an especially felicitous expression to newer understandings of the faith.

Many Christological issues raised by these medieval theologians continue to be issues for us—but then our world raises momentous and complex questions that were utterly beyond their ken. They differed among themselves in dealing with the key issue of their day, that of relating the rediscovered wisdom of Aristotelian philosophy with the revealed wisdom of revelation, but by and large they shared an attitude of critical openness. More and more our age is being described as the theater of a similar epochal shift. Our age harbors a plethora of pitfalls and opportunities for theology, as it brings Jesus Christ and the newer challenges of today to bear on one another. The organic, optimistic, and constructive bent of medieval theology has much to teach us as we move further along in our pilgrimage from the ''through a glass darkly'' of faith to the ''face to face'' of vision.

Chapter Seven
Christology at the Reformation

Clark H. Pinnock

In referring to Christology, I have in mind both the person and the work of Christ, both his identity and his significance for humankind. The subject is never properly addressed in a purely theoretical way but only when it is taken to refer to the human interest in salvation. Changes in the soteriological concern tend to raise new questions for Christological theory about the person of Jesus.[1]

Incarnation theology was not a battlefield in the time of the Reformation. The confession of Chalcedon had stood nearly unchallenged for 1,000 years, and the Reformers were firmly committed to it. Despite their emphasis on the Scriptures alone, they did not repudiate the theology of the church fathers or the creedal doctrine scheme produced by that early period. The great majority of Protestants expressed allegiance to the ecumenical creeds and incorporated them into their own confessions of faith.[2] While a few radical reformers (Servetus and Socinus) did challenge the orthodox doctrine, they were exceptions to the rule and did not command a large following. Not until the Enlightenment did the serious challenge to Chalcedon begin in earnest.[3] If there were new moves in Christology at the Reformation, they occurred in the area of soteriology and the work of Christ. In this chapter I first consider Christology in Luther and Calvin and then examine it in a few examples of the radical reformation.

---

[1]Wolfhart Pannenberg, *Jesus—God and Man* (Philadelphia: Westminster Press, 1968) 39.

[2]See the Formula of Concord, introductory Epitome 2.

[3]A. T. Hanson and R. P. C. Hanson, *Reasonable Belief: A Survey of the Christian Faith* (Oxford: Oxford University Press, 1980) 88-89.

The Christology
of the Conservative Reformation

Luther's Christology

Luther was an enthusiastic and adamant supporter of the Christological dogma of the early church. In his hymn based on John 1:14 he wrote, "'All praise to Thee, eternal God, who clothed in garb of flesh and blood, dost take a manger for thy throne, while worlds on worlds are thine alone.'" He used the two-natures terminology to describe the mystery of the Incarnation and also the patristic idea of an exchange of attributes between the two natures in the single person of Christ. No less than Athanasius and Anselm was Luther concerned for the true deity in humanity of Christ and for the same reason: he wrote, "If Christ is divested of his deity, there remains no help against the wrath of God and no rescue from his judgement."[4] He believed that Christ could not be our Redeemer if he were not true God and true man in one person. As Paul Althaus insists, "We may not modernise Luther at this point."[5] Luther accepted unequivocally the Christological dogma of the early church. In his conflict with Thomas Müntzer he even appealed to secular authority to maintain the teaching of sound doctrine on this point. Christological heresy ought not to be tolerated. It was profanity and blasphemy and ought to be punished accordingly. In this, Luther's attitude was identical to Calvin's in the Servetus incident to which we will return, and perhaps even more vehement.[6]

As regards his creedalism there was, however, a perceptible move from complexity to simplicity. While upholding Chalcedon, Luther had a decided dislike for speculations in theology such as occurred in Thomas, Scotus, and Ockham and preferred to place the emphasis on the practical soteriological concerns. This preference was not due, let me hasten to add, to any latent anti-Trinitarianism but rather to Luther's sense of what was really important in Christology, namely, the soteriological *why* not the metaphysical *how*.[7] For Luther and Calvin, one is saved not by getting the metaphysics right but by trusting in God, who was present personally in the Incarnation. The ontological and the functional, as we would say to-

---

[4]*Luther's Works,* ed. Jaroslav Pelikan (St. Louis: Concordia Publishing House, 1957) 22:22.

[5]Paul Althaus, *The Theology of Martin Luther* (Philadelphia: Fortress Press, 1966) 180.

[6]Bernard M. G. Reardon, *Religious Thought in the Reformation* (London: Longman Group, 1981) 86.

[7]Cf. Earl M. Wilbur, *A History of Unitarianism: Socinianism and Its Antecedents* (Cambridge: Harvard University Press, 1946) 1:15-16.

day, were wedded closely together, and the crucial matter is that one grasp the Lord Jesus Christ with the whole person unto salvation. Luther was deeply concerned to be practically evangelical, not to be philosophically precise. He placed the stress upon what Melanchthon would call "the benefits of Christ."

Thus in terms of his total Christology, the creed is important for Luther in that it specified the conditions that made the redemptive work of Christ on the cross possible and intelligible. God took our flesh and made the manger his throne in order to reveal his gracious will to reconcile us to himself. In what Luther calls "a happy exchange," Christ represented sinful humanity before God, bearing our guilt and enduring the wrath of God for our sakes. Like Anselm, Luther viewed Christ's work in terms of satisfaction—Christ brought satisfaction to God for our sins. God cannot simply forget about his wrath and show mercy to sinners unless his righteousness is satisfied. "Christ, the Son of God, stands in our place and has taken all our sins upon his shoulders. . . . He is the eternal satisfaction for our sin and reconciles us with God the Father."[8] Aulen was mistaken to suggest that, according to Luther, the decisive factor in the cross was the defeat of the powers of darkness. The victory motif was in fact dramatic imagery to describe the effect of the Atonement by Luther, but not his explanation of the death of Christ itself, which has to do with the removal of God's wrath against us, something that Satan is actually using against humankind. By taking away our guilt, Christ robbed the evil powers of their primary weapon against us. Luther uses the victory motif in the context of the Latin theory of atonement. By dealing with the condemnation of the law, Christ secured our justification and broke Satan's grip on us.[9] As the Augsburg Confession puts it, Christ suffered for us "that he might reconcile the Father to us, and might be a victim not only for original guilt but also for all actual sins of men." Chalcedon was important for Luther because it spelled out the conditions that made it possible for Christ to save us.[10]

In his treatment of the two natures of Christ, Luther got into theological trouble and placed tremendous strain upon the human nature of Jesus. Not that he denied or even diminished the excruciating reality of Jesus' hu-

---

[8]*Luther's Works* 51:92.

[9]Robert S. Franks, *The Work of Christ: A Historical Study of Christian Doctrine* (London: Thomas Nelson & Sons, 1962) 279-306; Althaus, *Theology of Martin Luther,* 218-23.

[10]Otto W. Heick, *A History of Christian Thought* (Philadelphia: Fortress Press, 1965) 1:332-34.

manity—he is very emphatic on precisely this point. More than half his sermons are based on the Synoptic Gospels, and he treats the details of Jesus' relationships with other people with care and vividness. As Dorner says, "The vigour and determination with which Luther insists on the reality of the humanity of Christ, even in the matter of growth, are worthy of note."[11] His emphasis is strong. The problem arose as a result of Luther's understanding of the exchange of attributes between the divine and the human, according to which whatever is assigned to one can be assigned to the other. Because he did not think in terms of a pretemporal decision on the part of the Logos to forego the uses of the divine attributes of majesty, Luther actually thought of the baby Jesus possessing omniscience, omnipotence, and omnipresence and conceived of Jesus making decisions in regard to the use of the divine attributes on a day-to-day basis. The danger in this way of thinking is a very real one that the humanity be swallowed up and absorbed into the divine nature. Luther, like Cyril before him, is running the risk of losing the genuinely human nature because of his belief in the *genus majestaticum,* the doctrine that Jesus possessed all the divine attributes at his birth.

Ironically, it may be that Luther's desire in the context of the eucharistic controversy to interpret literally the phrase "this is my body" pushed him in the direction of thinking in terms of the ubiquity of Christ's resurrection body, even in the case of his earthly experience. If so, it is a case of the tail wagging the dog! His Christology was shaped in part from its being drawn into the dispute over a different theological topic, which tended to make it adjacent to that subject rather than an independent topic of inquiry deserving of its own sovereign sphere of importance.[12] The same problem arose also when he came to treat the "cry of dereliction" from the cross. In answer to the question "How was Christ forsaken by God?" Luther said, "The deity withdrew and hid . . . the deity withdrew its power and let the humanity fight alone." Such a statement does not do much justice to the suffering of God in the sufferings of Christ but indicates a problem in the area of the two natures for Luther.[13] It was perhaps inevitable that, from within Lutheranism, someone like Gottfried Thomasius (1802–1875) would arise and move the logic in the other direction, to think in

---

[11]J. A. Dorner, *History of the Development of the Doctrine of the Person of Christ,* vol. 11, pt. 2 (Edinburgh: T. & T. Clark, 1866) 90.

[12]A. B. Bruce, *The Humiliation of Christ* (Edinburgh: T. & T. Clark, 1881) 82; Dorner, *History,* 116-40, 172.

[13]*Luther's Works* 12:126-27.

terms of the divine nature's being drawn into the sphere of the human, rather than the other way around. In his "kenotic" proposal Thomasius has the Son of God renouncing the divine attributes for the term of his incarnate life, thus preserving the true humanity intact, a solution holding attractions for those who wish to be orthodox and still respect the real humanity of Jesus. Luther himself almost made the same move in some remarks of his about the way in which God in Christ shared in the weakness, suffering, and humiliation of Jesus, how the Creator became a lowly creature and a servant subject to all people. But Luther's Christological theory of the two natures was never able to be rid of its inherent contradictions and tensions.

Calvin's Christology

Calvin too accepted the Chalcedon formulation about the person of Christ. The title to chapter 12 in book 2 of the *Institutes of the Christian Religion* is "Christ had to become man in order to fulfill the office of mediator." In Calvin's thinking, only one who was true God and true man could bridge the gulf between God and man. "Who could have done this had not the self-same Son of God become the Son of man, and had not so taken what was ours as to impart what was his to us, and to make what was his by nature ours by grace?" (2.12.2). In a statement that draws the person and the work together, Calvin says, "Accordingly, our Lord came forth as true man and took the person and the name of Adam in order to take Adam's place in obeying the Father, to present our flesh as the price of satisfaction to God's righteous judgement and in the same flesh to pay the penalty that we deserved" (2.12.3). Were one to diminish either the deity or the humanity of Christ, Calvin insists at length, one would weaken and overthrow the true faith (2.12-17).

In the course of these remarks Calvin refers to Michael Servetus as a "deadly monster" and refutes his opinions (2.14.5-8). Because the incident concerning Servetus illustrates so dramatically how seriously Calvin took the orthodox Christology and falls so unfavorably upon Calvin's reputation, let us pause briefly to consider it. The execution of Servetus for unorthodox views draws vivid attention to the fact that dark persecuting zeal flowed in Protestant as well as Catholic veins. Thousands of Anabaptists (most more scriptural in their faith than Servetus) were killed for the desire to see the work of reformation carried further. Usually the cause was their belief in the practice of baptism or in the separation of church and state, beliefs now very widely shared in all branches of the Reformation. In defense of Calvin, consider the following points, which help to put the picture in better perspective. First, hundreds of Calvinists, including Calvin's friend Étienne de la Forge, were killed by Catholics in France, and Calvin himself was a refugee from such terror. Second, by all accounts

Servetus seems to have been an ambitious and abusive fellow who, before his arrest in Geneva, had been sentenced to death twice by the Inquisition. His book entitled *The Restoration of Christianity* gives some indication that Servetus saw himself as the leading reformer of the period. Third, the court of Geneva, with the support of Zurich, Basel, and Bern, came to the decision about Servetus independently and not at the urging of Calvin. It is deeply ironical, I think, that Calvin should be plagued as much in death as in life by the one the court called "this pestilence." The point to note here is the great seriousness with which doctrines such as Christology were taken by Reformers like Calvin.[14]

For Calvin as for Luther, the Incarnation was not an intellectual puzzle but a profoundly religious issue. Christ had to be God and man in order to be our prophet, priest, and king, as Calvin expresses it in the *Institutes*. As priest in particular, this fact enabled him to put away our sins. Appealing to the Book of Hebrews, Calvin saw that Christ had to share in our flesh and blood (2:14) and come into the world in a body prepared for him (10:5) so as to save us by the sacrifice of himself (vv. 10, 12). In Calvin's words, "As a pure and stainless Mediator he is by his holiness to reconcile us to God. But God's righteous curse bars our access to him, and God in his capacity as judge is angry toward us. Hence an expiation must intervene in order that Christ as priest may obtain God's favor for us and appease his wrath" (2.15.6). As our Mediator, the God-man Jesus Christ stood in our place, paying the penalty we all deserved and brought about the reconciliation. "This is our acquittal: the guilt that held us liable for punishment has been transferred to the head of the Son of God (Isaiah 53:12). We must, above all, remember this substitution, lest we tremble and remain anxious throughout life—as if God's righteous vengeance, which the Son of God has taken upon himself, still hung over us" (2.16.5). Like Anselm, Calvin believed that the Incarnation took place for the purpose of redemption, which required the atoning death of the Mediator. He sweeps away the contrary opinion of Osiander for defending Scotus's view earlier that Christ was not originally predestinated to come into the world for the purposes of redemption but for some other higher purpose (2.12.5-7). But unlike Anselm, for whom the Atonement was a meritorious satisfaction, Calvin sees it as penal, a substitutionary punishment, in which Christ was wounded for our transgressions and experienced the wrath of God.[15]

---

[14]For an informative account of the Servetus incident, see T. H. L. Parker, *John Calvin, a Biography* (Philadelphia: Westminster Press, 1975) 117-24.

[15]Reardon, *Religious Thought in the Reformation,* 195.

As for the two natures of Christ, Calvin did not follow Luther's thinking on the communication of the attributes but chose to place great emphasis upon the lowliness and condescension of Christ in being willing to enter into the full reality of the human situation. In this way Calvin managed to avoid jeopardizing the genuine human experience of Christ. He held it to be important that the human nature not be diminished or impaired, or that the divine nature not transfer to the human nature its own majestic attributes. The human retains "its own distinctive nature" in the union, and the two natures are joined without being confused (2.14.1-2). Against the Lutherans he denied the ubiquity even of Christ's risen body, maintaining that, even after the Ascension, the flesh remains local while the Logos itself is omnipresent (4.17.29-30). For this view the Lutherans in turn invented the term *extra-Calvinisticum* and used it as a scourge. For Calvin, in effect, the two natures lie side by side without affecting the reality of the other. The human does not participate in the attributes of the divine nature. After the Incarnation the Logos exists, not only in his assumed flesh, but also outside it (*extra carnem*). Calvin does not really work this position out theologically but leaves us with the appearance that the natures are juxtaposed rather than profoundly united. In this regard his view suggests a Nestorian stance and is even protokenotic in that the divine nature seems to be appropriated to the human rather than the reverse. We really need to hear more about how Christ can be fully divine and not possess the attributes of majesty.

In conclusion, we cannot say that Luther and Calvin did a great deal of fresh thinking on Christology. They assumed that traditional theology was basically on the right track and needed to be defended. Even as regards soteriology, where they did orient the subject in a way more helpful to faith's function, they worked with categories of the Atonement available to them from the medieval churchmen, giving the topic a fresh Pauline flavor. But the difficulties they experienced trying to relate the two natures strongly suggest that there are some unexplained and unresolved issues there. By not going back to the New Testament afresh and thinking the subject through in a new way, they set themselves up as a target for anti-Trinitarians like Socinus. For me the most glaring question left unanswered is "How could Christ be truly human if he was at the same time creator of the universe?" Ironically, the very speculation in Christology that Luther and Calvin shunned would return soon in Protestant orthodoxy, rooted in part in Luther's own speculations about the ubiquity of Christ's body.[16]

---

[16]George H. Tavard, *Images of the Christ: An Enquiry into Christology* (Washington, D.C.: University Press of America, 1982) 67-69.

Without being novel, Luther and Calvin did feel very strongly about the received Christology. They were absolutely certain that the Savior would have to be the Creator of the world as well. Tied to an evangelical soteriology rather than to the sacramental theology of Athanasius, they saw it as a very vital question, one on which the church ought to be very clear-headed. They compel us to ask in theological education today: were they right? do the Scriptures teach what they believed? how is a person justified before God? Those we call conservative-evangelicals tend to feel with Luther and Calvin that clarity on this matter is essential and that theological institutions and denominations ought to enforce such beliefs and resist revisions to them. Their traditional standpoint comes into sharp conflict with the tendency since the Enlightenment to permit radical pluralism in theological inquiry and not to foreclose the issues prematurely, whatever the great tradition says.

The Christology
of the Radical Reformation

Brethren type of groups in the radical reformation desired a more complete restoration of primitive Christianity. Because of an orientation to religious experience and to issues of practical discipleship and their belief in the liberty of the individual conscience, they were not bound to creedal statements and were freer to innovate doctrinally and in other ways. Although the majority of them, called "the evangelical Anabaptists," including Menno Simons and Balthasar Hubmaier, were substantially in agreement with the received Christology, others in the rationalist wing such as Servetus and Socinus departed radically from it. The effect of the emphasis on religious liberty was to hasten the phenomenon of dissent in Christendom, a pluralism that Luther and Calvin had started but that the radical reformation carried much further, spelling doom for the relatively monolithic catholic culture of Europe. The new experiments in Christology among the Anabaptists in turn anticipated and sowed the seeds for widespread innovation in dogma that occurred three centuries later. To get a feeling for Christology among the Anabaptists and radical reformers, let us consider three thinkers: Menno Simons, Michael Servetus, and Faustus Socinus (Sozzini).

Menno Simons (1496–1561) was an evangelical Anabaptist from the generation following the events in Zurich in the 1520s. He was able to provide leadership first to the Dutch believers and then to a wider circle that eventually took his name. Although he spent much of his life preaching and evangelizing, he did a good deal of writing as well. On the subject of Christology Menno claimed to uphold the Nicene Creed and wrote a tract entitled "A Solemn Confession of the Triune, Eternal, and True God, Father, Son and Holy Ghost" (1550). But there also appeared in his thinking the doctrine of the "celestial flesh" of Christ, which was entertained widely among Anabaptists of the time and linked to a view of salvation that was more deificatory than forensic.[17] Though unusual to modern ears, the thinking behind this notion was quite orthodox in nature. It arose out of trying to explain the Incarnation and extended the logic in a novel direction: in order to save us, Christ cannot have been an ordinary man born of a sinful woman but must have possessed a pure humanity. It was the kind of thinking that would lead Roman Catholics to posit the Immaculate Conception of the Virgin Mary.

There were different versions of the celestial-flesh doctrine: some thought that Christ brought his body with him from heaven to become visible in Mary, while others supposed his human nature was a special creation in her. In respect to Menno, Calvin picked up on this twist in Christology and argued that it placed the true humanity of Christ in jeopardy and made him unlike us in important ways. He accused Menno of thinking that Christ's body was a mere appearance, being a kind of "heavenly flesh" (*Institutes* 2.13.1). But in the course of refuting it, Calvin gives evidence of grasping the motive that lay behind the doctrine in the first place: "They consider it shameful and dishonorable to Christ if he were to derive his origin from men, for he could not be exempted from the common rule, which includes under sin all of Adam's offspring without exception" (2.13.4). Though Calvin had a point in being concerned for the genuineness of the Incarnation under such a conception, nevertheless, he spoke of Menno in very harsh terms, calling him prouder than an ass and more impudent than a dog. (Menno indeed returned these compliments, calling Calvin a "man of blood.") For Calvin to lump Menno together with Servetus in his mind and not to see that Menno was much closer to his own theology and piety is difficult to understand or leave uncriticized.[18]

It seems that Menno, in order to explain how Christ became a sinless man, adopted a position expounded by Melchior Hoffman in an altered form. Hoffman had taken the view that Christ brought his body with him from heaven, taking nothing of the substance of Mary, but passing through her "as water through a pipe." The Incarnation then was entirely the work of God. He was quite specific in saying that "the eternal Word of God did

---

[17]George H. Williams, *The Radical Reformation* (Philadelphia: Westminster Press, 1962) 325-37.

[18]Willem Balke, *Calvin and the Anabaptist Radicals* (Grand Rapids: Eerdmans, 1981) 206-207.

not take our nature and flesh from the Virgin Mary but himself became flesh.'' Had he taken the flesh from Mary, he would not have been able to save us or serve us as food unto eternal life.[19] After wrestling with the doctrine, Menno resolved it in this way: the Logos came to Mary through the Spirit and became flesh and blood without taking it from Mary's body. Christ's birth was the result of the activity of neither father nor mother. Mary was, so to speak, only the one who fed him. It fitted in with his medical understanding stemming from Aristotle that the seed of the man caused conception, and not the contribution of both sexes, as Calvin thought. Menno thought, like the ancient monophysites, that the idea of two natures, one heavenly and one earthly, divided Christ, and that one would better think in terms of heavenly flesh as well. As he said, ''For Christ Jesus, as to his origin, is no earthly man, that is, a fruit of the flesh and blood of Adam. He is a heavenly fruit or man. For his beginning or origin is of the Father, like unto the first Adam, sin excepted.''[20] In a tract entitled The Incarnation of Our Lord,'' he goes on to say that the whole Christ came down from heaven, not the deity only. In adopting this view, Menno hoped to avoid the blasphemy of the usual rendition of classical Christology, which would, in his view, ''rob us of Christ, the Son of God, and direct us to an earthly, sinful creature, and a man born of Adam's impure and sinful flesh.''[21] He differed from Hoffman in being prepared to allow that Christ derived nourishment from Mary's body and in placing his emphasis on the church's receiving her nourishment from Christ and heavenly manna.[22]

In summary, Menno was concerned about the unity of the person of Christ and the threat posed to his heavenly nature by the evil that entered our nature through Adam. His answer to both problems was his doctrine of celestial flesh, whereby the heavenly origin of Christ was emphasized and the possibility of evil affecting him eliminated. His humanity must have had, he reasoned, a higher origin and sprung from God himself. Speculations such as these from within an essentially orthodox set of presuppositions surely alert us to the danger—indeed, the impossibility—of trying to unravel the mystery of the Incarnation. It is the kind of thing that led Karl Barth to emphasize that we cannot know the *how* of God's becoming

---

[19]See George Williams, *Radical Reformation*, 328-32, for translations of Hoffman's remarks.

[20]*The Complete Writings of Menno Simons* (Scottdale PA: Herald Press, 1956) 437.

[21]Ibid., 792-97.

[22]Williams, *Radical Reformation*, 395-96.

man but only *that* he has done so. The proper task of theology and the merit of Chalcedon itself is not to solve the mystery but to bear witness to it.[23]

Michael Servetus (1511–1553), a Spaniard, was the most famous of the anti-Trinitarians of the period because of his fatal encounter with Calvin and Geneva. He was a man of many talents and interests, being trained in law, medicine, and humanist studies.[24] But he is not easy to classify as one who was at once "a speculative brooder and a proponent of the redemptive significance of the sacraments."[25] His views in theology were decidedly unorthodox, and his zeal to propagate them unceasing. He was the author of a work entitled *Christianismi restitutio* (1553), in which he set forth his ideas and plans for a thorough reformation of the Christian faith. The book consists of six parts, including much material exposing the errors of Trinitarian thinking and the Christology that accompanies it. He believed that church doctrine needed to be revised from top to bottom in both its speculative and practical dimensions, and he set forth his proposal how to carry out such a reconstruction.[26]

His doctrine of God was much influenced by Platonic philosophy and by the reading of the Hermetic literature, from both of which sources he repeatedly quotes. The result is very nearly pantheistic. God transcends all things and fills all things. God is manifested in and is the essence of everything. The Logos Servetus distinguished from the personal Logos of orthodoxy, seeing it as the impersonal picture of the world and a shining forth of the mind of God. The Logos realized personhood and full reality in the person of Christ, not before, making the Messiah at the same time unique and very different from the Christ of the creeds. Christ came into the world not to redeem sinners but to reveal eternity and the nature of God as he really is. The eternal Word, which preexisted as an idea and potency in God, attained in Christ a personal existence.

There is no place in such theosophical thought for a Trinity except in a highly metaphorical way, as a pattern of the manifestation of divinity in three modes in the world. Servetus's way of thinking make it possible for him to use old terms in wholly new ways, enabling him to be flexible, at one moment denouncing the Trinity (in the creedal sense) and at another

[23]Karl Barth, *Church Dogmatics,* vol. 1, part 2 (Edinburgh: T. & T. Clark, 1956) 126.

[24]Wilbur, *History of Unitarianism,* vol. 1, chaps. 5-13.

[25]Williams, *Radical Reformation,* 854.

[26]R. H. Bainton, *Hunted Heretic: The Life and Death of Michael Servetus* (Boston: Beacon Press, 1953). The fullest account of his theological ideas remains H. Tollin, *Das Lehrsystem Michael Servets, genetisch dargestellt* (Gütersloh: 1876–1879).

moment defending it (in his own sense). He could as well deny the deity of Christ as orthodoxy conceived it, or affirm it in a pantheistic manner in which everything is God after all. For if all things are of the divine nature and substance, then of course Christ is divine also. In his earlier work Servetus laid down a lower view of Christ, treating him as mere man but constituted Son of God by divine grace. Afterward he characterized this view as foolishness when pantheistic thinking became more attractive to him and he found a better way to deny the two natures. He came to a neo-platonic Christology in the end in which Christ was the concentration of the rays of the glory of God that surrounded the universe and humankind with divine brightness. In Servetus's theology, persons were thus grounded in God and endowed with the divine nature and on a quest after deification.[27] His conception of Christ was not without grandeur. Jesus was no less than the manifested substance of God in a process of self-realization. On the other hand, it is not easy to differentiate the mode of the divine presence in Christ from its mode in every human soul, making "incarnation" a most common event. Since all things derive from God, Christ differs from us only in the supernatural mode of his birth and in his sinless character (neither of which Servetus denied). The Logos and the Spirit signify primal light and power and are understood to be the progressive disclosure of the one unitary personality of God.

Servetus was a fascinating figure, combining in his person elements of the Renaissance and the radical reformation, and his thought, not remembered for its own merit, raises two basic questions for us: why does orthodoxy put so much importance on creedal formulations that cannot easily be proven from Scripture and ought not to be placed over it? What is it in us and our zeal for truth that can entertain the death penalty for those who disagree with our mental constructions?

Faustus Socinus, son of Alexander Sozzini, was born in Siena, Italy, in 1539. His family was imbued with the spirit of the Renaissance and approached theology in a critical way. Already at the age of twenty-three, Faustus published a commentary on John's Gospel in which he denied the essential divinity of Christ and cast doubt upon the natural immortality of human beings. He spent his mature years in Poland, where he came into contact with a sect with unitarian leanings. In this context he found considerable toleration for his thought, and he was able to play a unifying role among the various sectarian groups in the area. Shortly after his death, in 1604, the Racovian Catechism was published, in the drafting of which he had played a major role.

---

[27]Dorner, *History,* 161-71.

A kind of ethical theist, the cast of his mind was rationalist and critical, and for him reformation meant chiefly the reconstruction of doctrine.[28] Drawing his inspiration largely from Italian humanism, Socinus had little appreciation for religious experience but a profound sense of the human person's inherent moral capacity. Religion for him was ethical through and through, anticipating Kant in his principle that what was not morally serviceable in Christian theology ought to be jettisoned. As the catechism puts it, "The Christian religion is the way of attaining eternal life which God has pointed out by Jesus Christ; or, in other words, it is the method of serving God, who will reward the obedient with eternal life, and punish the disobedient with death." This fundamental presupposition affected the whole of his Christology. It meant that no vicarious atonement was required and left Socinus free to attack the idea vigorously, as he did. God loves humankind and needs no appeasing to be willing to forgive us. Humankind does not suffer from the guilt or even bondage of original sin and has merely to open itself to God's grace and favor.[29] The entire superstructure of orthodoxy in its thinking about God and atonement is biblically fallacious and contrary to right reason and ought to be abandoned. Rather than thinking of grace and wrath as aspects of God, Socinus spoke of God's simple will to save humankind from death, for which he sent Jesus to us to make this plain. Humanity needs teaching and illumination, which is what God provided in Christ. Salvation depends upon the prophetic, and not any priestly, office of Christ. The miracles of Jesus (which Socinus did not deny) served to authenticate the truth of Christ's teachings and to underline the importance of observing them. Biblical revelation sets forth the pattern of a life pleasing to God, and salvation depends upon good works done in response to the revelation of his will. Christ's work was to make known God's grace, not to procure it. He is our supreme example, and we are saved by receiving his word and by following him.

For such a humanistic soteriology, only an adoptionist Christology is required, and Socinus thought of Jesus as a unique man, born of the Spirit and raised from the dead, but not divine in the orthodox sense. God alone is divine, and Christ was mortal as we are. His "divinity," if one may call it that, was bestowed on him at his ascension into heaven and really amounted only to divine honor for his successful probation. Christ became "God," though by nature only human, in the sense that God bestowed vindication and world government on him on account of the righteousness

---

[28]Reardon, *Religious Thought in the Reformation*, 230-36.

[29]Franks, *Work of Christ*, 362-77.

of his obedient suffering.[30] God shared his own power with the victorious Christ and welcomed him onto his throne as coregent in the ruling of the world. Christ did not have two natures, but only one—the human nature acquired from Mary and attained to a metaphorical divinity through the successful completion of his task on earth. In this way Socinus succeeded in producing a new doctrine of salvation and of Christ that in the not-to-distant future would become a standard paradigm. More than Servetus, who reminds us of the Valentinian Gnostics, Socinus anticipates and symbolizes the kind of revisionist Christology that came on the scene after Kant, when one heard little about the Trinity or preexistent Logos as the eternal Son but a good deal about the ideal humanity of Jesus as our contagious example.[31]

My own judgment is that the Anabaptists had every right to go back to the Bible afresh and to think of the Christ in terms that such study supplied and controlled. Indeed, one major result of their work is that even the followers of Luther and Calvin are now compelled to do the same thing themselves and not just defend tradition in Christology. At the same time, I think that when one does go back to weigh the New Testament witness in this regard and considers the strength of the incarnational model, he or she will end up closer to Calvin and Luther than to any of these radical reformers and Anabaptists I have surveyed. The witness, after all, of the filial consciousness of Jesus, coupled with the divine glory of Christ's postexistent reign and the strong hints about his preexistent glory, does carry tremendous weight and gives support to the old orthodox consensus in its major outlines.

Dialogue and Interaction

I would like to comment on some of the other chapters in this book. First, I am in full agreement with Russell Aldwinckle (chap. 9) when he assumes a classical Christology and then asks how one might defend it in the modern post-Darwinian context. Objections have been raised to our confession of Jesus Christ as God and Savior, and it is proper, rather than caving in under pressure, to attempt intellectually solid responses to them as Aldwinckle does. His essay is a happy apologetic counterpart to my own concerns here.

Second, I am disappointed with Iain Nicol's treatment of nineteenth-century Christology (chap. 8) in that he fails to register any serious objec-

---

[30]Williams, *Radical Reformation,* 749-56.

[31]Tavard, *Images of the Christ,* 73-94.

tion to the basic thrust of the projects of both Schleiermacher and Ritschl. Their moves, which were in the direction of an "ideal man" Christology, were not meant (in my understanding, at least) to complement incarnation thinking but to replace it. Had they only intended to supplement the received doctrine with a more serious treatment of the significance of the humanity of Jesus, then I would feel differently about them. But as it is, were they not undermining the foundations of the classical Christology that the Reformation broadly asserted and attempting to place the gospel of redemption on a new and different basis?

Third, I agree with Patrick Gray (chap. 4) on the organic connection between the person and the work of Christ, as the present chapter reveals early on and throughout. But I do object to his suggestion that doctrines are "forms giving expression to living experience" after the manner of Schleiermacher. It is one thing to say that revealed doctrine can and needs to be correlated with human experience, but quite another thing to say that these doctrines are themselves the products of human experience. Such a view of the matter condemns us to a radical diversity in theology we will not be able to survive and to the reduction of revelation content to the demands of the culture at the moment.

Fourth, in response to J. A. T. Robinson (chap. 11), I am fully sympathetic with the need to say something helpful about the finality of Christ in the context of religious pluralism. It is a responsibility of ours in the twentieth century, with which the Reformation offers us little help. But his apparent answer is unacceptable to me. He rejects and even stoops to ridicule the classical doctrine of the Incarnation, even while hanging on to the respected term himself. His Christology consists in an adoptionist model: Jesus is all human persons were meant to be by God. God is seen and best defined in him. Recognizing the subtleness of Robinson's theology and his tendency to turn up on both extremes rather than in the middle, I am forced to admit that I might be wrong to read this chapter too literally, as if it said all the late bishop would want to say. Nevertheless, I must protest the inadequacy of the incarnational dimension of chapter 11, as it stands. By now the author will know heaven's verdict on it.

A Final Reflection
on Theological Education Today

For better or worse, Christianity developed in the early centuries of its existence an authoritative commentary on the meaning of the New Testament and its Christology. It was felt necessary in the face of religious pluralism to promulgate in the form of a *regula fidei* and creedal formulations the true understanding of who Jesus Christ was and is. For all its emphasis on the Scriptures, the majority of Protestants went along with this decision and endorsed the results. Even the nonconfessional Anabaptists remained in the framework of the patristic Christology for the most part and with few exceptions did not break away from it. Authentic Christianity was known in relation to its definitive Christological statements. Luther and Calvin evidently believed that one could not go beyond Chalcedon on scriptural grounds and should hold the line firmly on this question. But other voices at the Reformation began to raise the possibility that this ancient formulation could use some updating and rethinking, a point of view that in the centuries since then has only increased tenfold in gaining acceptance. Why must Christians be tied so tightly to a Greek formulation, however excellent in its day, that no longer carries the conviction and intelligibility it once did? A formulation that tilts more to the ontological side than the New Testament itself, that presupposes some Hellenistic ideals of perfection in relation to God that seem to skew the biblical witness, and that pushes us in the direction of a dualism in the person of Christ and even to a Docetism? Surely it is possible to go back to the Bible and to come up with a doctrinal model more suitable to our time and more scriptural in substance. The Christology of the Reformation strongly suggests that this is necessary.[32]

At the same time, we do not need to equate incarnational Christology with Chalcedon, as if there is only one way to state it. Biblical truth is not as easily overturned as ecclesiastical commentary is. A question for theological education today might be ''How shall we express the New Testament faith in the Lord Jesus Christ about which the Reformers were so concerned, and how should we regard heterodox viewpoints such as they and we face?'' Should we remain wide open to the humanistic proposal of a Socinus or the Gnostic-like musings of a Servetus? Or should we take our stand in the channel of the ancient Christology and work out from there? It drives us back in the last analysis to the truly vital question of Christology: ''How do we obtain right standing with God, by whom was it provided, and how?'' The answers must be found in the New Testament, and the Reformation can serve to alert us to the issues and inform us of their deep evangelical concerns.

---

[32]Tony Lane makes a good attempt to do this in ''Christology beyond Chalcedon,'' in *Christ the Lord: Studies in Christology Presented to Donald Guthrie,* ed. Harold H. Rowden (London: Inter-Varsity Press, 1982) 257-81.

Chapter Eight

Schleiermacher and Ritschl: Two Nineteenth-Century Revisionary Christologies

Iain G. Nicol

Since Schleiermacher's response to the Enlightenment criticism of religion in the *Reden* of 1799, and less directly in the *Glaubenslehre* of 1821, many theologians are persuaded that the normative expressions of Christology as derived from dogma and tradition are sufficiently problematic as to warrant their reformulation or, more drastically, their replacement. Philosophical and theological victims of the Enlightenment criticism of religion included the traditional arguments for the existence of God, the notion of causality, and the proofs from miracle and prophecy for the deity of Christ. While these attacks were severe enough, those which have since proved to be most far-reaching and insistent were the criticisms that focused upon the appropriateness and credibility of the Chalcedonian language of nature and substance. In part due to Kant and to the tests to which it had been earlier subjected by the British empiricists, most notably Locke and Hume, this language became a philosophical casualty of the Enlightenment. An example indicative of an age that had become impatient with metaphysical speculation was Locke's well-known attempt to formulate a definition of substance: "something . . . we know not what," which underlies the accidents, or properties, of things.[1] If terms such as *substance* and *consubstantiality* had not become entirely unintelligible in the theological and philosophical circles of post-Enlightenment Germany, it was certainly open to serious question as to what clear meaning could be at-

---

[1]John Locke, *Essay concerning Human Understanding,* ed. A. C. Fraser (New York, Dover Publications, 1959) 2:23.3.

tached to them. For some Protestant theologians at least, the challenge was clear.

I

Schleiermacher and Ritschl responded to the challenge in different ways. However, it is possible to enumerate at least three broad features of their work in which they are comparable as revisionary theologians.

The first is their insistence that the familiar question "Who do you say that I am?" is one that cannot adequately be answered apart from the question of the significance of what Christ did. For both Schleiermacher and Ritschl, though for Ritschl in particular, the question about the being of Jesus in himself cannot and should not be distinguished from the question concerning the meaning of his work. As Pinnock has already noted, this is not a radically new departure.[2] It echoes the Christological *pro me* of the early Luther, and it retrieves Melanchthon's emphasis upon true knowledge of Christ as knowledge of his "benefits." These Reformation precedents for a Christology "from below" find their respective transformations in Schleiermacher's "consciousness-Christology" and in Ritschl's key concept of a Christology of vocation (*Beruf*). In designating Christ's God-consciousness as "the very being of God in him," Schleiermacher's concession to an ontology is unhesitating. Ritschl, by contrast, and sometimes with tedious insistence, will not permit the question of the being of God in Christ to arise at all. As Christologies from below, and at this stage quite apart from any question of their respective validity, it is clear that Ritschl's is the more consistent.

The second comparable aspect of their Christologies is implied in the first but is made more explicit for the sake of clearer emphasis. The subject of Christology, the Jesus who is the Christ, is identified by both theologians as the actual Jesus of history, the Jesus who is accessible to historical inquiry. If we were to express this basic assumption in the terms of contemporary theological debate about the question, both would no doubt wish to argue that a quest of the historical Jesus is as historically possible as it is theologically necessary. Expressed in equally contemporary terms, their Christologies involve no radical discontinuity between the historical Jesus and the kerygmatic Christ. For both Schleiermacher and Ritschl, as *Gemeindetheologen,* the Christ of the community's remembrance, worship,

---

[2]See the opening paragraphs of his chapter in this volume. His subsequent criticism of my treatment of Schleiermacher and Ritschl is rather surprising, especially in the light of my critical analysis of and negative conclusions about their use of the language of archetype and prototype.

and proclamation is the actual Jesus of history. The Christ who acts in and through the Christian community is continuous with the Christ who once acted in history.

A third element common to their Christologies makes comparison possible. While their assumptions about the starting point from which a revisionary Christology may be developed differ in significant ways, the Christological and soteriological rubric under which certain characteristics common to both their positions may be gathered is *archetype* or *prototype*. For Schleiermacher, following a Pauline theme, Christ is the Second Adam, the one in whom creation is fulfilled. He is the historical actualization of the archetypal ideal of the truly human. It is not because of his consubstantiality with the Father that he is divine. He is divine because he is sinless, because the constancy and potency of his God-consciousness as it effectively dominates and informs all other knowledge and action is the very existence of God in him. In the uninterrupted constancy and potency of his God-consciousness, Christ is to be distinguished from all others both in degree and kind. He is the epitome of the God-man relationship.

For Ritschl, the leitmotiv is similar, although again the emphasis is quite different. As the one whose purpose it was to found the kingdom of God in the world as a universal, supramundane, spiritual, and moral community, Jesus is the prototype of the ethical-religious person. His deity is manifest in a personal aim coincident and concurrent with God's own purpose of actualizing his kingship over all humankind. To affirm Christ's deity is to affirm him in the historical exercise and realization of his kingly office in founding a society that transcends all earthly ties. One makes this affirmation not in the form of an assent to what Ritschl termed metaphysical propositions, but rather as an affirmation that involves a value judgment of a direct kind, a judgment rooted in and informed by one's religious-ethical interest and intentionality.

Both of these theologies are theologies of the church. In different respects they are also Christocentric. Formulated in response to specific cultural contexts and historical movements, they are also apologetic theologies. Schleiermacher addressed himself to a public that was experiencing the Romantic reaction to the Enlightenment and to a nation in the throes of mixed political fortunes. He was sensitive to the new knowledge and methods of the natural sciences and could perceive that new terms and conditions were about to be set for theological dialogue and debate. Ritschl's time was different. Together with his contemporaries he experienced the complete breakdown of the Hegelian synthesis. In addressing himself to the intellectual and spiritual vacuum left in its wake, he seriously contended with the theories of evolution and of reductionist materialism that competed to fill it.[3] If we have become accustomed to characterizing the spirit of the middle and late nineteenth century as progressive and as naively optimistic, then it must be clearly emphasized that Ritschl was by no means so sanguine. Nor, for that matter, was the earlier Schleiermacher. Both were fighting apologists. If Schleiermacher's struggle was for the restoration of the anarchic freedom of the human spirit in a religious integrity, Ritschl's was for the conviction that spirit is constitutive of what it means to be human, to be a creature named and graced with a vocation and not merely the product or the extension of an evolving impersonal nature. These are some of the basic assumptions correlative to their respective theologies and Christologies, and it will be useful to keep them in mind as we now turn our attention to a brief analysis first of Schleiermacher's then of Ritschl's position.

II

According to the Chalcedonian definition, Christ unites the divine and the human natures in one person and one hypostasis. Perfect in both deity and humanity, coessential with the Father with respect to his divinity, coessential with us with respect to his humanity, he is without sin. This is the formula with which Schleiermacher's difficulties began, and in proposition 96 of *The Christian Faith,* he discusses them at some length.[4] We shall attempt to summarize them.

The first question he raises is aimed at the indifferent use of the term *nature* as it is applied to both human and divine. Setting etymological considerations of Greek and Latin aside for the moment, Schleiermacher bases his formal logical criticisms of its use upon the current understanding of the term. *Nature,* he argues, is a term we normally employ to denote at least two things. It denotes that which is divided or conditioned. Alter-

---

[3]For a more detailed analysis, see Aldwinckle's chapter in this book. For the moment it is of interest to note that in 1850, nine years before the publication of Darwin's *Origin of Species,* when Ritschl was twenty-eight, Tennyson wrote:

> Are God and nature then at strife,
> That nature lends such evil dreams?
> So careful of the type she seems,
> So careless of the single life
>
> . . . .
>
> I falter where I firmly trod.
>
> *(In Memoriam)*

[4]Friedrich Schleiermacher, *The Christian Faith,* trans. H. R. Mackintosh and J. S. Stewart (Edinburgh: T. & T. Clark, 1928) 391-98. Subsequent references to this work are cited in the text as *CF,* followed by proposition and page number.

natively, we normally use it to denote "the summary of all finite existence." Consequently, he continues, it is a mistake (perhaps we would say "a category mistake") to attribute nature or *a* nature to the God who is "the unconditioned and the absolutely simple" (*CF* 96:392). In a brief discussion of etymology, Schleiermacher then goes on to suggest that the Greek term *physis* may not have been completely divested of its pagan and therefore polytheistic connotations prior to its adoption into the dogmatic tradition.

His second criticism is concerned with the way in which the Chalcedonian definition relates the terms *nature* and *person*. He writes, "In utter contradition to the use elsewhere, according to which the same nature belongs to many individuals and persons, here one person is to share two quite different natures" (*CF* 96:393). How then can a duality of two different natures concur in the unity of one person? Schleiermacher's response to this question is to suggest that, on the basis of the definition itself, no clear explanation is possible. Attempts to resolve the dilemma on the conditions set by the formula issue either in an explanation that succeeds only in fusing the two natures into a third that is neither divine nor human but rather a curious mixture of both or in an explanation that effects the complete separation of the natures at the expense of their unity in the one person.

While it is not so much our concern here, a third problem arises when the nature language of the Christological dogma invades the essence language appropriate to the doctrine of the Trinity. As Schleiermacher points out, the Trinity is a unity in essence, not in nature. What place, then, has Christ's divine nature in the context of Trinitarian coessentiality? Or are we to suppose that, like Christ, both God and the Holy Spirit also have a nature outside their participation in the divine essence? (*CF* 96:395).

According to Schleiermacher, then, these are the dilemmas with which the two-nature doctrine confronts us. He made no attempt to deny the fact that the language of orthodoxy sought to express the profound truth of the oneness of Christ with God and humanity. His quarrel was much more with the alleged appropriateness of the terminology in which that truth had been traditionally stated. A similar but much more provocative question of meaning for contemporary Christological debate is raised by John Hick. He writes, "To say, without explanation, that the historical Jesus of Nazareth was also God is as devoid of meaning as to say that this circle drawn with a pencil on paper is also a square."[5] This extreme statement is one with which Schleiermacher could not have agreed. Nevertheless, he was

---

[5]John Hick, *The Myth of God Incarnate* (London: SCM Press, 1977) 178.

convinced that his reservations about the Christology of tradition and dogma were sufficiently serious as to warrant a revision in which what he terms "the exceeding inconvenience" of the expressions "divine nature" and the notion of the duality of natures in one person would be studiously avoided (*CF* 96:397).

Since Schleiermacher was convinced that he could no longer construct a Christology on the foundation of the traditional language of orthodoxy, and since he was hesitant about the status of Scripture as a regulative norm, which basic criterion could he use to develop and measure a revised Christology? Where was Schleiermacher to begin? His answer to this question is essential to a proper understanding of his entire theology. The regulative principle of, and the means of access to, a revised Christology is his definition of the essence of Christianity as the faith distinguishable from all other faiths "by the fact that in it everything is related to the redemption accomplished by Jesus of Nazareth" (*CF* 11:52).

The definition has a wide range of vitally important implications for his Christology. He was confident, for example, that it provided the fixed point from which he could steer a straight course between the ancient yet recurrent heresies of Ebionism and Docetism (*CF* 96:396, 398). However, its principal implication for our present purposes is that, in placing the primary emphasis upon soteriology, upon the redemptive work of the historical Jesus in imparting the true consciousness of God to the Christian community, Schleiermacher was clearly attempting to create a Christology "from below to above." Given this definition, and given his approach to Christian faith as a reality accessible to phenomenological analysis, it nevertheless must be asked where, precisely, the starting point of Schleiermacher's Christology is to be located? Not in psychologized objectifications or in the God-consciousness of the Redeemer as such or in the redemption-consciousness of the community of believers as such, as though these distinguishable consciousnesses were actually separable. Its locus, rather, is the dynamic relationship between them, between the mediation of the God-consciousness through Jesus of Nazareth and its historical appropriation by the community in liturgy and proclamation.

A further step is required. It involves the important transition from soteriology to Christology. The community's consciousness of its relationship to God as one of absolute dependence is archetypally reflected in Jesus of Nazareth. As the exclusive mediatorial source of the God-consciousness, Christ is also the archetype of the relationship between God and human beings by virtue of the constancy and potency of his own God-consciousness. Schleiermacher's reformulation of the classical two-nature doctrine is succinct in its conclusions: "The Redeemer, then, is like all men in virtue of the identity of the human nature, but distinguished from them all by the constant potency of his God-consciousness, which was a veritable existence of God in him (*CF* 94:385).

In summary, then, Schleiermacher in this way, with his revolutionary definition of the essence of Christianity, sought to establish a firm conjunction between soteriology and Christology, or as he himself preferred to express it, between Christ's "activity" and his "exclusive dignity," and in a variety of similar statements he continues to address this same question. As we have seen, the God-consciousness of the Redeemer is the very being of God in him. It is also, as Schleiermacher emphatically stated, "the innermost fundamental *power* within him" (*CF* 96:397). As the very being and power of God in him, Christ's archetypal God-consciousness is therefore to be qualitatively distinguished from all other human God-consciousnesses. As a given of human nature, given with our common, immediate self-consciousness, the "natural" God-consciousness can never become the being and power of God in us. The reason is that our God-consciousness, unlike Christ's, is continually exposed to the arrestment effected by sin. It constantly succumbs to the attraction of its opposite, the world-consciousness, and is powerless to resist it. Nevertheless, God-consciousness does become the power of God in us when the generative power of the God-consciousness of Christ overcomes and transforms the consciousness of the world, or, to express it in more traditional terms, when our human incapacity is overcome and transformed by the divine capacity.[6]

The transformation is the experience that Christ both initiates and sustains in the power and constancy of his God-consciousness. Apart from Christ, men and women cannot recognize or acknowledge their incapacity, nor are they able to acknowledge the capacity that belongs exclusively to Christ. Such is the experience of the active antithesis between sin and grace, flesh and spirit, God and the world. Schleiermacher's description of the existential resolution of the antithesis is presented in the form of a phenomenological analysis of Christian piety and of the experience of the

---

[6]The development of Schleiermacher's position to this point, together with this reference to a linguistic affinity with earlier tradition, prompts at least two very brief comparisons. It is possible that Schleiermacher would not have objected too strongly to the suggestion that here there are clear echoes of Athanasius's idea that God became man in order that man might become divine. On the other hand, it is more likely that he would not at all have objected to the suggestion that his treatment of the antithesis between world-consciousness and God-consciousness finds its closest parallel in Augustine's discussion of the Incarnation and of the capacity of Christ to transform a disordered love of the world into an ordered love for God.

process of conversion, never complete, from one form of consciousness to the other.

Before we conclude this brief exposition, at least one central question must be addressed: Is Schleiermacher's Christology merely the *product* of Christian religious experience? Certain further considerations might well lead us to the conviction that this conclusion is inevitable. We have seen that, on the basis of his definition of the essence of Christianity, everything in it must be "related to the redemption accomplished by Jesus of Nazareth." Correspondingly, like all other Christian doctrines, a Christology must also consist in an account of "the Christian religious affections set forth in speech" (*CF* 15:76). It is a Christology that begins from below and that gives priority to Christ's activity. Nor can there be any doubt that the correlative starting point for Schleiermacher's Christology is the God-consciousness of the Christian community and its experience of redemption. Are we not, then, compelled to conclude that his Christology is exhaustively reducible to soteriology, or that it is indeed no more than a transcript of the subjective Christian religious affections?

There is a measure of truth in this objection. However, in response to it, it must be emphasized that Schleiermacher certainly never intended to insist that Christology is reducible to a phenomenological analysis of Christian religious experience, or that it is simply the retrospective projection of the God-consciousness of the Christian community. The God-consciousness of the Christian community, its "feeling of utter dependence," from Schleiermacher's point of view, has its objective ontological correlative in the God-consciousness of the historical Jesus. It is from the historical Jesus that the authentic God-consciousness is mediated to the Christian community. It is to the historical Jesus that the God-consciousness of the community is bound. The God-consciousness of the community is therefore dependent upon an event that has taken place in our history, upon the God-consciousness of Christ as the being and power of God in this actual historical individual. The shift, then, from phenomenological analysis to ontology in the endeavor to effect their dialectical correlation is made without hesitation.

Unfortunately, however, this move cannot be made as easily as Schleiermacher apparently assumed, and it is really at this point that some of the more serious difficulties involved in his position begin to arise. And while it must immediately be emphasized that these deficiencies bear little resemblance to those of which objectors to his alleged subjectivist Christology accuse him, they do nevertheless emerge in conjunction with his ontological statements about the historical Jesus and in particular with his assertion that the historical individual, Jesus of Nazareth, was also ideal.

He writes, "The ideal must have become completely historical in him, and each historical moment of his experience must at the same time have borne within it the ideal" (*CF* 93:377). As the one who completes and fulfills creation, as the Second Adam, Christ is *Urbild*. As a historical individual, he is also the archetypal ideal of the God-man relationship.

A number of questions arise at this point, and, having posed them, this very brief summary must be concluded. How, for example, can it be asserted that Christ is archetype and yet that redemption is related to and dependent upon the activity of a specific historical individual? Or similarly, what kind of relationship, if any, is possible between archetype and historical individuality? Is it possible that archetypal perfection can develop and unfold in time and history and yet at the same time be unconditioned by time and history?

It is not at all easy to understand, Schleiermacher writes, "just how the ideal can have been revealed and manifested in a truly historically-conditioned individual" (*CF* 93:380). He was thus by no means insensitive to the difficulties involved in asserting the historical actuality of the archetype of humanity in Jesus Christ. Nevertheless, he was unable to resolve these problems in any satisfactory way. He was not an unhistorical thinker, as some have suggested. Allowances must also be made for the fact that he did not experience the full impact of the implications for biblical study of the later nineteenth-century historical criticism. Yet what we now perceive to be among the most serious difficulties presented by his Christology are his unusually uncritical assumptions about the capacity of history to yield the kind of answers that he required of it and, in this same connection, his unswerving allegiance to the Fourth Gospel as the most authentic and reliable source document for his *Das Leben Jesu*.

While similar assumptions were shared by many of his contemporaries, the results of Schleiermacher's research on the life of Jesus should not really surprise us. Schleiermacher concluded, "He must have been . . . ideal"; "the ideal must have been completely historical in him." These must-haves collide with the more recent and widely shared conviction that history has no place for archetypal ideals or for absolutes. In spite of his sincere attempt to do justice to Jesus' historical individuality, the most remarkable thing about much of his historical exegesis is that it is powerfully determined by his assumptions about ideality and the possible form of its historical manifestation. One of the consequences of this bias is that specific historical questions tend to be prematurely resolved in accordance with the dogmatic requirement that "he must have." If he "must have," and if the ideal is somehow to be fitted into a historical mold, then the possibilities that Jesus was exposed to conflict and temptation or that he could have erred are stringently excluded. Thus, contrary to Schleiermacher's best intentions, the humanity of Christ is seriously diminished.

Must we then conclude that the notion of archetype is so limited in its validity and application that it must be excluded from honest Christological discussion? Do we have to admit that it is finally redundant? We shall return to this question in a brief conclusion.

III

Turning now to the Christology of Ritschl, one immediately notes that he fully endorsed Schleiermacher's criticisms of the language of the two-nature doctrine. He also took these criticisms somewhat further when he characterized its formulations as disinterested, speculative, or, as he most frequently preferred to express it, metaphysical, by which he meant that such language is inappropriate to religion and to religious discourse. Second, it is notable that, like Schleiermacher again, yet in a more consistent manner, Ritschl set out to build a Christology from below.[7] For Schleiermacher, as we have already noted, the historical Jesus of Nazareth is the Redeemer, who effects the victory and ascendance of the God-consciousness over world-consciousness. In Ritschl's case the reference to the Jesus of history is similar, yet the emphasis is quite different in that Christ is viewed as one who possesses the power to resolve "the contradiction in which man finds himself, as both a part of the world of nature and a spiritual personality claiming to dominate nature."[8] As Ritschl understands it, the resolution of this contradiction has to be effected in and through Christ's human achievement. Quoting the views of the early Luther and of Melanchthon, he therefore insists that to know Christ is to know him in what he does for us in his action toward us. As one who considered himself to be an authentic interpreter of the authentic Luther, he could write, for example, "According to Luther, the Godhead of Christ is not exhausted by maintaining the existence in Christ of the divine nature; the chief point is that in his exertions as man his Godhead is manifest and savingly effective" (JR, 393).

With these references to "Christ's human achievement" and to "his exertions as man," we reach the focal point of Ritschl's Christology. Its basis and regulative principle is a historical one, namely, the fact of Christ's loyalty and obedience to the purpose of God, his allegiance to his historical

---

[7]Wolfhart Pannenberg, *Jesus-God and Man* (Philadelphia: Westminster Press, 1969) 36-37.

[8]Albrecht Ritschl, *Justification and Reconciliation,* vol. 3 (Edinburgh: T. & T. Clark, 1902) 199. Subsequent references to this volume are cited in the text as *JR.*

vocation (*Beruf*) to be the founder and head of God's kingdom in the world. This will not be the Christ of the two-nature formula, nor will it be the Enlightenment or Kantian Jesus, who is merely the accidental vehicle for the communication of timeless truths that have no necessary connection with specific historical events. Nor will it be the Hegelian Christ, who symbolizes the universal truth of the oneness of human and divine. It will be none of these, for, as Ritschl repeatedly insists, the *historical* Jesus must be normative for Christian faith and for Christian theology and not a Christ adorned in inappropriate "metaphysical" properties.

What, then, did Ritschl understand by "the historical Jesus"? It is immediately clear, for one thing, that he did not mean the historical Jesus as distinct from the Christ of faith, or the Jesus of history understood as some figure behind the Gospels or behind the church's kergyma. Nor did he mean the Jesus of the biographer. On this popular and academic theme of nineteenth-century theology, Ritschl's position has often been misunderstood and misinterpreted. It is of some interest to note, for example, that his views on this question cannot be included under the generalizations that James M. Robinson makes about nineteenth-century historiography in his influential book *A New Quest of the Historical Jesus.*[9] In the following short passage Ritschl in fact expresses a view that differs quite radically from that of Robinson:

> It is no mere accident that the subversion of Jesus' religious importance has been undertaken under the guise of writing his life, for this very understanding implies the surrender of the conviction that Jesus, as the founder of the perfect moral and spiritual religion, belonged to a higher order than all other men. But for that reason, it is likewise vain to attempt to reestabish the importance of Christ by the same biographical expedient. We can discover the full compass of his historical actuality solely from the faith of the Christian community. (*JR* 3)

Thus, according to Ritschl, the real Jesus is accessible to us only through the witness of the church. He does not hesitate to assert that the Christ of the community's remembrance, worship, and proclamation is the actual Jesus of history. Nor is it possible to discover any evidence to suggest that Ritschl ever expressed any methodological doubts with regard either to his initial assumptions about historical method or to the conclusions to which he was led. His exegesis is therefore by no means presuppositionless and it enables him to posit a direct continuity between the Jesus who once acted in history and who "belonged to a higher order than all other men" and

---

[9]James M. Robinson, *A New Question of the Historical Jesus* (London: S. C. M. Press, 1959) 26-32.

the Christ who continues to act through the church and who is the object of its worship. Expressed in the language of contemporary theology, one would say, then, that there is a direct continuity between the Jesus of history and the kerygmatic Christ.

If Ritschl is to sustain this thesis, then clearly the nature of this continuity has to be demonstrated. The fundamental key to it is Ritschl's notion of Christ's lifework (*Lebenswerk*). Christ's lifework is his vocation to be the founder and head of the kingdom of God as a supramundane, universal, ethical fellowship. In this fellowship the contradiction between nature and spirit is overcome in and through the human achievement of the Christ who has overcome the world (John 16:33). His lifework can be summed up in another of Ritschl's favorite Johannine texts: "My meat is to do the will of him that sent me, and to finish his work" (4:34). His historical vocation, his purpose to establish the kingdom in history, coincides and concurs with the Father's own purpose for human beings. Between the Father and the Son there is therefore an identity of will and purpose expressive of their essential solidarity, and this solidarity is revealed in Christ's history and in his human "exertions" and "achievement."

The relationship of solidarity between the Father and the Son is consummated in Christ's steadfast endurance and in his obedience unto death. In the eventfulness of this relationship Christ's vocation is fulfilled. To found the kingdom is his singular ethical-religious vocation. He had no other vocations. He did not marry, had no children, and apparently relinquished any occupation he might have had in the interest of pursuing this singular, personal aim. His every word and action are intimately related to this one end (*Zweck*).

Not unlike Bultmann, Ritschl did not believe that exegesis could ever be presuppositionless. Nor, as we have already noted, did he hesitate to admit it. With regard to the question of continuity, he seems to be suggesting that if we read the Gospels from a historical-ethical perspective or on the basis of a historical-ethical interest and intentionality, then these are the conclusions to which we shall inevitably come. Possibly reflecting the influence of Kant, he proposes that to read the Gospels properly is to read them with the expectation that our question about the chief end of human life will be answered. We are thus bound to conclude that Christ's self-end (*Selbstzweck*) is also God's, and that the exalted Christ who exercises his lordship over the community and who is the object of the community's remembrance and worship is continuous and identical with the actual Jesus of history who exercised lordship over the world in his historical vocation. In his attempt to substantiate this conclusion further, Ritschl reverses the traditional dogmatic order of the doctrines of humiliation and exaltation.

In the traditional pattern, humiliation precedes exaltation. He attempts to show, therefore, that Jesus' earthly life is already a manifestation of his exaltation by virtue of the fact that he exercised his lordship over the world in and through his earthly ministry. His exaltation, then, is not to be understood as exclusively related to the confession of the post-Easter community. And as Ritschl reminds his readers again and again, the basis for this conviction is the fact that "*every* form of influence exerted by Christ must find its criterion in the historical figure presented by his life" (*JR,* 406; italics mine).

As we confess Jesus as the Christ, or as Ritschl often expresses it, honoring Christ as God, our historical-ethical judgment issues in a religious one. Properly understood, the Christological confession is, in Ritschl's controversial phrase, "a religious value-judgment [*Werturteil*] of a direct kind" (*JR,* 398). This is not the kind of judgment that belongs to the sphere of disinterested scientific knowledge. It is a judgment prompted by the existential condition of human life, by the contradiction between nature and spirit in which we find ourselves. It is equally prompted by the human need and will to resolve the contradiction. Ritschl's notion of value-judgment therefore presupposes this specific interest and intentionality, and it is in relation to these existential considerations that he wishes it to be understood. To honor Christ as God is primarily to express an attitude. It is to give expression to a "blik." Unlike the formula of Chalcedon, therefore, it is not to be regarded as equivalent to the kind of knowledge that involves disinterested, metaphysical speculation. Here, as frequently elsewhere, Ritschl again proclaims his metaphysical agnosticism. In his recent book on Ritschl, James Richmond expresses this point well when he writes, "Along the scale from below upwards Ritschl rather abruptly imposes an upper epistemological limit beyond which he forbids others or himself to travel."[10]

It is therefore God in his self-revelation that we encounter in the historical Jesus, not a divine incognito. The passage in which Ritschl best expresses this view is as follows:

> That Christ overcomes his fate, reveals to us in him the Creator of the world; that he endures indignities which he has not deserved, of course for the good of men, reveals in him the Creator, the wise ruler, the gracious protector of the world; finally, that he does not withhold his benefits from the unthankful and unbelieving, that he prays for those who crucify him, proves his connection with the perfect God, who bestows his favours both on the evil and the good. The God-man has all the divine attributes. (*JR,* 416)

---

[10]James Richmond, *Ritschl—a Reappraisal* (London: Collins, 1978) 179.

As we contemplate this historical pattern of "grace and truth," the dynamic movement of Christ's love as it confronts every hindrance and rejection, and as we permit that same grace and truth to impact upon us, then we share in Christ's victory and lordship. In this same historical pattern of grace and truth, the kingdom of God is realized in history as the universal, world-transcending fellowship of those for whom all worldly impediments are overcome. The community's essential conviction is that nothing in all creation shall be able to separate (it) from the love of God, which is in Jesus Christ (its) Lord (Rom. 8:38-39). This, finally, is the community's value-judgment about the Christ who has overcome the world and who gives his people God's kingdom as their gift and task.[11]

We may now sum up this very brief exposition of Ritschl's Christology. To assert that Christ is God or to value Christ as God is to make two confessions simultaneously. It is to acknowledge him as the perfect revealer of God and as the manifest type of spiritual lordship over the world (*JR,* 389). It is as man without sin that one honors him as God. For Ritschl, then, Christ is prototypical in the sense that what we are destined to become is already prefigured in his work and person. He is the prototype of our vocation, and as prototype he can be neither surpassed nor transcended.

IV

For those who have become accustomed to the view that human existence is through and through historical and to the idea that all our thinking is equally historical, designations of Christ as either archetype or prototype are uncommonly difficult to explain and to justify. (Further problems are raised by Ritschl's Christology in particular, in which the one notion shades into the other.) However, in the following remarks my comments will first focus very briefly upon certain broad features of the Christologies of Schleiermacher and Ritschl that constitute permanent insights for Christian education. We shall then conclude with a more extensive but by no means exhaustive examination of the appropriateness of the Christological terminology of archetype and prototype and its importance for the new em-

---

[11]Ritschl's "social gospel" presents some interesting parallels with contemporary liberation theologies. The following passage indicates the extent to which he was by no means the post-Kantian bourgeois moralist of theological caricature: "The kingdom of God which thus presents the spiritual and ethical task of mankind as it is gathered in the christian community is supernatural, insofar as in it the ethical forms of society are surpassed (such as marriage, family, vocation, private and public justice, of the state), which are conditioned by the natural endowment of man (differences in sex, birth, class, nationality) and also offer occasion for self-seeking" ("Instruction in the Christian Religion," in *Three Essays,* trans. P. Hefner [Philadelphia: Fortress Press, 1972] par. 8).

phasis upon exploratory approaches to "spirituality" and "formation" now to be found in many Protestant colleges and seminaries, especially in those that form an integral part of our various academic and ecumenical contexts of theological education.

In seeking to fulfill its primary purpose, theological education will strive after the cultivation of the habitus of theological reflection or of the aptitude for theological judgment as necessarily and vitally informative of the practice of ministry.[12] How is such a habitus or such an aptitude formed? It may be suggested that, in any educational venture shaped to these specific ends, there are at least three primary moments. Although they are certainly also to be found elsewhere, they are integral to the processes that led to the development of the two Christological positions outlined above.

First, in developing their respective Christologies, both Schleiermacher and Ritschl demonstrated a profound attentiveness to the comprehensive historical context of their times. This stance involved sensitive analysis of, and serious dialogue with, the various philosophical, scientific, social, and political influences that shaped the future of the post-Enlightenment era. In different ways, and like the Christologies of other historical periods, their conclusions reflect these developments. Like ourselves, they were persons of their time. Yet as correlative responses to the formative dynamics of their respective situations, their Christologies are not to be viewed as representative of a craven abandonment of tradition or as an abject accommodation of Christian truth to the spirit of the times. They are rather to be understood as Christologies appropriate to specific situations of active *Christian witness*. In seeking to cultivate a habitus and a capacity for theological judgment, theological education will view the analysis and critique of those influences determining the future of our own historical context in the same way and not as ends in themselves, ends that may certainly enhance our understanding of the world but that may as easily anesthetize any Christian praxis toward its possible change.

The habitus of theological reflection and the cultivation of an aptitude for theological judgment also call for more than assent to the classical Christological dogmas or to the theological party line. A second component in this educational process will therefore involve a critical engagement with the biblical and theological traditions. This lesson we may also learn from Schleiermacher and Ritschl. We do no honor to the biblical tes-

---

[12]The need for theological reflection is the central theme of Edward Farley, *Theologia: The Fragmentation and Unity of Theological Education* (Philadelphia: Fortress Press, 1983). On the aptitude for theological judgment, see Charles M. Wood, *Vision and Discernment* (Atlanta: Scholars Press, 1985) chaps. 2, 5.

timonies or to the Christological tradition by classifying them with Lot's wife. It is rather through the mutual interaction of past and present that whatever is of enduring validity in the tradition comes to life and is made manifest as fitting for contemporary Christian witness. Through a fusion of the horizons of past and present, we may also develop responsible judgments about the appropriate criteria for such witness as involving not only what to think but also what to do and how to do it.

Third, as *Gemeindetheologen,* the Christologies of Schleiermacher and Ritschl are also compatible with an understanding of the universality of the people of God and their corporate vocation.[13] This view finds explicit emphasis in Ritschl's ethical doctrine of *Beruf,* while for Schleiermacher, the God-consciousness mediated by Christ is a consciousness of and in community, a consciousness of the self as a unique yet integral part of the totality of the *laos theou.* Education toward Christian maturity in reflection and judgment will also recognize the importance of this aspect of their thought and its relevance for Christian witness. One of the most saddening and distressing characteristics of so much contemporary Christian witness is to hear such frequent reference to *my* faith, *my* theology, *my* Christology. The formation of judgment and of a habitus for theological reflection properly understood nevertheless includes the recognition that such processes take place in community. Whether that community is the theological college or seminary or the local church, such properly Christian capacities will be developed on the basis of the understanding that "we are members of one another" (e.g., Eph. 4:25).

We turn now to a final consideration, namely, to the aspect of Christian education that involves formation, conformation, and education toward that which in some traditions is specifically and without hesitation understood as imitation of the person and work of Christ, and in others as a somewhat vaguer conception of what it means to be Christlike, or to "grow in grace." Two points may be selected for our further reflection.

The first is that any Christology that appeals to a typology, whether an archetypology or a prototypology, presupposes some analogical relationship (or a combination of analogical relationships) between the human and the divine. This kind of Christology tended to predominate in the patristic era, and in particular in the Eastern tradition. Emphasis is placed upon the typological and analogical relationships between a Christology and an anthropology in which Christ's communion with God is viewed not as the absolute exception to the rule but as a relationship to which others can at

---

[13]See the opening pages of the chapter by Joseph Ban in this volume.

least approximate or perhaps instantiate. Such Christologies are therefore developed from a perspective that assumes that the complete, undivided archetype or prototype embraces and includes related types not necessarily equal to the archetype or prototype but at least comparable to them in both degree and kind. Stated in somewhat different terms, what is presupposed is an analogical relationship between the one and the many whereby the many are at least capable in principle of relating themselves to the divine *Logos*. Corresponding to this is the additional assumption that the finite has the capacity for the infinite. It should, however, not be concluded that with respect to the classical Christologies, the participation of the human in the divine is ever possible without the assistance of divine grace and divine revelation.

However, from the point of view of many modern Protestant theologians, especially those of the Reformed tradition, these Christologies are in constant danger of casting themselves adrift from their focal and exclusive reference to Jesus Christ. Consequently, much of modern Protestant theology has reflected a disposition to make use of the classical Christologies only as negative foils to its own kind of Christocentrism or possibly even its Christomonism. However, it is essentially for this reason that the theologies and the Christologies of archetype and prototype of Schleiermacher and Ritschl have become targets of attack and sometimes of scornful dismissal. Schleiermacher's interpretation and use of the Pauline Second Adam motif, it is sometimes argued, cannot be defended against the objection that history may yet produce a third, a fourth, or an infinite series. Ritschl's Christ as the prototype of our vocation, it is objected, represents a view that is equally defenseless against the criticism that such a position presupposes a possible emergence of a subsequent instance or instances of improvements upon the original.

Once again, there is certainly some truth in these criticisms. However, even though it is most unlikely that one's advocacy of Schleiermacher and Ritschl will assist in exonerating them, one should nevertheless be prepared to defend them at least in the interest of their receiving a fair hearing. It is immediately apparent, for one thing, that they can both be defended against the accusation that their respective Christologies imply a correspondingly triumphalist anthropology, a view that was otherwise typical of many thinkers in the late eighteenth and nineteenth centuries. This incident has nevertheless proved to be a powerful ingredient in the arguments against them developed by some of their modern Protestant successors. Yet perhaps more emphatically than Ritschl, Schleiermacher did not hesitate to confirm the human incapacity for the divine or to stress the fact that men and women suffer from a seriously vitiated God-consciousness. Human life is saturated with guilt, and with the sin that is "in each the work of all, and in all the work of each" (*CF* 71:288).[14] Perhaps Ritschl is more mildly optimistic than this, nevertheless one should not judge too hastily, for as we have already had occasion to note, one of the basic cornerstones of his anthropology is the conviction that, apart from the reconciliation effected by Christ, human life is an ineradicable and stultifying contradiction. In some of his references to the church regarding the actual ethical fruits of organized Christianity, Ritschl also offers the quite scathing observation that the Church community, by the fact that it has carried so much actual sin in the course of its history, may well have to be judged totally unfit to be the mediator of Christ's benefits (*JR*, 500). In these particular respects, therefore, there is very little evidence to suggest that analogies between the divine and the human that might encourage a triumphalist anthropology can be readily derived from the theologies of either the one or the other.

Second, Christologies of archetype and prototype are also more specifically characterized by the various ways in which they make use of the analogy of being and of analogies of attribution. The *imago Dei* presupposes an *analogia entis*. The infinite "I am" and the finite "I am" are not the same, but neither are they totally dissimilar. It follows that, if the finite in some sense participates in the infinite by virtue of the analogy of being, it also participates in the perfections of the infinite by virtue of the analogy of attribution. (For example, God's goodness is not the same as human goodness but is nevertheless in certain aspects reflected in human goodness.) Once again, however, in their assessment of this particular theological tradition, many modern Protestant theologians have generally been disposed to employ a hermeneutic of suspicion. Christologies that depend upon a doctrine of analogy for their articulation, it is sometimes suggested, reflect another dangerous variation of the assumption that the human, by its very nature, somehow has the capacity to participate in the divine. Consequently, it has often been in direct opposition to this tendency that much of modern Protestant theology has reflected an insistence that there can be no continuity between the human and the divine, or that between finite and infinite there is an absolute qualitative hiatus. The search for this being or for that infinite quality or attribute as somehow analogously inherent in finite human life is bound to end in frustration and disappointment, for such an entity or such allegedly analogous qualities or

---

[14]Schleiermacher also commented, "A trace of the consciousness of sin lurks even in the most exalted moments of religious experience, just because the God-consciousness does not permeate our whole being uniformly" (*CF* 68:277).

attributes are always incommensurably other than God and radically discontinuous with the divine.

Again it must be conceded that such criticisms do have a certain validity. However, even if it is agreed that ontological and attributive analogies between the divine and the human do have serious limitations, the question concerning the sense, if any, in which finite existence may yet be open to and thereby capable of participating in the infinite, the human in the divine, is one that should not feel compelled to surrender too prematurely. It does not have to be surrendered, nor should it be. However, a satisfactory answer to this question will not be readily available if we continue to think that one can be derived from a definition of human "nature" and its attributes. Nevertheless, it can and also should be maintained that, on the grounds of the historicity and subjectivity of human existence, on the basis of our interest, intentionality, and our disposition toward the future in desire and hope, our finite human existence *is* open to the infinite horizon of life, open to the boundary with the infinite at which transcendence encounters us. Continuities between a this-worldly transcendence and immanent historical existence are therefore discernible, and it is to the credit of both Schleiermacher and Ritschl that, to some extent, their revisionary attempts at a reformulation of Christology prompted the realization that, even in theology, thought about transcendence can no longer begin "from above." For this aspect of their theologies at least, one should therefore be prepared to defend them.

Nevertheless, against Schleiermacher and to a lesser extent also Ritschl, it must be said, that, on any assessment of their Christologies, it is difficult to know how, and just as difficult to know that, the archetypal or prototypical ideal of humanity became historical in the individual Jesus of Nazareth. The fact that Schleiermacher asserted and attempted to prove that this ideal was historicized in Jesus, and also that Ritschl had no reason to question his assumption that the same ideal was prototypically realized in the historical vocation of Jesus to found the kingdom of God, leaves one with serious reservations about the adequacy of their respective historical methodologies.

However, for fairly obvious reasons, they should not be blamed too much for this limitation. On the other hand, both of them really failed to see clearly that however he may have understood himself and however the Christian community may have understood him, Jesus announced that there was still more to come, and this more to come was apparently not to be flatly identified with his person. Therefore even if the archetype or the prototype of humanity was in some sense actualized in Jesus, and even if he is to be understood as the historical fulfillment and completion of the ideal of humanity and thereby of creation itself, he was also the one who proclaimed the kingdom of God. While we may thus rightly be mildly critical of their understanding of history and of what they seemed to assume history could yield by way of satisfying our hunger for objective verification, we should perhaps be more critical of their limited perception of the fuller implications of Jesus' eschatological proclamation of the kingdom of God for their Christologies of archetype and prototype.[15] More so than Schleiermacher, Ritschl had a keener understanding of the distinction between Jesus' realization of the ideal as prototype and his commitment to the eschatological kingdom of God and its future realization as an ongoing task. The basic difference between Schleiermacher's Christology of archetype and Ritschl's Christology of prototype is thus directly related to the difference between the platonically inspired realized eschatology of the former, and the inaugurated eschatology of the latter.

Thus it is difficult to see how a Christology of archetype could be combined with the eschatological "not yet" of Jesus' proclamation of the kingdom, or that it could be properly correlated with the fact of history's openness toward the kingdom's universal realization. One of the implications of Schleiermacher's Christology, then, is that it seems to require history's foreclosure. Ritschl's Christology can more adequately accommodate this correlation. Yet, on the other hand, the correlation of Christological prototype with a corresponding typological anthropology makes it difficult to account for the fact of historical individuality and contingency.

While these, then, constitute at least some of the difficulties inherent in this particlar sphere of Christological discussion, and while the language of type has become somewhat inappropriate in the context of subsequent Christological debate, the question nevertheless arises as to whether any sound Protestant theology of formation, or of what it means to be Christlike, can survive without it, or at least without some form of an equivalent language. Whatever their deficiencies, the Christologies of Schleiermacher and Ritschl could and did provide firm bases for what we would now classify as corresponding theologies of formation. In Schleiermacher's case, as evidenced in his *Brief Outline on the Study of Theology*,[16] an implicit Christology of archetype could also lend support to a theology of theological education itself.

---

[15]In his *Die Predigt Jesu vom Reiche Gottes* (Göttingen: Vandenhoeck and Ruprecht, 1892), Johannes Weiss offered this criticism of Ritschl's position. However, its implications for Ritschl's Christology of prototype were not made explicit.

[16]Friedrich Schleiermacher, *Brief Outline on the Study of Theology*, trans. T. Tice (Richmond: John Knox Press, 1966).

Is there such an equivalent language? It may only be suggested that a now questionable theology of formation according to the Christological archetype or prototype might find more adequate expression in the form of a Christology and teleology of process,[17] or alternatively in a narrative Christology that enables us to articulate an understanding of conformity with the story of the One who is actively present in the world. Each offers different possibilities for effecting the necessary correlations between the image of Christ and the formation of that image in those who seek to be his followers. However, a detailed discussion of these alternatives properly belongs to our twentieth-century theological agenda.

---

[17]In this form it may possibly meet some of the ''central concerns'' enumerated in Aldwinckle's concluding remarks in his chapter in this book.

Chapter Nine
Christology after Darwin

R. F. Aldwinckle

Has the impact of Charles Darwin's thought upon Christian theology raised any special new issues in the area of Christology? Some will immediately reply, None at all! All the basic questions and all the possible answers have already been anticipated in the age-old attempt of Christian thinkers to articulate the significance of Jesus Christ for the Christian experience of redemption in Christ and for theological reflection on the meaning of that experience both in the past and the present. While in a certain sense this answer may be true, it is equally a fact that Darwin was one of those seminal thinkers who, whether intentionally or not, has changed the total perspective in which the role and status of human beings is now regarded. Any change in the way we regard men and women must affect the way we deal with the Christological issue. Classical Christology, which spoke of the Word made flesh (John 1:14) or of God becoming man, obviously has a vested interest in arriving at an adequate understanding of what it means to be human. Of course, not only Christology but the whole doctrine of God is also involved. All God-talk depends upon the responsible use of analogies or models taken from some facet of human experience. Our anthropology, in the theological sense of our view of the human being, will determine how we think of God. There is no implication here of Feuerbach's dictum that "all theology is anthropology," which he took to mean that God is only the projection of human attributes and human idealism upon a supposed transcendent reality. We are simply emphasizing that no doctrine of God can be constructed that is not at the same time a doctrine of man and vice versa.

In choosing Darwin (1809–1882) as our starting point, it needs to be emphasized that more is involved than geology and biology as special sciences with limited goals and aims. While Darwin himself was not inclined to metaphysical speculation, those who claimed to be his followers in his lifetime, T. H. Huxley, Herbert Spencer, and others, were not so re-strained. It was not long before extrapolations were made from Darwin's natural selection that resulted in what is sometimes called "the evolution-ary worldview." The noun *evolution* is totally absent from the *Origin of Species* (1859), which should perhaps put us on our guard. Inasmuch as Darwin's work in biology placed the human being fairly and squarely in a cosmic process of continuous change, no hard and fast distinction could henceforth be made between "nature" and "history." Physics, geology, biology, and history now were taken to describe one unified and contin-uous process. Henceforth, human beings are parts of nature and organic to nature now conceived as dynamic process.

Prior to Darwin, some philosophers had indeed arrived at the idea of a developing and creative cosmic process. Hegel (1770–1831) is a notable case of a major philosopher alive and influential in Darwin's early years, though there is no evidence that Darwin was acquainted with Hegel. In the restricted field of biology itself, the idea of a dynamic process, including the transformation of species, was anticipated by Lamarck (1744–1829) and Buffon (1707–1788). The idea of continuous change and development was not new, even when applied to human beings. What Darwin did was to give, in the eyes of many, an empirical and scientific grounding for what up to that time could be regarded as a possible speculation but no more. It is safe to say, however, that after Darwin, an evolutionary worldview gradually came to dominate Western thinking, despite vigorous dissent-ers.[1] Its influence has been pervasive, not only in science but also in phi-losophy, theology, and indeed in general literature.[2] The recent appearance and attractiveness to many of process philosophy and theology is hardly intelligible apart from the long-term results of Darwin's work upon our thinking.

The effect of all this influence has been to raise again in the most acute form questions concerning the nature and status of the human being in the general scheme of things. What are the theological and Christological im-plications? Let us note the basic assumptions that traditional theology has made.

---

[1]J. R. Moore, *The Post-Darwinian Controversies* (Cambridge: Cambridge University Press, 1979); J. Durant, ed., *Darwinism and Divinity* (Oxford: Basil Blackwell, 1985).

[2]H. H. J. Nesbitt, ed., *Darwin in Retrospect* (Toronto: Ryerson Press, 1960) 67-69.

1. Nature and history are not self-explanatory but become intelligible only when interpreted as the result of the intentional and purposive activity of God the Creator, who brought all things into being and sustains them in being.
2. Nature is oriented to the emergence of human beings and must, therefore, be understood teleologically. Nature on the physical level is designed (i.e., by God). On the human level, God has given to human beings freedom of will, although limited in its scope.
3. Authentic human existence is possible only through a right relationship to God, who established a created order and still guides it to his chosen ends.
4. Human beings have misused their freedom, fallen into sin, and now inherit the painful consequences.
5. God, however, is love and is concerned for his creation, especially those made in his image. He has actively intervened in human history from the beginning but especially in the history of Israel, through which he prepared the way for his definitive saving action.
6. In the fullness of time, God became man in his Son Jesus Christ. The incarnate Christ is both truly man and truly God, of the same nature as God (*homoousios*) and of the same nature as man.

Despite reservations about his overall view, we agree with Schubert Ogden that Christology cannot be exclusively concerned with the question "Who is Jesus?" if by Jesus is meant the historical figure who lived in Palestine 2,000 years ago interpreted apart from his relationship to God. The question "Who is God?" is equally important. Indeed, there can be no Christology in the strict sense that is not at the same time a doctrine of the reality and nature of God.[3]

Without the above assumptions, traditional Christianity could hardly be said to have either a doctrine of God or a Christology. Can these assumptions still be defended in the light of Darwin and Darwinism?[4] In four

---

[3]Schubert Ogden, *The Point of Christology* (San Francisco: Harper & Row, 1973) 15ff. and chap. 7.

[4]When the name *Darwin* is used, I refer to the specific biological views expressed by him in his published work. The term *Darwinism* (some have coined the term *Darwinisticism*) refers to later developments in biology as well as to philosophical speculations claiming support from the work of Darwin, even though he himself did draw all these same conclusions from his own work.

areas there appears to be a direct conflict between Darwinism and the above Christological and theological assumptions.

Darwin, Darwinism, and God. Does the theory of natural selection, as expounded by Darwin, rule out theology? More specifically, if we can read the natural and historical sequence as the sphere of activity of a sovereign and personal teleology completely, then what becomes of God as Creator, Redeemer, and Sanctifier? Is a personal God in any sense still possible or even credible? If teleology is rigorously eliminated, then can we any longer talk of the "acts of God"? Is Darwin and Darwinism committed to the view that chance and unguided forces are solely responsible for the process that has produced the human race? In short, can a strict Darwinism believe in God in the Christian sense? It is not implied in what has just been said that any form of the teleological argument, taken alone, can demonstrate the existence of a personal Creator. The point here is that, if the work of Darwin renders all appeal to design and purposiveness illegitimate, then further appeals to other types of evidence, such as moral and religious experience, cannot be properly made.

Darwin and the divine image in man. Is Darwin's thought and Darwinism consistent with the Christian view that we are made in the divine image and are the objects of God's special care and concern? Darwin did grant a special status to human beings but did he go far enough?

Orthogenesis, sin, and the Fall. At no point does the conflict between evolutionary views and some forms of Christian doctrine appear to be as crucial as in regard to this question. If a literal Adam and Eve and a historical fall from a state of original righteousness and perfection are insisted upon, then there is no reconciliation possible between such a view and the claim that human beings emerged from the animal world by a process of gradual change and transformation.

Darwin and eschatology. If Darwinism of necessity excludes God, then obviously the final end of man cannot be to know God and enjoy him forever. All talk of the beatific vision, the communion of saints, and even prayer seems to be beside the point. If Darwinism excludes a sovereign, intelligent, holy, and loving will, responsible for the world and presently active in it, then there can be no eschatology in the Christian sense. We cannot speak of a goal or end either for the human race as a whole or for individuals for the simple reason that evolution does not know where it is going. Still less can we conceive of a life after death on the basis of such an agnostic Darwinism.

These, then, are what appear to be the points of basic conflict. Certain questions now arise as to how this situation has arisen. In stating these issues, it will be noted how often I have used the word *if*. An examination of the assumptions made by Darwinism and those who appeal to Scripture is obviously needed. Does Darwinism necessarily involve the abandonment of teleology and purpose and, therefore, of God in the theistic sense? Does the Christian view of God as Creator ex nihilo necessarily involve a literal interpretation of the Genesis narratives, and do these narratives, however interpreted, commit us to a specific scientific theory—for example, the fixity of species and, therefore, the impossibility of the production of the different species by gradual change and transformation? The way these questions are answered will influence the form and shape of our anthropology and the Christology we seek to construct—that is, if we still believe that the Christological question can be meaningfully raised in such a context. I comment briefly upon the points of conflict listed above, indicate my own understanding of these questions, and then reassess the Christological issues.

Darwin, Darwinism, and God

In taking up this question, there is a need to disentangle the distinct issues that are involved. First, how did Darwin understand his own theory, and what did he actually say, as distinct from what people then and now thought he had said? Second, how was Darwin's work understood and used by those who came after him, whether biologists or Christian thinkers? In this chapter we must be content with only a rough outline of the possible answers.[5]

Dissatisfied as a medical student in Edinburgh, Darwin went to Cambridge at the suggestion of his father to study divinity. He tells us in his autobiography that he rather liked the thought of being a country clergyman and that, after reading some books on divinity, he did not doubt the literal truth of the Bible or of the creeds.[6] He adds the significant qualification, however, that "I never was such a fool as to feel and say 'credo quia incredibile.' "[7] Even after the return of the *Beagle,* he seriously pondered for a time whether he should be ordained. It would be a fascinating study to examine the intellectual and spiritual process by which Darwin's original faith became attenuated to the point where he felt he must be con-

[5]For a brief summary of the recent literature, the following are especially useful: J. C. Livingston, "Darwin, Darwinism, and Theology," *Religious Studies Review* 8:2 (April 1982); Moore, *Post-Darwininian Controversies.*

[6]Nora Barlow, ed., *The Autobiography of Charles Darwin, 1809–1882* (London: Collins, 1958).

[7]Ibid., 57.

tent to remain an agnostic.[8] He was never aggressively anti-Christian and anti-theistic, and in spite of his growing agnosticism, he could say in a letter years after the *Origin of Species,* ''Perhaps I deserve to be called a theist.''[9] I do not suggest that Darwin was a Christian in spite of himself, a tactic that would throw doubt on his integrity.

More important is the question concerning the connection between his love of science and biology in particular and this erosion of his former faith. If we are to trust his own account, Darwin seems to have experienced the kind of intellectual doubt and moral and spiritual crisis that many thoughtful men and women undergo. Many difficulties that he had with the Old Testament came from historical and ethical questions rather than from his scientific work. Parts of the Old Testament seemed to present a picture of God as a revengeful tyrant, and this offended his moral sense. As with many moderns, he was not unaware of the problem of religious pluralism and speculated about the claims for a unique revelation.[10] Discussing the defense of belief in God on the basis of inward convictions and feelings, he observes that ''it cannot be doubted that Hindoos, Mahomedans and others might argue in the same manner and with equal force in favour of the existence of one God, or of many Gods, or as with the Buddhists of no God.''[11] He also tells us how unwilling he was to give up his belief and how he had daydreams about the discovery of old letters and manuscripts that would confirm what was written in the Gospels. He was deeply troubled by the doctrine of eternal punishment of unbelievers, which, if true, would have included ''my Father, Brother and almost all my best friends.'' ''And this,'' he says in an unusual passionate outburst, ''is a damnable doctrine.''[12]

These are the reactions not primarily of a scientist qua scientist but of a morally sensitive and humane person who found grave difficulties in some forms of inherited Christian doctrine. One could have such reactions as Darwin had whether one was a biologist or not. With respect to immortality, he conceded it to be an instinctive belief and was troubled by the view of the physicists of his day that the sun and the planets will one day be too cold for life. ''Believing as I do that man in the distant future will

---

[8]Ibid., 94.

[9]Francis Darwin, ed., *Life and Letters of Charles Darwin* (New York: Appleton and Co., 1888) 282.

[10]Ibid., 85.

[11]Ibid., 90.

[12]Ibid., 87.

be a far more perfect creature than he now is, it is an intolerable thought that he and other sentient beings are doomed to complete annihilation after such long-continued slow progress. To those who fully admit the immortality of the human soul, the destruction of our world will not appear so dreadful.''[13] He also deplored in his later years the decline in his aesthetic sensibility. Poetry, music, the sublimity of natural scenery no longer moved him as they once did. Darwin emerges from his autobiography as a warm and sensitive human being. His difficulties with some aspects of Christian belief did not arise from what would be called today scientism or a brash positivism. Any attempt to commend Jesus Christ as the best clue we have to the nature of God will have to take into account some of Darwinism's difficulties with some aspects of theological tradition and whether that tradition faithfully reflects ''the mind of Christ.''

We now turn to the effects of his specific scientific interests upon his general views about the world and the status of human beings within it. By the time of the *Origin,* he had certainly rejected the fixity of species, held at that time by influential scientists as well as some orthodox Christians. A literal interpretation of Genesis was also rejected. He had not, however, decisively abandoned the notion of a Creator working through general laws rather than by ad hoc interventions. The residual influence of Paley is still to be detected in 1859 as well as later in 1879. He was, however, deeply influenced by Lyell's *Principles of Geology* (1830–1833), which had substituted the idea of general and uniform law in geology for the popular theory of successive geological catastrophes. It was easy, as Darwin himself admitted, to carry over this idea of general law into the area of his own biological research. ''There is grandeur in this view of life, with its several powers, having been originally breathed by the Creator into a few forms or into one: and that, whilst this planet has gone cycling on according to the fixed law of gravity, from so simple a beginning endless forms most beautiful and most wonderful have been, and are being evolved.''[14]

As far as the authority of Scripture is concerned, I would simply affirm that, in my view, the Bible is not a scientific textbook. It is, therefore, improper to look to Scripture for scientific answers to strictly scientific questions. Darwin then cannot be faulted for seeking an account of biological phenomena on the basis of the criteria that biologists consider to be normative for their discipline. Having said this, however, it is still legitimate to ask

---

[13]Ibid., 282.

[14]Charles Darwin, *The Origin of Species and the Descent of Man* (New York: Modern Library, 1936) 374.

whether the factors operative in evolution require the exclusion of teleology and the purposive activity of God. We have seen that Darwin himself was not dogmatic in answering these questions. It is generally accepted that he emphasized the combined effects of chance variations weeded out by natural selection, so that the fittest—that is, those best adapted to their environment—survive. Darwin himself recognized that there were some basic mysteries to which science in his day had not yet found a convincing or plausible account. Mention need only be made of the origin of life itself and why organisms vary in the way they do and produce the results they do. Another remarkable fact is the existence prior to life of a universe and an earthly environment with just the needed chemical elements and the required structure that made the emergence of life possible and its continuing survival and development once it had appeared. A modern biologist, Jacques Monod, has dogmatically stated that we have no option but to acknowledge "pure chance, absolutely free but blind" as the only conceivable hypothesis as to how the world came to be."[15] Yet, taking this posture, as A. R. Peacocke has observed, is to erect the admission of randomness and unpredictable spontaneity into a metaphysical dogma for interpreting the world process as a whole.[16] This is surely an extraordinary extrapolation if it is implied that such a metaphysical dogma inevitably emerges from the science of biology as carried on by professional scientists.[17]

Limited space allows us to say at this point only that the question of the existence of God cannot be responsibly discussed without taking into account every dimension of human existence.[18] The question of teleology in evolution is by no means a dead issue. Tennant appeals to such facts as the adaptation of thought to things and of the inorganic environment to organic life, to aesthetic arguments based on beauty and sublimity in nature, and to human moral consciousness and status and its presuppositions. All these remain as strong testimony to the possibility of restating the teleological argument after Darwin.[19] Richard Swinburne's recent impressive trilogy in theism is further confirmation, particularly the second volume.[20]

---

[15]Jacques Monod, *Chance and Necessity* (London: Collins, 1972).

[16]A. R. Peacocke, *Creation and the World of Science* (London: Clarendon Press, 1979) 94.

[17]I. T. Ramsay, ed., *Biology and Personality* (Oxford: Blackwell, 1965).

[18]J. E. Smith, *Experience and God* (New York: Oxford University Press, 1968).

[19]F. R. Tennant, *Philosophical Theology,* vol. 2 (Cambridge: University Press, 1937).

[20]Richard Swinburne, *The Existence of God* (Oxford: Clarendon, 1979); Ninian Smart, *Philosophers and Religious Truth* (London: SCM Press, 1964).

The point of these references is simply to emphasize that the case for theism is still being made forcefully in the post-Darwinian period. Christians, of course, would want to add to this purely philosophical discussion a more careful consideration of history, revelatory disclosures in history, and the special significance of Jesus Christ.[21]

Darwin and the Divine Image in Man

Here we come to an issue crucial in its relationship to Christology. As the creeds affirm Jesus to be "truly man," it is important to have some reasonably clear idea about what constitutes human existence. Popular but uninformed thinking talks loosely about our coming from monkeys or of man "the naked ape" and assumes that this is what Darwin said. He sometimes did make statements to the effect that the difference between animal and human was only a matter of degree and that he sometimes had doubts as to whether the human mind, descended from a long line of animal ancestors, could be trusted. Yet Darwin never believed that men and women were no more than apes. He acknowledges that the difference is immense, while insisting that animals act in ways remarkably analogous to human intelligent activity and that, even on the emotional level, there are remarkable similarities.[22] Nor did he fail to stress self-consciousness, reason, the power of abstraction, language, the sense of beauty, and even belief in God as characteristic and distinguishing features of the human race.

T. H. Huxley, Darwin's most devoted and loyal defender, stressed the fact that biological had now taken second place to social evolution and that, in the latter, man's nature and capacities became clearly revealed. His grandson, Sir Julian Huxley, contrary to the opinion of some biologists, revived the idea that there is direction in evolution and that the human being is the goal of the process. "Before man, that process was merely animal. After his emergence on to life's stage, it became possible to introduce faith, courage, love of truth, goodness—in a word, moral purpose into evolution."[23] Teilhard de Chardin also stressed the importance of the stage in human development that resulted in the rise of consciousness and the self-consciousness that marks the emergence of the distinctively human being.[24] Existentialists, with their emphasis on freedom likewise see human existence as unique and distinctive. John Macquarrie has written, "To be free

---

[21]H. P. Owen, *The Christian Knowledge of God* (London: Athlone Press, 1969).

[22]Philip Appleman, ed., *Darwin: Selected Writings* (New York: Norton, 1979) 176ff.

[23]Ibid., 331.

[24]Teilhard de Chardin, *The Phenomenon of Man* (New York: Harper Torch, 1971) 141ff.

is to have laid upon one human care and human responsibility, in place of the unthinking irresponsibility of the animal.''[25] While the view of man's creation in the image of God is not an isolated affirmation but depends upon the developed Christian understanding of God, perhaps enough has been said to reinforce the point that Darwin has not led all biologists, still less thinkers in other disciplines, to deny the distinctive features of human existence. To talk glibly of the naked ape does not give a fair reflection of modern scientific and philosophical thinking.

Sin and the Fall

As already indicated, the impact of Darwin seemed most devastating to many in regard to the historic doctrine of the Fall. The implication of Darwin's thought for Christology is obviously far-reaching. If man is not responsible for his fall into sin and alienation from God, then there seems no obvious reason why he needs a Savior or a Redeemer in the traditional sense. If this is so, the classic views of the Atonement and the Incarnation seem to be prescribing a divine cure for a disorder for which human beings are not in any case responsible. Are these inevitable consequences of the changed status of the human being in the Darwinian worldview? It has to be admitted that not all of the tradition can be preserved on this issue. The Augustinian picture of Adam and Eve as emerging from the hand of God in mature perfection and original righteousness cannot now be affirmed as strict historical fact. Neither modern anthropology nor biology can give plausibility to such a beginning of the human race in untarnished perfection. Joanne McWilliam has shown that, despite Augustine's emphasis on the original righteousness of the original pair, he nevertheless rejected the docetic Christ of the Manichaeans, while retaining the stress on compassion as the motive for the eternal Son's becoming man.

It needs to be remembered, however, that Augustinianism does not constitute the whole of the Christian tradition. John Hick has rightly called attention to the view of the Greek father Irenaeus (130–c.A.D.202) that Adam and Eve in the garden were like children. ''So also it was possible for Himself to have made man perfect from the first but man could not receive this [perfection], being as yet an infant.''[26] This ancient view of the first man as truly human but still immature is obviously easier to reconcile with the Darwinian view of human emergence from a long prehuman ancestry. Nevertheless, this view still leaves us with the mystery of the emer-

---

[25]John Macquarrie, *In Search of Humanity* (London: SCM Press, 1982) 20.

[26]Cited by John Hick in *Evil and the God of Love* (London: Collins, 1970) 218.

gence of the truly human, with all that that involves in the way of moral awareness, freedom, and responsibility, the possibility of deviation from the will of God—not to mention language, culture, and the whole range of conceptual and symbolic thinking. It is not impossible on the Darwinian view to give full weight to the truly human when it does appear and, therefore, to the emergence of freedom, sin, guilt, alienation, and all their fateful consequences. These considerations led even Tillich to declare that the story of the Fall "cannot be completely demythologized"[27] and that the transition "from essence to existence" still contains a temporal element, a once upon a time.[28] In short, the fact of man's lowly origin does not change the character and nature of what the human being now is. History is not simply the continuation of biology alone but has its own distinctive human characteristics.

Darwin, Orthogenesis, and Eschatology

It seems clear once again that the crucial issue is whether Darwinism must necessarily exclude teleology and all idea of God's working in and through the natural and historical developments. Presumably God, if we believe in God at all, could have produced human beings through a slow and gradual process rather then by a fiat in a single moment. Which method he adopted is a question in regard to which scientists must be allowed their rightful say. More important, however, is the question whether the evolutionary process can be said to have goals or whether it had the specific goal of producing human beings. There is obviously no unanimity on this question, just because the question involves more than purely scientific considerations. Some biologists, such as Julian Huxley, have been stout defenders of orthogenesis, namely, that evolution has proceeded in a more or less straight line to a culminating point: that point being the emergence of the human race. Others equally strongly resist, arguing that evolution might have many ends or goals and that we are only one such end, and perhaps not the most significant one.

Jacques Monod stands at this other extreme. Of course, it may be asked whether we can speak of goals in regard to a process that is determined basically by physical conditions and elements. How can an unconscious or an unintelligent physical process be said to have aims or goals? My own view is that an "unconscious teleology" is a contradiction in terms, but then we are back to the theistic hypothesis as the most intelligible inter-

---

[27]Paul Tillich, *Systematic Theology,* vol. 2 (Chicago: University of Chicago Press, 1957) 29.

[28]Ibid.

pretation of the cosmic process as a whole. If Darwin's position excludes teleology completely, then the idea that the emergence of the human race was in some meaningful sense planned has to be given up. It is not at all clear that either Darwin himself or later biological research compels us to this conclusion.

Evolutionary Thought and the Incarnation

Having examined the basic Christian assumptions and the points of apparent conflict between them and the work of Darwin, we shall now consider the doctrine of the Incarnation in an evolutionary worldview. This paper may perhaps be justly criticized for hardly dealing with Christology at all. Yet I believe that the issues discussed must constitute the framework within which modern attempts to express the significance of Jesus Christ must be carried on. Unless theological education is to be pursued in a kind of intellectual vacuum, we shall have to talk of Jesus in the cultural context that has been briefly described in the previous pages. It is clear, of course, that the Incarnation, in the classic language of the patristic period, or any talk about God's becoming man, cannot be a simple deduction from science or any specific scientific cosmology. I fully agree with Karl Rahner on this point.[29] Even if we can make out a convincing case for a revised form of the teleological argument in the manner of F. R. Tennant or Richard Swinburne, this is a far cry from the affirmation made in the historic creeds and the Definition of Chalcedon.

Several observations may be made concerning modern attempts either to state or restate the doctrine of the Incarnation. The first concerns the hesitation to speak about specific acts of God. This springs from the tendency to emphasize the continuity in both biological and historical development. Whatever incarnation means, it cannot mean, so it is contended, an absolute break in this continuity. Jesus was at least a Jew of the first century, and this fact places him fairly and squarely in a specific historical and cultural context. This point is made abundantly clear in Paul Dekar's discussion of Jesus the Jew (see chap. 10). That Jesus had a genuine physical body also places him in the context of a long process of biological evolution. His body, like ours, was not an isolated phenomenon but the result of the total cosmic process up to the time of his appearance. The Hebraic emphasis on the whole person, as against Greek dualism, seems to be more consonant with the scientific view of the human person as a psychosomatic unity. All this means that Jesus, whatever theology of the Incarnation we develop, was not simply a bolt from the blue. If he was *homoousios* with

---

[29]Karl Rahner, *Theological Investigations,* vol. 5 (Baltimore: Helicon Press, 1966) 157.

us according to his manhood, as Chalcedon says, then he was really one of us both in his biological and historical antecedents.

This view finds expression in Donald Baillie's "No More Docetism" as well as in J. A. T. Robinson's assertion that any talk about God's embodiment in a human being must give full weight to the fact that "Jesus was born and bred and evolved from within it (i.e. the biological and historical process), a product of it rather than an invader of it."[30] This same emphasis is found in such a process thinker as Norman Pittenger as well as in G. W. H. Lampe's Bampton lectures.[31] The latter warns us against overemphasizing the radical break with the past involved in the appearance of Jesus. "We should try to set the process of the Christ-event within the perspective of a continuous process of which we can discern neither the beginning nor the end and to avoid the idea that in Christ God has broken into the process in which He is always immanent and radically altered his own relationship to his human creation."[32] It is no exaggeration to say that this emphasis on the universal, immanent activity of God in the cosmic process as a whole owes much to the changed perspective induced by Darwin's work. The status of humankind in that process is perceived in a new way, which has implications for the way we interpret the "truly man" and the relationship of Jesus' humanity to ours.

Nothing in all this line of thinking is basically inconsistent with what Christian theology has always affirmed about the real humanity of Jesus. Nevertheless, this strong emphasis on divine immanence and uniformity of action does raise special problems with which modern Christology is still grappling. If Jesus is so completely one of us (*totus in nostris,* as J. A. T. Robinson affirms), is any room left for specific and even unique acts or act of God in a process regarded as evidence of God's universal activity? God appears to be doing everything but nothing in particular. Should we abandon altogether the language of uniqueness, of the once-for-all, not to mention the language of finality? Can any event or any person be unique and final in a process that is without beginning or end and that is moving continually into the future? We are driven back to the doctrine of God and his relation to the world he has made and is still sustaining. It is doubtful whether the phrase *act of God* can be given an intelligible meaning without a more thorough view of God as personal than much modern theology is willing to concede. Austin Farrer roundly declares that theology of the

---

[30]J. A. T. Robinson, *The Human Face of God* (London: SCM Press, 1973) 203.

[31]G. W. H. Lampe, *God and Spirit* (Oxford: Clarendon, 1977).

[32]Ibid.

Christian type is cosmic personalism.[33] William Temple, nearly two generations ago, in a perceptive critique of A. N. Whitehead's *Process and Reality,* argued that "personality is always transcendent in relation to Process."[34] The category of organism is thus inadequate to express the distinctive nature of both human and divine personality. Furthermore, the most impressive feature of human personality at its highest is not unalterable uniformity of conduct but constancy of purpose, perpetual and delicate self-adjustment to different and changing circumstances.[35] There is, therefore, no basic contradiction between God's uniform activity in the cosmic process and the possibility of specific divine action or acts in which God's loving and saving purpose is more fully disclosed. The task of any modern Christology that is in real continuity with our Christian past must be its success in combining these two emphases and doing justice to both.

In this latter part of the chapter, I take a brief look at the shape of some modern Christologies and try to identify the issues with which a future Christology must grapple. We shall, of necessity, have to move far beyond Darwin to consider wider philosophical and historical issues. It needs to be said, however, that there can be no return to a pre-Darwinian view, if this means a total denial of any or all forms of biological evolution. This restriction does not mean that we are committed to speculative philosophical constructions claimed as legitimate extrapolations from Darwin's work. This latter must be seen in the context of the total scientific enterprise and in particular the radical developments of modern physics.[36]

Nor can Darwin's work be properly assessed while ignoring such recent restatements of the case for theism by F. R. Tennant, E. L. Mascall, Richard Swinburne, and Keith Ward, to name only a few. In other words, we cannot consider the work of Darwin in isolation from the total field of modern knowledge. As this influence bears on Christology, however, it is clear that Jesus must be seen as an "emergent" from one unified cosmic process, although this position in no way cancels what has just been said

----

[33]Austin Farrer, *Saving Belief* (London: Hodder & Stoughton, 1964) 63.

[34]William Temple, *Nature, Man, and God* (London: Macmillan, 1934) 261.

[35]Ibid., 267.

[36]Ian Barbour, *Issues of Science and Religion* (London: SCM Press, 1966); S. L. Jaki, *The Road of Science and the Ways to God* (Chicago: University of Chicago Press, 1978); idem, *Cosmos and Creator* (Edinburgh: Scottish Academic Press, 1980); A. R. Peacocke, *Creation and the World of Science* (Oxford: Clarendon, 1979); A. R. Peacocke, ed., *The Sciences and Theology in the Twentieth Century* (London: Oriel Press, Routledge & Kegan Paul, 1981).

about God's uniform and specific action. I list briefly the basic issues that confront any contemporary Christology.

1. If Jesus is *homoousios* with us according to the manhood, as Chalcedon affirms, is it any longer possible to use of him the language of divinity, uniqueness, and finality?

2. Do we know enough of Jesus of Nazareth by modern historical research to be able to restate the basic intention of the classical Christology? Denis Nineham has underlined the quandary of those forms of liberal theology that strip Jesus of the dogmatic categories of patristic thinking and yet wish to give a central place to Jesus on the basis of his sinlessness and moral perfection. He asks whether historical evidence can never substantiate this attribute, whether from a negative or positive point of view.[37]

3. Is the emphasis on process and dynamic and creative becoming, one of the consequences of Darwin's influence, consistent with a theism that confidently describes God by personal analogies and uses language about acts of God or a specific act of God? This becomes a crucial issue in the recent attempts to use the philosophy of A. N. Whitehead and Charles Hartshorne as the basis for a so-called modern Christology, despite the relative silence of these two thinkers on this issue.

4. Can we single out one specific "act of God" (i.e., Jesus as the Christ or the Word made flesh) as giving us the clue to the meaning of the cosmic process up to now, as well as being an anticipation of a divine goal to be reached in the future?

These are the fundamental questions, and the rest of this chapter is simply a tentative effort to suggest ways in which these questions are being answered at the present time and might be answered in the future. As has often happened in the history of Christian thought, there is a tendency for certain types of language to become fixed and often to be used in an unquestioned way. Modern Christology is no exception. One example would be the current talk of Christology "from below" and "from above" to indicate two distinct and distinguishable methods of approach. What exactly is such language intended to convey? Does a Christology from below mean a so-called Jesus of history, reached by modern historical research governed by the assumptions of the Enlightenment? Is the result of this process supposed to be the "real" Jesus, as distinct from later theological and doctrinal developments? One big assumption often made is that the real Jesus

---

[37]John Hick, ed., *The Myth of God Incarnate* (London: SCM Press, 1977) chapter 10.

could not possibly be the Christ of faith and Christian dogmatic reflection. It is often contended that miracle, notoriously difficult to define, can no longer be taken as historical evidence of events or happenings that should be allowed to dictate the shape of a Christology. This question concerns not only a few healings or one or two questionable nature miracles but the resurrection of Jesus, which seems to be the presupposition of all the New Testament writings. To come to grips with the implications of all this, it would be necessary to consider in detail the appeal of Troeltsch to the principles of criticism, analogy, and correlation. I refer the reader to recent discussions of this as well as to Troeltsch himself. Certainly, if the historian must rule out as not factually historical anything that does not have a significant analogy in his or her own present experience,[38] then not only must the Resurrection appear extremely questionable, but even Jesus himself can hardly be said to be analogous to anything in contemporary experience. Nevertheless, the attempt to free Jesus from dogmatic swaddling clothes is by no means confined to what some would regard as outdated liberal theology.

One of the fascinating features of the contemporary situation is the way in which Roman Catholic thinkers such as Hans Küng, Karl Rahner, and Edward Schillebeeckx have tried to penetrate behind the dogmas to Jesus of Nazareth as the norm and criterion. Schillebeeckx, for example, observes that the traditional Christology has fallen apart in our time.[39] One is accustomed to emphasis on experience in Protestant theologies stemming from Schleiermacher. Many are surprised to find this same emphasis appearing again in some modern Catholic Christology.[40] Schillebeeckx in his second volume tries to recover or retrieve the original Christian experience of salvation prior to the dogmatic development that resulted in the creeds and the Chalcedonian Definition. Certainly he does not believe that historical research can of itself generate that experience or produce saving faith. Yet in his historical investigation of the New Testament documents and the Gospels in particular, he is influenced by some of the Enlightenment assumptions. One example would be his treatment of the Resurrection and his preference for exaltation rather than resurrection as a symbol

[38]R. Morgan and Michael Pye, trans. and eds., *Ernst Troeltsch: Writings on Theology and Religion* (Atlanta: John Knox Press, 1982). See also W. J. Abraham, *Divine Revelation and the Limits of Historical Criticism* (Oxford: Oxford University Press, 1982); and Van A. Harvey, *The Historian and the Believer* (New York: Macmillan, 1966).

[39]Edward Schillebeeckx, *Jesus,* trans. Hubert Hoskins (New York: Seabury, 1979).

[40]Edward Schillebeeckx, *Christ* (New York: Seabury, 1980) 29ff.

of Jesus' true status after his earthly life had ended.[41] Again, while he is anxious to emphasize that the appeal to experience is not an emotional capacity or sheerly subjective and that the peculiarly Christian experience is productive of new experience, the point to be noted here is his conviction that it is possible to get back to a preconceptual and predogmatic existential experience. We admittedly cannot remain there, since all experience calls for some interpretation, with guesses, hypotheses, theories, and the use of various models in order to interpret adequately the intrinsic meaning of the experience. This interpretation, he says, is not the denial of the objectivity of the revelation but only of a stunted and limiting scientific (i.e., conceptual) objectivity.[42]

We may properly welcome this appeal to experience in the Catholic thinkers named, provided experience is carefully defined as to its different meanings and provided it is realized that the role of reflection in faith and the interpretive models used demand for their justification a far more extensive philosophical analysis than Schillebeeckx has yet attempted. We must await yet a third volume from him before we are in a position to say how exactly he relates experience in detail to the dogmatic tradition of the church. We find in Rahner this same emphasis on unthematized experience—that is, experience not yet interpreted in terms of fixed and abstract categories and concepts. The goal of the world is God's communicating of himself to it.[43] This communication, however, is not primarily in propositions, concepts, or dogmatic formulas but rather in experience understood existentially. It would be unfair to these thinkers to imply that they have no use for reflective and conceptual thinking. Their long and subtly argued works bear ample testimony to such thought. It is important for us to recognize that such conceptualizing has no relevant practical bearing apart from the prior experience that the concepts and dogmatic statements are trying to articulate in human language. It is evident that this method of approach is vastly different from those attempts to do theology deductively by arguing from self-evident axioms given by either infallible Scripture or the authoritative dogmatic tradition established by the church's magisterium.

What, then, is meant by Christology from above? Such Christologies tend to start, not from a Jesus stripped of all interpretation and doctrinal

---

[41]Schillebeeckx, *Jesus,* 516ff.

[42]Schillebeeckx, *Christ,* 48.

[43]Rahner, *Theological Investigations,* 173; and idem, *Foundations of Christian Faith* (New York: Seabury, 1978), emphasize divine presence in unthematized form. Hans Küng, *On Being a Christian* (New York: Doubleday, 1976) 83, defends starting from below.

significance, but from Jesus identified with the Christ of faith and the later church's conceptualizing of the meaning of this identity in the two-nature doctrine and the doctrine of the Trinity. Melvyn Hillmer, in chapter 3, insists that the unity must not be lost, despite the justifiable emphasis on the variety of the Christological viewpoints of the different Gospels. The criterion of the historical Jesus, who is the Christ, the Son of God, is essential. This latter affirmation is not simply the result of literary analysis and historical study. It is an interpretation of faith by both the early disciples and the writers of the Gospels. It implies a Christology from above if one intends to make a statement, not only about the faith of the early church, but about the nature of Jesus' relationship to the Father. The theological tradition assumed that Jesus is the Second ''Person'' of the Trinity, who became man for us human beings and our salvation. The Eternal Son or Word preexists the historical Jesus as a distinct hypostasis in the Godhead. In short, the divinity of Jesus Christ is assumed—and not only any view of divinity but a view conceptualized in a very specific way.

Barth's statement affirms that ''the mystery of the revelation of God in Jesus Christ consists in the fact that the eternal Word of God chose, sanctified and assumed human nature and existence into oneness with Himself in order that, as very God and very Man, to become the word of Reconciliation spoken by God to man.''[44] How does Barth know this fact with sufficient certainty to make it the starting point of his whole dogmatic enterprise? The key is to be found in his treatment of Anselm and his contention that ''theological science is for Anselm the science of the Credo: *intelligere* comes about by reflection on the Credo that has already been spoken and affirmed.''[45] Barth's given is not, like Hartshorne's, ''a matter of mutual logical implication of a limited number of key concepts'' derived from an analysis of the structure of general experience.[46] Nor is the given an innate intellectual equipment of men and women but a gift of God in Christ in the mystery of the Incarnation. Especially significant is Barth's comment that ''Anselm always has the solution of his problems already behind him (through faith in the impartial good sense of the decisions of ecclesiastical authority).''[47] This is the crux of the matter for all Christologies from above. Can we assume that Barth shares Anselm's confidence in the decisions made by the church in its development of the doctrine

---

[44]Karl Barth, *Church Dogmatics,* vol. 1, pt. 2 (Edinburgh: T. & T. Clark, 1956) 122.

[45]Karl Barth, *Anselm: Fides Quaerens Intellectum* (London: SCM Press, 1930) 27.

[46]C. E. Gunton, *Becoming and Being* (Oxford: Oxford University Press, 1978) 11.

[47]Barth, *Anselm,* 25-26.

of the Incarnation? The answer would appear to be yes, in marked contrast to such men as Pannenberg, Wiles, Schillebeeckx, Rahner, and others. All of these do not necessarily deny the validity of the church's Christological decisions, but such validity can be established only at the end of the theological inquiry. They cannot be the unquestioned starting point for a contemporary Christology. Barth, however, will not accept this prohibition but rather starts with the affirmation of the Credo—that is, faith's interpretation of the event of Jesus Christ not only in the New Testament but in the mainstream doctrinal development of the church's theologians.

At first sight it might seem as if Barth is simply taking over traditional theological propositions and concepts and then deriving his Christology and indeed his whole theology from the axioms contained in these received statements. For example, in regard to the appeal to a precritical or unthematic experience already considered, Barth is wholly opposed if this means an appeal to the religious consciousness in general. His approach is consistently a posteriori and not a priori; that is, he starts from the way in which God has made himself known in the three ways of being in which God functions in his becoming. Yet God's becoming is not a metaphysical term to characterize the universal character of the cosmic process as a whole, as in Hartshorne. It is concrete and temporal but specific and assumes the incarnation of the Eternal Word in Jesus of Nazareth and the response to this event in faith in the biblical witness and its continuation in the church, where this witness is appropriated and reaffirmed by the community of believers through the inner witness of the Holy Spirit. No one comes to such an affirmation by one's own historical and theological investigation. Barth was fond of Calvin's dictum that we have God as our Father and the church as our Mother. His *Church Dogmatics* is full of concepts both theological and indeed philosophical, which has led some to assume that he has lost himself in abstractions and rarefied concepts that are remote from the realities of personal communion and fellowship with God.

Yet this view is probably a serious misunderstanding. Words like *being* and *essence* are not in Barth what they signify in more metaphysical theologies or in pure philosophy. Barth rejects the view that we cannot speak of God in himself but insists, "For deity does not exist at all in itself and as such but only in the modes of existence of Father, Son and Spirit."[48] This statement confirms our earlier comment about his a posteriori approach. The above is further borne out by his view of language and his attitude to the classical natural theology. Human language, even the biblical

---

[48]Barth, *Church Dogmatics,* 133.

language, is open textured, and words in themselves, not even in Scripture, are to be identified without further ado as revelation. We achieve responsible speech about God only to the degree that the words of Scripture and of the church's witness are taken by the Holy Spirit and to enable us to make the affirmation that Jesus is Lord. From this confession everything flows, whether it be the doctrine of creation as deriving its meaning from the covenant or the covenant deriving its meaning from the new covenant in Jesus Christ.

From these basic assumptions derive also Barth's distrust of a natural theology based on the *analogia entis*. The danger of the latter lies in the hidden assumption that knowledge of the true God may be gained, at least in part, from the analysis of the structure of being or existence in general. This assumption Barth forcefully repudiates. We cannot develop a theological anthropology independently of the revelation of authentic humanity in the Word made flesh. Nor can we reach a doctrine of creation, in the specific biblical and Christian sense, by studying nature or the cosmic process apart from the knowledge of God given to faith. Nor can we develop a doctrine of the Trinity by psychological analysis of the human person. Barth rejects the *vestigia Trinitatis* in the human psyche. This method of approach lacks the fundamental knowledge that Jesus is Lord and that the Eternal Word was made flesh in a real happening or event independent of anything that a merely human psychology could show. The analogy of faith, as distinct from the analogy of being, is rooted in the three ways of being in the temporal manifestations of the one God. There is no a priori method of getting to this point. We can know God in this way only insofar as we are taken out of ourselves into the divine action in creation, covenant, election, and the Word made flesh. Into some grasp of this mystery only the Spirit can guide us. Accordingly, we cannot decide a priori or on the basis of any set of philosophical assumptions what God can or cannot do.

Some theology of the tradition, mixed with certain philosophical assumptions, may have reached false conclusions in regard to the nature of God. The apathetic or impassible God is reached by philosophical speculation, not by attending to what God has actually done in Jesus Christ. If we ask how can the transcendent God be immanent in that which is other than himself (e.g., in creation or in the humanity of Jesus), Barth's reply is that God has actually done this. God is subject, and in his sovereign freedom, he is free to become immanent if he so chooses, even to the point of becoming fully one with Jesus of Nazareth. Furthermore, he does so without ceasing in the slightest to be God.[49]

---

[49]Ibid.

These few comments on Barth are not, of course, adequate to the theme, but we do find here an impressive example of one form that a Christology from above can take. Nor have we attempted a critique of some of the more controversial issues that Barth raises. When he was once asked what he was trying to do in the *Church Dogmatics,* he replied, ''It is to listen to what Scripture is saying and tell you what I hear.''[50] As Sykes puts it, the very use of the word *God* depends on the story of Jesus' death and resurrection.[51] The proof of God's existence is in his ''Self-Expression in history as told in the Bible.''[52] I hope this very concise summary has not obscured the fact that much criticism of Barth has missed the point because of its failure to give full weight to the centrality of the Incarnation as the actual becoming of God in a human existence. Not that critical questions cannot be raised. Has Barth really heard all that Scripture says? How is his theological reconstruction related to modern historical criticism of the Scriptures? Why does he say so little about the relation of the biblical story to history outside this context? Is his sharp distinction between religion and revelation tenable if we take a wider view of history? Is all natural and philosophical theology irrelevant because it does not start with the Word made flesh? And specifically, does his Christology really do justice to the full humanity of Jesus and the responsible freedom of persons? There will no doubt be continued debate about these and other issues. It is clear, however, that Barth cannot simply be dismissed as a naive fundamentalist or an obscurantist conservative. He may not have said the last word, but it is difficult to believe that any future grappling with Christological issues can simply ignore him.

Perhaps the very distinction between Christologies from below and from above should be questioned if further progress is to be made. Otto Weber has said that ''no one can ascend from a 'below', which is somehow given, to an 'above' without holding this 'above' to be at least partially given in or with the 'below.' ''[53] Pannenberg, despite his sympathy with this point, still prefers a Christology from below, that is, rising from the historical man Jesus to the recognition of his divinity.[54] In other words, the concept

---

[50]S. Sykes, *Karl Barth: Studies in His Theological Method* (Oxford: Clarendon, 1979) 55.

[51]Ibid., 58.

[52]Ibid., 59.

[53]Otto Weber, *Grundlagen der Dogmatick* (Neukirchen: Kreismoers Verlag der Buchhandlung des Eriziehensvereins, 1962) 2:20-25. See also W. Pannenberg, *Jesus-God and Man* (London: SCM Press, 1968) 33.

[54]Pannenberg, *Jesus-God and Man,* 33.

of Incarnation belongs to the end of theological inquiry. It is not an un-questioned assumption prior to the study of Jesus' message and fate by modern historical methods. Bearing this understanding in mind, we shall now proceed to other modern attempts to deal with the Christological issue in the light of modern critical history developed since the Enlightenment.

Kenosis and Modern Thought

Another major issue for a contemporary Christology is whether the idea of divine self-limitation, freely chosen by God, can be invoked as a way of reconciling the true humanity of Jesus with the claims for his divinity expressed in the church's creeds. Insofar as the nineteenth-century quest of the historical Jesus made it more and more impossible to ascribe to Jesus of Nazareth unqualified omnipotence, omniscience, and omnipresence, any interpretation of the two-nature doctrine that seemed to imply this position becomes correspondingly suspect. That Jesus was limited in both power and knowledge became widely, though not universally, recognized. It is well known that, from Thomasius onward, a significant number of Christian thinkers tried to reconcile this fact with traditional Christological orthodoxy by appealing to the idea of *kenosis,* or self-emptying. While not claiming that Paul had all this in mind in the hymn of Philippians 2:5-11, they found in the suggestion of a self-emptying and, therefore, self-limitation of the Eternal Son a useful concept for combining the claim for the divinity of Jesus with the limitations of the historical figure that the modern historical approach was emphasizing.[55] Some who were reluctant to accept the idea of a total self-emptying on the part of the Eternal Son preferred to appeal to the idea of latency in regard to the so-called metaphysical attributes. Jesus had these powers but did not exercise them in the full sense and perhaps was not always in conscious possession of them.

It is also well known that the various forms of kenotic Christology evoked a critical response. The more the distinctions of the "persons" of the Trinity were emphasized, the more it seemed that the self-emptying of the Eternal Son left us with a Jesus as a finite and limited historical person with no assurance as to his divinity. On the other hand, the more the unity of the triune God was emphasized, the more perplexing it became to conceive of a God who divested himself of those metaphysical attributes or

---

[55]For further historical detail about this development, the reader may consult H. R. Mackintosh, *The Person of Christ* (Edinburgh: T. & T. Clark, 1937); J. S. Lawton, *Conflict in Christology* (London: S. P. C. K. 1947); Oliver Quick, *Doctrines of the Creed* (London: Nisbet, 1938); Vincent Taylor, *The Person of Christ in New Testament Teaching* (London: Macmillan, 1958).

properties that seemed to be involved in any definition of Godhead. As William Temple asked. "What was happening to the rest of the universe during the period of our Lord's earthly life?"[56] Was the universe no longer under divine control when Jesus was an infant in the cradle or during the period of finite limitation of his thirty-odd years on this planet? Certainly the critics had raised some grave difficulties with some forms of kenotic Christology, even though they did not wish to return to the claim that Jesus of Nazareth had the metaphysical attributes in an unqualified sense, whether consciously known by Jesus or merely latent. The effect of Darwin's work and the development of an evolutionary worldview has only rendered the problem more acute. The more emphasis is placed upon the fact that "Jesus was completely one of us" in every sense,[57] the more it seemed impossible to doubt the limitations inherent in any form of finite manhood. The problem of divine self-limitation, even if we do not use the word *kenosis*, still remains. Modern grappling with the Christological issue makes this clear. A persuasive attempt to show that a Logos and a *kenosis* Christology can be combined is to be found in Walter Kasper's recent impressive work.[58]

Thomas Altizer has offered us a very radical form of *kenosis*. The transcendent God of Old Testament faith appears in Jesus in a "totally empty or kenotic form."[59] There is obviously a dangerous ambiguity in this kind of language. Does Altizer really mean that the transcendent God has ceased to be and has no other reality than in the crucified Jesus? Here the breach of continuity with the historic Christian faith seems absolute.[60] Somewhat similar problems arise in the title of Jürgen Moltmann's well-known book *The Crucified God*. His concern is a doctrine of God that does full justice to God's real participation in the cross and suffering of Jesus. This view involves a radical change in Christian thought about the impassibility of God, or God's inability to suffer. Moltmann does not wish to go to the extreme of Altizer and distinguishes his own position from the "death of God"

---

[56]W. Temple, *Christus Veritas* (London: Macmillan, 1934) 142.

[57]Robinson, *Human Face of God*, 89.

[58]Walter Kasper, *The God of Jesus Christ*, trans. J. O'Connell (London: SCM Press, 1984) 189.

[59]T. J. J. Altizer, *The Gospel of Christian Atheism* (Philadelphia: Westminster Press, 1966) 87.

[60]R. F. Aldwinckle, *The Living God and Radical Theology*, idem, McMaster Divinity College Bulletin no. 2, (May 1967); idem, *Did Jesus Believe in God?* New Theology no. 5 (New York: Macmillan, 1968).

movement of some years ago. ''Jesus' death cannot be understood as 'the death of God' but only as death in God.''[61] Even more recently, Don Cupitt has reached similar conclusions in his *Taking Leave of God,* to which Keith Ward has made an effective reply in his *Holding Fast to God.*[62] Any attempt to preserve the genuine humanity of Jesus by eliminating God would seem to be a hopeless dead end as far as an intelligible Christian theology is concerned. The problem raised by the kenoticists remains.

Another attempt to deal with this issue is found in Pannenberg's comprehensive study.[63] In his discussion of the history of the kenotic idea, he rejects any view of the God-man as one who possessed all the divine attributes but simply refused to use them. ''Jesus would remain an almighty, omniscient, omnipotent man, even though the humbly hides his glory.''[64] It is not possible here to go into all the details of Pannenberg's subtle argumentation. His solution appears to be as follows. Until the Resurrection, the essential unity of Jesus with God (interpreted as the real presence of God in him) was hidden not only from other men but also from Jesus himself.[65] Only from the vantage point of the Resurrection, defended by Pannenberg as a historical reality or event, and its retroactive significance can we see that Jesus was really at one with God, even in his pre-Easter existence. This unity was hidden from Jesus because the ultimate decision about his earthly life had not yet been given. Presumably the implication of this view is that Jesus himself became aware of his ultimate vindication by God only at the Resurrection. This view enables Pannenberg to admit the full extent of the limitations of Jesus' earthly existence and to come to terms with the more radical forms of New Testament scholarship. Jesus, for example, did not claim to be Messiah, Son of Man, or even Son of God in a way that would distinguish him uniquely from all other men. To have had absolute certain knowledge of his unique sonship to God or his preexistence would have meant the surrender of his true humanity. He walked by faith in God's ultimate purpose and not by sight. Pannenberg thus rejects any view of the two-nature doctrine as involving a synthesis of divine and human in one human person, nor does he favor any of the existing kenotic Christologies from Thomasius onward.

---

[61]J. Moltmann, *The Crucified God* (London: SCM Press, 1974) 207.

[62]Keith Ward, *Holding Fast to God* (London: S.P.C.K., 1982).

[63]Pannenberg, *Jesus-God and Man,* 307ff.

[64]Ibid., 319.

[65]Ibid., 321.

At first sight, it appears as if Pannenberg has simply eliminated the divinity in the traditional sense, but such does not appear to be his intention. That Jesus was one with the God of the Old Testament, whom Jesus called Father, can be derived only from the historical particularity of this man Jesus, his message and his fate. Yet we cannot evade the problem of Jesus' self-consciousness. We cannot penetrate to this self-consciousness from the titles (Messiah, etc.) because we do not have any historical certainty that he applied these to his own person and action. Nevertheless, "Jesus' self-consciousness was decisively stamped by his message of the nearness of God and his kingdom."[66] This latter tack does not entitle us, however, to begin to interpret the meaning of this in terms of an incarnational doctrine taken as a self-evident premise from which to start. If the Incarnation as a unique personal unity with God is theologically correct (and Pannenberg thinks it is) it can be arrived at only from the perspective of the Resurrection and the latter's proleptic guarantee to faith that God's purpose, manifest in Jesus, will be finally accomplished at the consummation of history. It cannot simply be read off from the account of the life and death of Jesus in his pre-Easter existence.

There is no space here to develop a critical assessment of the many debatable aspects of Pannenberg's thought. The general direction, however, is clear. A contemporary Christology cannot assume an incarnational Christology as its starting point. It must first of all inquire as "to the determinative significance inherent in the distinctive features of the real historical man Jesus of Nazareth,"[67] in particular, his relationship to the Judaism of his time, which enabled Jesus to clarify his openness to God in terms of a special vocation. Pannenberg is nonetheless emphatic that such an inquiry into the historical career of Jesus cannot reach a Jesus independent of his relationship to God mediated through the Jewish tradition. This construction would result in a crass distortion of the historical reality, for the brute facts of a positivist thought are pure abstractions.

The question still remains as to whether we can still believe in the God of Israel, whose agent Jesus believed himself to be. This God-question cannot be resolved in terms of absolute demonstration here and now but only when the totality of history is seen to have a certain significance in the light of God's fulfilled purposes. The deity of God is his rule, and only when that rule has

---

[66]Ibid., 332.
[67]Ibid., 34.

been universally established can it be known with certainty.[68] Hence the ontological priority of the future. Just as Jesus did not know in his earthly existence with absolute knowledge who he was and would be, so too with us. While faith has the assurance that comes from the anticipatory or proleptic faith of the Resurrection as historical event, absolute certainty about the God of Jesus must remain problematic until the final summing up of all things. Faith has enough to live and die by, but it is still faith, not full and complete knowledge. A Christology from below may lead to a Christology from above, but this possibility is a deduction of faith, not the result of an assumed two-nature doctrine taken as the first axiom. Pannenberg, therefore, does not need to use the concept of a divine self-emptying, because the incarnation of the Logos is not his starting point. Nor is the question of his authentic humanity open to debate, for this characteristic is assumed as a self-evident result of modern historical research into the life and career of Jesus of Nazareth. If, however, we are led to affirm in faith the real unity of Jesus and God, even in his pre-Easter existence seen from the perspective of the Resurrection, this unity remains the final mystery and cannot be made more intelligible by invoking the two-nature doctrine of the classical Christology. Nevertheless, faith assures us that this man Jesus was God in all the ways required for revelation and redemption.

Another form of kenotic Christology is to be found in the work of Austin Farrer (though he may not be very happy with the word *kenotic*). Farrer admits that the unbelieving historian is not being simply pig headed in not admitting a unique divine presence in Jesus.[69] While the Christian faith cannot dispense with some historical fact in the hard headed post-Enlightenment sense, it is not believed on historical grounds only. The problem of the Incarnation, as he sees it, is not how to combine two determinate sorts of being in one person (the two-nature doctrine again). Rather it concerns how we are to believe and express the fact that the infinite Godhead can finitize his personal action in a unique way "so that he is purely divine in being purely human."[70] "God's Incarnation consists precisely in being the man Jesus and not in being anything else."[71] But what was incarnate in Jesus? Not simply Godhead but "the divine Sonship in the Godhead."[72]

---

[68]W. Pannenberg, *Theology and the Kingdom of God* (Philadelphia: Westminster Press, 1969) 55-56.

[69]Austin Farrer, *Interpretation and Belief* (London: S.P.C.K., 1976) 127.

[70]Ibid., 137.

[71]Ibid., 130.

[72]Ibid., 137.

This view, says Farrer, is unintelligible apart from some doctrine of the Trinity. In a very broad sense, Farrer is kenotic in affirming that it was not necessary for Jesus to know his role in terms of the metaphysical attributes, whether possession of them or clear knowledge that he possessed them. Jesus knew how to play his role as the divine Son without the metaphysical elaborations of later doctrine. His mental furniture was derived from his local rabbi, and that was sufficient. ''He had all that was needed to be the Son of God.''[73] The defining of this doctrine was the task of later hands and Christian thinkers. The process of developing a theology of his person was begun by the apostles and continued later, but there is no need to claim that all this was a necessary part of Jesus' self-consciousness and certain knowledge. Farrer was fully aware that, if any claim to divinity in any sense was to be retained, the problem of double agency must be faced, even if a complete understanding of this duality eludes us as far as precise conceptualization is concerned. By *double agency* is meant the relation of the will of God to the will of the Son, interpreted as freely chosen obedience. Obviously the relation of the two wills is not exactly the same as in the relationship between two human beings. Yet if we eliminate the presence and the activity of the divine will, we cannot talk of a unique divine presence as informing the activity of Jesus the man. Unless Jesus could know and be confronted with the will of his Father in some significant sense and be free to give real and total obedience, then all Christological claims must be abandoned. There must have been some element of reflection and interpretation in Jesus' awareness of the will of God and its absolute claim upon his obedience. There is no such thing as a ''pure datum of revelation prior to those necessary evils reflection and communication.''[74] This fact must be as true for Jesus as it is for all later Christian reflection upon his significance.

H. D. Lewis has objected that taking this position is to open the door to the possible canonization of everything said or written by apostles or church fathers.[75] Farrer, however, objects in turn that, if all reflection is exposed to negative criticism that doubts all such reflective activity as a means of knowing the will of God, then we are left with no revelation at all. If Paul or John or the other New Testament witnesses are completely untrustworthy as media of the revelation in Jesus, then we have no means of ascertaining what was the original witness of Jesus to the will of the

---

[73]Farrer, *Saving Belief,* 80.

[74]Austin Farrer, *Faith and Speculation* (London: Adam & Charles Black, 1967) 101.

[75]Ibid.

heavenly Father. We must accept the paradox that God authoritatively reveals himself through fallible human thought.[76] This is as true for Jesus as for the interpretations of later Christian witnesses as they gave their witness and formulated their doctrines. "The paradigm is Christ's ability to play his part with a mental furniture acquired from his village rabbi."[77] If we question this possibility, what other requirements would have helped Jesus better to fulfill his mission? Would he have been better equipped if he had had the philosophical training of a Platonist, an Aristotelian, or a Stoic—or had the knowledge of a Newton or an Einstein? To this suggestion Farrer would no doubt have given a decisive no. Jesus had all that was necessary to be the Son and therefore the perfect and adequate revealer in word and action of the saving presence and will of God his Father, whose unique Son he knew himself to be. Such knowledge of the Father was not mediated to him through a sophisticated philosophy or theological conceptual scheme, but it was no worse and none the less real for that.

There would appear to be some resemblance here between Farrer's point and the distinction later made by Karl Rahner between thematic and unthematic knowledge. "There is in man an inseparable unity in difference between one's original self-possession and reflection."[78] We cannot identify true knowledge only with the objectifying concept or with an original self-possession totally devoid of the reflective element. This original unity of reality and self-presence is not totally mediated by the concept that objectifies in so-called scientific knowledge.[79] It is an existentiell experience, a free, personal, and subjective appropriation and actualization. This can also be spoken of in abstract theory or objective concepts without having lived through the existentiell experience. As these considerations bear upon Christology, Rahner wishes to distinguish between Jesus' existentiell awareness of his unity with God and a reflective expression of this relation in concepts (e.g., the two natures, a metaphysical sonship, a conscious use of the concept of preexistence). Says Rahner, "God's self-revelation in the depths of the spiritual person is an *a priori* determination coming from grace and is in itself unreflective."[80]

Both Farrer and Rahner do not believe it possible to exclude reflection and interpretation from the existentiell experience. Even in the case of Je-

---

[76]Ibid., 102.

[77]Ibid., 103.

[78]Rahner, *Foundations of Christian Faith*, 15.

[79]Ibid., 16.

[80]Ibid., 172.

sus, he could understand his calling and role only by the use of images and concepts, such as *kingdom,* taken from the Jewish tradition in which he was nurtured. Nevertheless, the relation between experience and reflection and the degree and sophistication of the latter is important. If we ask whether Jesus was consciously preoccupied with the question as to how the two natures were combined or what was the nature of his preexistent life, we sense at once how artificial such an inquiry is and how alien it all is to the Jesus of the Gospels, unless we insist that some of the reflections of the Fourth Gospel are the ipsissima verba of Jesus of Nazareth. As Farrer also insists, popular Jewish theology had no set terms "in which incarnation or metaphysical divine sonship could be stated."[81] By the very nature of the case, therefore, Jesus could not have reflectively interpreted who he was in terms of a vocabulary and set of concepts quite lacking in the tradition that produced him.

Yet both Farrer and Rahner would say that this fact does not rule out an awareness of what it meant to be the Father's only Son and obey his will gladly. It does not even rule out an experiential identity of the Father and the Son through "interpretation, interrelatedness and the indwelling of the Holy Spirit."[82] These terms are important because they indicate the difference between Jesus and his Father. His prayers to his Father must involve his awareness of the difference. In the normal human case of parenthood, a son may become like a father, but the separation and the distinction clearly remains. Farrer apparently sees the uniqueness of Jesus in the fact that in him, the two become one in more than a formal sense. "In the person of Christ the mutual interpenetration is complete; it is necessary to talk of personal identity."[83] It is necessary to stress again that, in talking like this, Farrer and predominantly Rahner too are talking of Jesus' existentiell apprehension of spiritual realities, not a reflection upon or a conceptualization of that apprehension in the more sophisticated language and concepts of later Christian thought.

Farrer's Christology is, therefore, kenotic in the sense that Jesus knew how to be the Son of God in action without having a systematic conceptual scheme claiming to explain his unity with the Father and what this relationship involved for his obedience and sacrificial self-giving for the world.

---

[81]B. Mitchell, ed., *Faith and Logic* (London: Allen & Unwin, 1957) 103.

[82]M. P. Wilson, "Austin Farrer and the Paradox of Christology," *Scottish Journal of Theology* 35:2 (1982): 145-63.

[83]Farrer, *Saving Belief,* 75; idem, *A Faith of Our Own* [American title, *Said or Sung*] (New York: World Publishing, 1960) 23.

What the earlier kenoticists were claiming in regard to the limitations of Jesus of Nazareth could, therefore, be fully accepted by Farrer. Jesus was not Man in general. He was a man, a Galilean carpenter turned free-lance rabbi.[84] He was born in a specific place, Palestine, in the reign of Caesar Augustus. "He was not saved from factual errors in matters irrelevant: he was not prevented from supposing that Moses wrote the whole Pentateuch or that the world had begun five thousand years ago. But he saw in detail day to day how to be a true Son to his Father and a true saviour of his people."[85] It must be confessed that many Christians, both past and present, would find this position hard to take. They would see it as the surrender of the essentials of the faith. Jesus could not have been limited in such matters as Farrer calls irrelevant and still be the living Lord and Savior of the world. Yet Farrer refuses this alternative. The fact that Jesus walked "in factual darkness by spiritual light"[86] does not alter the fact that he knew how to be a true Son of the Father. "Where knowledge was not available, love and candour steered him through."[87]

It is one of the striking features of Farrer's view that, despite this full admission of the limitations of objective knowledge and power in Jesus, he is still able to affirm the unique beginning and end of the career of Jesus of Nazareth in the Virgin Birth and the Resurrection. He is careful, however, to distinguish his position from some popular forms of theological logic. "Jesus is not the Son of God because he had no human father."[88] It is conceivable that the Son of God might have been the offspring of an ordinary union. All we can say—and this reveals the weight that Farrer gives to the New Testament records and the Catholic tradition—is that God chose to do it this way. So too with the bodily resurrection. Whether God could have set the seal of approval upon Jesus and vindicated him in some other way is an idle, speculative question. God did it in this way, and unlike Bultmann, Farrer is not prepared to accept the dogmatic prohibition that "God never bends physical fact into special conformity with divine intention."[89]

Many other aspects of Farrer's thought would need to be considered if this were a full-scale treatment. It is hoped that enough has been said to show that there are still some modern defenses of a kenotic Christology,

---

[84]Farrer, *Saving Belief,* 69.

[85]A. Farrer, *The Brink of Mystery* (London: S.P.C.K., 1976) 20.

[86]Ibid., 21.

[87]Ibid., 21.

[88]Ibid.

[89]H. W. Bartsch, *Kerygma and Myth* (London: S.P.C.K., 1953) 216.

bearing in mind that not all forms of such Christology are either coherent or satisfactory. We seem to have traveled a long way from Darwin. Inasmuch as Darwin and later historical research have strengthened the claim that Jesus was *totus in nostris,* wholly one of us, then a modern Christology must work on that assumption. Nevertheless, it is not necessary to deduce from this premise that Jesus can be accounted for solely in terms of his historical and cultural conditioning. Nor does the Incarnation, properly understood, have to be ruled out a priori. To affirm that Jesus is *the* Son in the only sense that really matters is neither a scientific nor a historical judgment, especially if the latter is understood in the post-Enlightenment sense. Yet it is not incompatible with scientific or historical fact as distinct from speculative scientific cosmologies or philosophies of history that exclude the possibility of divine action from the start. So much attention has been devoted to Austin Farrer because, in my view, he has answered many of the criticisms of the doctrine of the Incarnation to be found in *The Myth of God Incarnate* and in the later discussion this volume has provoked.[90] He also gives a clear indication as to the proper use of the language of uniqueness in regard to Jesus.

There is no space in this study for a careful review of the work of the process theologians in relation to the Incarnation.[91] This would require extended treatment to be fair to the different thinkers involved. John B. Cobb, Jr., in spite of his emphasis on the centrality of Jesus for specific Christian faith, falls back in the last analysis upon "creative transformation" as the essence of the Christ principle, or Logos. This principle may or may not be linked to Jesus of Nazareth. In any case, the door must be left open for the possibility of divine saving action through creative transformation other than that produced through the person of Christ. This view is also shared by Schubert Ogden and Lewis Ford. Nor can an adequate discussion be given here in answer to Rosemary Ruether's question as to whether "a male Savior can save women."[92] The present writer hopes to take up this issue in another study entitled "The Logic of the Believing Mind." It needs to be observed, however, that all these thinkers, however divergent their views as to the role of Jesus or his uniqueness, are post-Darwinians who take the evolutionary assumption for granted, even when there is critical appraisal

---

[90]Hick, *Myth of God Incarnate;* Michael Goulder, ed., *Incarnation and Myth* (London: SCM Press, 1979).

[91]David Griffin, *A Process Christology* (Philadelphia: Westminster Press, 1973); Schubert Ogden, *The Point of Christology;* (San Francisco: Harper & Row, 1982) J. B. Cobb, Jr., *Christ in a Pluralistic World* (Philadelphia: Westminster Press, 1967).

[92]Rosemary Ruether, *Sexism and God Talk* (London: SCM Press, 1983).

of Darwin's natural selection as the only or the sufficient explanation as to why the evolutionary development has taken the course it did.

It should not be forgotten also that Darwin's theory is only one theory among others, and it is not an assumption to be taken for granted. For much extreme conservative theology, for example, the first human couple, Adam and Eve, are historical figures, and the Fall is a historical event. This position, however, is not typical of most modern theological thinking as a whole, in spite of the religious and political influence of fundamentalism, especially in the United States. We shall return now once again to a vital issue that the influence of Darwin has rendered more acute—namely, is it possible to think of God's action in specific ways as well as in his general and universal activity in nature and history?

Final Concerns

We may now sum up by offering a few remarks on the theistic claim that God works, not only through uniform law, but through distinctive personal actions. Inasmuch as Darwin has now compelled us to see human beings as part of a continuous process—physical, biological, and historical—it has also forced us to raise again the question of the character and possible direction, if any, of the total process. Only if a satisfactory answer can be given to this latter question can we go on to talk of divine action and of such specific divine action as the doctrine of the Incarnation involves. It is well known that, in recent years, there has been a vigorous debate on this issue as to whether the concept of incarnation is a coherent one and whether it is implicit, if not always explicit, in the New Testament witness.[93] This matter will be dealt with briefly here, not in order to reply to nontheists but rather to assess more critically those who still wish to consider themselves theists but who are unhappy with language about divine action or specific acts of God.

By his insistence on the uniformity of law in biological processes, even if a limited role is given to randomness or so-called chance,[94] Darwin has thrown into relief again the question as whether history, as the story of human action, is itself also subject to inviolable law. The age-old debate between determinism and free will in regard to human action is still with us. The reader may be referred to more modern substantial discussions of this

---

[93]Hick, *Myth of God Incarnate;* Goulder, *Incarnation and Myth;* Abraham, *Divine Revelation.*

[94]Peacocke, *Creation and the Word of Science,* 86ff.

issue.[95] If it is conceded that human beings are personal agents who have creative choice, even if within limits, then we can ask whether God can be intelligibly considered to have creative choice, only in this case they are the choices of a personal agent who is also the Creator and Sustainer of the universe. If we say yes to this question, then the way in which we conceive this possibility can take two forms. We can understand God as having made a creative choice "in the beginning" to make a world and establish the uniform laws by which it will operate. It has been noted that Darwin hints at something like this in *The Origin of Species* before he moved to the more settled agnosticism of his later years. On the other hand, we can argue that God's causal activity is not incompatible with a divine free act to give some of his creatures real, if limited, creative choice. "Thus, if God is free and Almighty, he can bring into being creatures which are free and therefore not sufficiently determined in all their acts by Him or anything else."[96]

As far as Christology is concerned, the crucial question remains as to whether God can freely choose to do a specific action such as "becoming man for us men and our salvation." If again our conception of God permits us to use such language, then we must turn to history for evidence as to such distinctive personal action on God's part. Here again we could argue for God's personal action through prophets, wise men, and mystics without necessarily implying such an action as the Incarnation would seem to involve. In either case, however, we can hardly talk of God's more general activity in human beings or in one decisive act of becoming man without some reasonable historical evidence to support the instances on which we choose to concentrate. For example, if God is said to be uniquely and distinctively present in Jesus, we must know at least enough about Jesus of Nazareth to make such a claim plausible. W. J. Abraham has recently entered the lists with a vigorous defense of the idea of direct divine communication and action in human history.[97] The inadequacies of certain types of fundamentalist literalism and the associated claims for inerrancy and infallibility does not mean that the idea of a divine speaking and action has to be dispensed with altogether. Indeed, one cannot remove this element without emasculating the Bible to a point where its central message dissolves into a precarious dependence on human insight alone. "It is simply

---

[95]C. A. Campbell, *On Selfhood and Godhood* (London: Allen & Unwin, 1957) 86-88.; Austin Farrer, *Freedom of the Will* (London: Adam & Charles Black, 1958); Keith Ward, *Rational Theology and the Creativity of God*, 78-79.

[96]Keith Ward, *Rational Theology and the Creativity of God* (Oxford: Blackwell, 1982) 82.

[97]W. J. Abraham, *Divine Revelation and the Limits of Historical Criticism* (New York: Oxford University Press, 1982).

impossible to replace the direct disclosure of God's will with surplus amounts of profound human insight."[98] Furthermore, we cannot talk of God's action in events and deeds, as distinct from some kind of verbal communication, unless we can specify the particular deeds in which God has so acted.

Abraham is especially critical of the tendency of much theology and biblical interpretation to evade this issue. While conceding Maurice Wiles does not intend to remove the figure of Jesus from some kind of centrality for Christian faith, he is critical of some of Wiles's assumptions that beg the question as to the possibility of such divine action as the Incarnation involves. Wiles has contended that no particular section of experience within the world can be given the kind of absolute authority or final normativeness that the classic doctrine of the Incarnation presupposes. The reason for this conclusion is his belief that modern critical historical methods have made it impossible to isolate one man or one event or series of events in this way. "No such Jesus is available to us or likely to become available to us."[99] The "tentativeness of our knowledge of [Jesus] life and works" makes any such absolutistic claims impossible.[100] Obviously, Wiles's presuppositions depend upon a particular view of the relation of God to the created order. At this point, I can only refer the reader back to my earlier remarks about process philosophy and theology as well as to Troeltsch.

I am fully aware that the above remarks are not an adequate treatment of the controversial issues raised. It must suffice to indicate in a brief conclusion what in my view must be the central concerns of any Christology after Darwin.

The history of the human race can no longer be separated from its biological antecedents or the continuing influence of biological factors in any estimate of what it means to be human. Therefore, any claim for special as well as general divine activity in the cosmic process, including history, requires a restatement and defense of theism as involving a view of God as transcendent personal Agent, related to his creatures not only through general law but also through specific divine communication and action.

While the problem of historical warrants still remains, it would be premature to claim, despite the alleged failure of nineteenth-century attempts, that the quest of the historical Jesus has failed in every respect. It is still possible to speak, as T. W. Manson does, of "The Quest of the Historical

---

[98]Ibid., 19, 45.

[99]Maurice Wiles, *The Remaking of Christian Doctrine* (London: SCM Press, 1974) 48-49.

[100]Ibid., 49.

Jesus—Continued.''[101] While no full-blooded doctrine of the Incarnation can dispense with historical warrants for the career of Jesus of Nazareth, the discernment of God's unique action in him is not the result of a historical judgment alone (i.e., not as history is understood in the post-Enlightenment period). Spiritual things are spiritually discerned. Otherwise, all serious historical students of the New Testament would inevitably emerge as believing Christians with the confession ''Jesus is Lord.''

The conclusion must be that the Christian doctrine of the Incarnation cannot be reasonably affirmed as if it were an isolated fact in a world from which God is otherwise absent. In the last resort, it depends upon a cumulative series of factors: the plausibility of theistic claims, the role of absolute values in human experience, the ability of Christian theology to assimilate the contribution of the sciences, the freeing of historical study from an all-embracing relativism, the continuing quest of the historical Jesus, and the present activity of the Spirit of God in enabling us to have the spiritual discernment to interpret properly the evidence that history supplies.

In my judgment, in all these areas today there are significant and helpful developments that may soon lead us beyond the fragmentary conjectures that so often seem to exhaust what modern theology has to say. The work and value of Darwin's contribution may then be seen in a wider and more satisfying perspective and not as a premature and negative dismissal of the hopes and spiritual aspirations of humankind.

One final question concerns the significance of this study of Christology after Darwin for theological education. The latter is usually carried on in seminaries that have a confessional allegiance of some kind, even where the seminary is closely linked to a university and where its students are in continuous contact with the so-called secular disciplines, the teaching of which is in no way committed to a religious perspective, still less to a specific Christian confession of faith. Insofar as the seminaries are concerned with the preparation of men and women for ordination or some form of Christian service, they are committed to the shaping of the whole person for the work of ministry. While this mission includes academic and intellectual training, more is needed for the proper fulfillment of the Christian vocation. The seminary must be concerned with the growth and development of the whole person. What the Catholics call spirituality or spiritual formation is as important as the academic study of religion. How to combine these two aspects of personal development in a satisfactory synthesis has been the continuing problem of theological faculties and their students. This is nowhere more true than in the

---

[101]T. W. Manson, *Studies in the Gospels and Epistles* (Manchester: Manchester University Press, 1962) pt. 1, ch. 1.

realm of Christology. All teachers at some time or other have become aware of the impatience and sometimes the rebellion of students against what they regard as the spiritual aridity of the traditional theological disciplines, even when these are dealing with the Bible or the history of the church or the theological work of past Christian thinkers. These studies seem to offer a stone instead of bread, intellectual abstractions rather than spiritual meat and drink for the living of the Christian life.

From our study of Christology in this chapter, certain conclusions seem to follow. Christians in general, and ordained ministers in particular, need to be fully familiar with the cultural situation that is the context of the Christian ministry in the modern world. Otherwise, the church will tend to become an intellectual ghetto divorced from the mainstream of modern life. On the other hand, the Christian must know the rock from which he or she has been hewn in order to escape uncritical bondage to the limited and transient experience of a modernity that lives only in the present and lacks roots in an abiding and saving eternal truth. Only such a faith can present an effective challenge to the contemporary world.

It has to be admitted, however, that the traditional theological disciplines, studied in an academic context, do not automatically produce faith. One can have extensive biblical knowledge and know much about church history and the development of theological ideas and the rise and fall of philosophical systems without ever coming to an authentic conversion and the personal knowledge of God in Christ through saving faith. Nor can we make the assumption today that those who come for theological training necessarily have this kind of faith, so that the task of the theological teacher is to help the student understand better and more fully the faith that he or she already has. Some students develop their present faith, but most theological teachers have had students who appear to be searching for a satisfactory faith rather than confident that they have found it. This fact presents the teacher of Christology with special problems. Much of the Christological debate of the early centuries seems remote and irrelevant if taken out of an experiential context. Students also experience a tension between the proper commitment to academic and intellectual integrity and the personal convictions of the teacher. These latter can hardly be suppressed altogether. The theological teacher is not an evangelist, as this term is usually understood, but he or she cannot be content with what Ninian Smart has called "methodological neutrality." This problem, however, is not confined to those who teach in theological seminaries. In the humanities and the social sciences, value-judgments are constantly being made or implied. Even in the natural sciences, such as physics, the elimination of what Michael Polanyi has called "personal knowledge" is no longer a possibility. No easy and glib solution to this problem is available at the moment. The fact remains that theological education cannot evade or be indifferent to the intellectual, moral, spiritual, and personal development of the whole person. This issue is going to remain with us with increasing urgency, and some hard and painful agonizing will be an inevitable part of all theological education in the days to come.

Chapter Ten

Christ in the Light of Contemporary Jewish-Christian Relations

Paul R. Dekar

Jesus was a Jew. What does it mean, Christologically and for teaching mission theology in a Christian seminary curriculum, to affirm the Jewishness of Jesus? The question arises generally from recognition that members of the Christian community cannot discuss theology in isolation from adherents of the other world religions. Christians today must articulate their faith concerning the person and work of Jesus in a religiously plural world.[1] In itself this task is not new. In this century it has assumed greater urgency for two reasons. First, the enormous expansion of Christianity has greatly intensified the encounter of Christians with non-Christians. Second, the waning of the colonial era, with which that expansion of Christianity was often (rightly or wrongly) associated, and the present increase in scale of global poverty and of militarism have motivated Christians to seek to create a more just and peaceful world in cooperation with all members of the human community.

More specifically, the question arises from the context of contemporary dialogue among Christians and Jews. Two recent historical events, the holocaust and the establishment of the State of Israel, have prompted Christians to examine afresh their understanding of the person and work

---

[1]In an excellent study entitled *Jesus—a Savior or the Savior? Religious Pluralism in Christian Perspective* (Macon GA: Mercer University Press, 1982), Russell F. Aldwinckle observes that two major issues presently shape Christian discussion—the question of unity and diversity in the Christian faith, and the matter of religious pluralism. For a basic bibliography of books in English, see Gerald H. Anderson and Thomas F. Stransky, eds., *Faith Meets Faith*, Mission Trends 5 (New York: Paulist Press; Grand Rapids: Eerdmans, 1981).

of Jesus. The first, the holocaust, has definite Christological significance. Rosemary Ruether has argued convincingly that anti-Judaism and anti-Semitism, culminating in the holocaust, are the "left-hand" of Christology.[2] By this term she means that there is a definite relationship between Christian attitudes toward Jews and Judaism and the traditional affirmation that Jesus was the Christ. Because Jews, for the most part, reject this belief, Christians have developed a polemic against Jews and their religion, a polemic that Hitler claimed motivated and gave substance to his "final solution." Ruether's research has been supported and challenged; whatever one's position, one can acknowledge that she is raising a crucial question when she asks, "Is it possible to say 'Jesus is Messiah' without, implicitly or explicitly, saying at the same time 'and the Jews be damned'?"[3]

The holocaust was evil and has generated theological reflection and reconstruction. For many Christians the second historical event, the establishment of the State of Israel, has been equally challenging. All too easily, Christians have made exclusive claims to the knowledge of truth and assumed, in the nettlesome case of the religion from which Christianity sprang, that after the life, death, and resurrection of Jesus, Judaism ceased to have any importance in God's purposes for humanity. Indeed, part of the Christian-Jewish polemic centered upon the conviction of many Christians that the church had become the true Israel. Judaism was allowed to exist not as a religion in its own right but as evidence of willful disobedience against God. Only recently has this situation begun to change, in part because the State of Israel provides an unavoidable and powerful symbol of Jewish survival, a context where Christians experience Jews and Judaism as vibrant realities. There, in a land holy to adherents of several world religions, Christians have had to grapple with the need to provide theological space for the continuing experience of Jews and Judaism.[4]

---

[2]Rosemary Radford Ruether, *Faith and Fratricide: The Theological Roots of Anti-Semitism* (New York: Seabury Press, 1974).

[3]Ibid., 246. Supportive scholarship includes Charlotte Klein, *Anti-Judaism in Christian Theology,* trans. Edward Quinn (Philadelphia: Fortress Press, 1978); and Alan T. Davies, ed., *Anti-Semitism and the Foundation of Christianity* (New York: Paulist Press, 1979). Alternative views are presented by Thomas A. Idinopulos and Roy Bowen Ward, "Is Christology Inherently Anti-Semitic? A Critical Review of Rosemary Ruether's *Faith and Fratricide,*" *Journal of the American Academy of Religion* 45 (June 1977): 193-214; and David Rokeah, *Jews, Pagans, and Christians in Conflict* (Jerusalem: Magnes Press; Leiden: E. J. Brill, 1982).

[4]See my "Does the State of Israel Have Theological Significance?" *Theodolite* 7:1 (Fall

The contemporary Jewish-Christian dialogue often focuses on these two contemporary events. Some Christians, especially Arab Christians, consider such focus theologically inappropriate and politically motivated.[5] To the extent that guilt for the holocaust and a nonprophetic stance toward the State of Israel, coupled with nonrecognition of the sufferings of other peoples including the Palestinians, frequently do characterize the dialogue, I am hesitant to explore the issue of Christ in the light of contemporary Jewish-Christian relations in isolation from the larger, world religious dialogue. Nonetheless, it is an important undertaking. Provided one is aware of some of the larger issues, one may legitimately limit and focus reflection in this manner with, one advantage that, by and large, Christians and Jews coexist under conditions of cultural, ideological, and material homogeneity. Many of the issues are the same when Christians encounter other world religions. It is hoped that any conclusions may prove paradigmatic for the theme generally.

There are unique issues, however, with which Christians and Jews must wrestle. Jesus was a Jew and took for granted a Jewish understanding of God, faith, sin, repentance, grace, the kingdom of God, and so on. The Jewishness of Jesus does have implications for Christians. The same holds true for Jews as well. It is no surprise that the contemporary Jewish-Christian dialogue, perhaps the most fruitful in the history of Jewish-Christian relations, has resulted in considerable Jewish scholarly interest in Jesus. The more Jews explore Jesus as one of their own, the more Christians are obligated to formulate their understanding of Jesus with awareness of Jewish insights.[6]

1983). Judaism provides theological space for Christianity through such concepts as the Covenant of Noah and the "righteous among the Gentiles" and through its self-conscious universalism to bear witness to God to all nations. By contrast, only a few Christian theologians have undertaken formally to formulate a Christian theology of Judaism.

[5]For example, Gabriel Habib, "A Statement," in *Auschwitz: Beginning of a New Era? Reflections on the Holocaust,* ed. Eva Fleischner (New York: KTAV, 1977). Habib is general secretary of the Middle East Council of Churches. To the view that the Jewish-Christian dialogue is politically motivated, it should be stressed that it springs in considerable measure from biblical scholarship. See Eugene Fisher, "The Impact of the Church on a Jewish Dialogue on Biblical Studies," in *Christianity and Judaism, the Deepening Dialogue,* ed. Richard W. Rousseau (Scranton PA: Ridge Row Press, 1983).

[6]Aldwinckle, *Jesus,* 39. The following comments of David Flusser, Jewish author of a major study on Jesus (see n. 20), are suggestive: "If with the help of Jewish knowledge it were possible to draw a picture, however incomplete, of the self-perception of Jesus, we would find, I am sure, the historical fulcrum of the Christian faith. That would partially bridge the age-old dichotomy between the historical Jesus and the Christ of faith. Consid-

A final introductory note is in order concerning the audience to whom this chapter is directed. The theme involves a matter of considerable controversy in missiological circles. Scholars in many disciplines need to relate their own work to the issues raised in other disciplines. Because relatively few Christians are involved in the Jewish-Christian dialogue, itself a subdisciplines within the discipline of missiology and theology, it is hoped that this chapter will encourage further reflection within the wider academic community. The benefits will be very real in terms not only of enhanced human understanding but also of creative inquiry into areas not discussed such as the content of Jesus' teaching, the relationship of the old to the new covenant, and the question of missionary presence among Jews.

Jesus the Jew

I began by observing that Jesus was a Jew. It would seem unnecessary to state this fact, but it is often forgotten, ignored, or (sometimes) disputed. So I emphasize the Jewishness of Jesus. He had a Jewish mother, spoke Hebrew and/or Aramaic, received Jewish education (including study of Hebrew Scripture), worshiped the Holy One of Israel, prayed as a Jew, observed Torah, and so on. Despite centuries of Jewish-Christian dispute, and notwithstanding their Jewish ways of interpreting what this fact means, Jews have always recognized Jesus as a fellow Jew. Few have gone as far as Martin Buber, who, at the end of his fruitful life of scholarship, wrote, "From my youth onwards I have found in Jesus my great brother."[7] But few would challenge the words of Israeli biblical scholar David Flusser, who stated, "I do not think many Jews would object if the Messiah when he came again was the Jew Jesus. . . . Judaism has never rejected Jesus. . . . Was Jesus a good Jew? Anyone who reads the synoptic gospels without prejudice must answer yes."[8]

---

ering furthermore how much post-Easter Christology was enriched by Jewish motifs, a new path opens up for the writing of a 'Jewish' Christology, from Jesus to Paul . . . faith which stamped Jesus becomes a part of Christian faith and morality" ("Foreword: Reflections of a Jew on a Christian Theology of Judaism," in *A Christian Theology of Judaism,* by Clemens Thoma, trans. Helga Croner [New York: Paulist Press, Stimulus Book, 1980] 16).

[7]Martin Buber, *Two Types of Faith,* trans. Norman P. Goldhawk (New York: Harper Torchbook, 1951) 12. See Donald L. Berry, "Buber's View of Jesus as Brother," *Journal of Ecumenical Studies* 14 (1977): 203-18.

[8]David Flusser, "To What Extent Is Jesus a Question for the Jews?" in *Christians and Jews,* ed. Hans Küng and Walter Kasper (New York: Seabury Press, Crossroad Book, 1974), 71. See also the important scholarship of E. P. Sanders, especially his *Jesus and Judaism* (Philadelphia: Fortress Press, 1985), and Ben F. Meyer, *The Aims of Jesus* (London: SCM Press, 1979).

Jesus was not a Gentile. At this point we are starting to interpret consequences of the fact that Jesus was a Jew. When Jesus taught, he did so as a Jew faithful to the law and the teachings of the prophets. He had no intention of starting a new religion. He was committed to Jewish observance of his day. When he taught his followers to pray, he used a language that any Jew could recognize and in principle, even today, join in using.[9] According to Matthew, when Jesus was asked about the law (Matt. 22:36-40), he cited the great Jewish affirmation of faith, the Shema (Deut. 6:4-5), and a passage from Leviticus (19:18) concerning love for one's neighbor. Matthew also records that, another time, Jesus urged his followers to keep the law "till heaven and earth passes away. . . . Whoever relaxes one of the least of these commandments and teaches men so, shall be called least in the kingdom of heaven" (Matt. 5:17-19). The pericope ends not, as Christians might read the text, with an attack on Jewish religious authorities but with the command that his followers exceed the scribes and Pharisees in faithfulness to the law.[10]

The gospel narratives and some modern writers refer to Jesus as a rabbi. In the first century, that designation was not an official title but referred simply to a teacher. Apart from the Bible very generally, did any specific strain of Jewish thought influence Jesus? Did Jesus belong to one of the number of Jewish parties that existed then? Some contemporary scholars have suggested that Jesus may have been a Pharisee. This claim may be contested but, at the very least, he was greatly influenced by the Pharisees. Quite in contrast with the negative image most Christians have of the Pharisees, the Pharisaic movement was not a dark, evil force. As Catholic scholar John T. Pawlikowski summarizes, at the heart of this movement lay a new perspective on the divine-human relationship, one far more personal and intimate than previously characteristic of Judaism.[11] Animated by this perspective, the Pharisees introduced revolutionary changes into

---

[9]Alfons Beissler, "The Spirit of the Lord's Prayer in the Faith and Worship of the Old Testament," in *The Lord's Prayer and Jewish Liturgy,* ed. Jacob L. Petuchowski and Michael Brocke (New York: Seabury Press, Crossroad Book, 1978) 17.

[10]Neil J. McEleney, "The Principles of the Sermon on the Mount," *Catholic Biblical Quarterly* 41 (1979): 552-67. Jewish perception of Christian ethics as taught by Jesus generally centers on the two love commandments and the Sermon on the Mount, which basis is considered inadequate. See Eugene B. Borowitz, *Contemporary Christologies: A Jewish Response* (New York: Paulist Press, 1980) 100.

[11]John T. Pawlikowski, *What Are They Saying about Christian-Jewish Relations?* (New York: Paulist Press, 1980) 93-107; idem, *Christ in the Light of the Christian-Jewish Dialogue* (New York: Paulist Press, Stimulus Book, 1982) 76-107. See also Harvey Falk, *Jesus the Pharisee* (New York: Paulist Press, 1985).

second temple Judaism, including the development of the synagogue, the emergence of the rabbi as a lay teacher, a greater emphasis on table fellowship, the addition of oral teaching to Scripture as a source of revelation, a fuller notion of the resurrection of the individual, and new moral teaching.

The above corrective to a distorted portrait of the Pharisees held generally by the Christians at the popular and scholarly levels is essential. It enables us to understand better the Jewish context of Jesus' teachings, both those that were characteristically Jewish and those that led to a parting of the ways by first-century Christians and Jews. Here, historical accuracy, to the extent that we can know the past, is at stake. Even more, it enables us to respect the Pharisees and religious Judaism shaped by Pharisaism.[12] All too easily, Christian awareness of Judaism is frozen in the first century of the common era. In fairness, Christians must acknowledge that, for 1,900 years, Judaism has had a history paralleling that of Christianity. Christians must open to the possibility that we have had something to learn from Jews. As Christians we have much to gain from asking what we have lost when, after the first century, we ceased to have meaningful contact with Judaism as a living religion.

Other areas of modern scholarship challenge Christians honestly to reformulate their understandings of Jews and Judaism. Perhaps most far-reaching is the deicide charge, that is, the accusation that the Jews killed Jesus, the very Son of God. The reason this area is so important is that every year, during Holy Week, Jews are depicted centrally and negatively. Liturgically and through such popular expressions as the Oberammergau Passion Play and *Jesus Christ Superstar,* Christians are led to regard Jews as responsible for the death of Jesus. Was this so? Allowing that Jews have different views on this, as on most questions, we may discern consensus among modern Jewish scholars that (1) Jesus did not claim to be God, but Messiah, a claim that did not entail self-representation as divine, whatever interpretation subsequent generations of Christians may have given it; (2) therefore, Jesus did not commit an offense of blasphemy or idolatry; (3) Jesus did not abrogate Jewish law and was not opposed by the Pharisees, at least not to the degree described in the New Testament; (4) the trial of Jesus before the Sanhedrin, as described in the New Testament, did not take place; (5) Jesus died at the hands of the Romans; and (6) in seeking to placate Roman officialdom, the New Testament writers shifted the fo-

---

[12]Klein, *Anti-Judaism in Christian Theology,* chap. 4.

cus of responsibility for the death of Jesus to the Jews.[13] That this move occured at a time of intense Jewish-Christian polemic had especially disastrous consequences.

This reconstruction obviously confronts Christians with many issues. If Jesus was a good, first-century Jew whose wrongs brought him into conflict primarily with the political authorities of his day, why the separation between Judaism and Christianity? One approach to this question is to hold Paul responsible. As a result, the denigrating picture Christians have of Judaism often has been supported by appeal to Paul. Jesus was not a Christian but became one through Paul, who severed Jesus' teaching from its Jewish moorings.[14] Such an attempt to establish a dichotomy between Jesus and Paul cannot be sustained. Paul was indeed a creative religious genius engaged in theological controversy with his fellow Jews after his conversion to Christianity. But Judaism left no less an imprint upon him than upon Jesus, and Paul faithfully interpreted the teachings of Jesus.

Another approach stresses the early church foundations of anti-Judaism and anti-Semitism. By focusing upon early Christian apologetics, this

---

[13]Hyam Maccoby, "Is the Political Jesus Dead?" *Encounter* 46:2 (February 1976): 80-89. For a fuller study, see his *Revolution in Judaea: Jesus and the Jewish Resistance* (New York: Taplinger, 1973). Important studies by Jews of the trial of Jesus include Paul Winter, *On the Trial of Jesus* (Berlin: Walter de Gruyter, 1961); Haim Cohn, *The Trial and Death of Jesus* (New York: Harper & Row, 1971); and Ellis Rivkin, *What Crucified Jesus?* (Nashville: Abingdon Press, 1984). For Jewish historiography, see David R. Catchpole, *The Trial of Jesus: A Study in the Gospels and Jewish Historiography from 1770 to the Present* (Leiden: E. J. Brill, 1971). Recent Christian scholarship includes Ernst Bammel, ed., *The Trial of Jesus* (London: SCM Press, 1970).

[14]H. J. Schoeps, *Paul: The Theology of the Apostle in the Light of Jewish Religious History,* trans. Harold Knight (London: Lutterworth Press, 1961) 261-62: "The Christian church has received a completely distorted view of the Jewish law at the hands of a Diaspora Jew who had become alienated from the faith-ideas of the fathers. . . . Paul could gain no audience with the Jews because from the start he misunderstood Jewish theology." For a Christian example, see Friedrich Heer, *God's First Love: Christian and Jews over Two Thousand Years,* trans. Geoffrey Skelton (New York: Weybright & Talley, 1970) 30-31: "Through St. Paul Jews and Christians were set on completely different paths. . . . Christianity after St. Paul denounced the fleshly earthbound hope of the Jews and branded the Jews as lascivious, fleshly and sexually obsessed. . . . Christ moves further and further away from the Jew Jesus, the Jewish man on earth." For similar statements, see Joseph Klausner, *Jesus of Nazareth: His Life, Times, and Teaching,* trans. Herbert Danby (New York: Macmillan, 1925) 413 ; and Martin Buber, *Two Types of Faith,* 34, where Buber distinguishes between the "Jesus of the genuine tradition" and the "Jesus of Theology," a transformation for which he holds Paul primarily responsible. Recent scholarship by Jews (Richard Rubenstein, Samuel Sandmel, and others) and by Christians (E. P. Sanders, Krister Stendahl, and others) has appraised Paul, like Jesus, as in continuity with first-century Palestinian Judaism.

approach seeks to minimize the role of the Bible—or at least of Jesus and Paul—for whatever happened later. Some would even go as far as to remove certain passages from the Bible, for example 1 Thessalonians 2:14-16, Matthew 23 and 27: 24-26, and the frequent references in John to "the Jews." This approach has one advantage. It uncovers the situation that existed after relations between Christians and Jews became strained, and it encourages Christians to grapple with the biblical and early church roots of modern anti-Judaism and anti-Semitism. The difficulty with this approach is that it is disingenuous. As David Flusser quips, "Practically everyone these days attempt to prove that there is no anti-Jewishness in the New Testament."[15] Why cannot Christians admit that the New Testament contains passages, such as those mentioned above, that express conflict and hostility toward some Jews? Jews may wish similarly to admit that there are Talmudic passages that contain expressions of Jewish hostility against Jesus and Christians. Jesus, Paul, and most of the New Testament Christians were Jews. They did not attack Jews radically or Judaism per se. Just because later generations misused parts of the Bible, we need not continue to do so. It is neither possible nor acceptable to most Christians to discount the Bible and the inherited teachings of the church on such themes as Incarnation and the cross, themes that clearly set Jew and Christian apart.

A third approach is to examine the separation of Christianity from Judaism in a positive way. For example, one may treat the New Testament as a sort of midrash upon Torah. From this perspective Christianity may be understood as an outgrowth of Jewish universalism, that is, Judaism for Gentiles, as fully valid for Christians as Judaism is valid for Jews. In the words of Paul van Buren, perhaps the most radical of Christian theologians of Judaism, Christianity "is how some Gentiles have come to a manner of walking in the Way to which they [the Jews] already walk. To ask them to come walk as we do would be a denial that, along *with* Israel's way, there is *also* a way for the Gentiles."[16] The strength of this approach is to shatter

---

[15]Flusser, "Reflections of a Jew," 17. An example of this approach is Clark M. Williamson, *Has God Rejected His People? Anti-Judaism in the Christian Church* (Nashville: Abingdon Press, 1982). Williamson rejects the view that Jesus was in constant conflict with his Jewish context. For Williamson, the alleged anti-Judaism of Jesus reflects the way the gospel writers dealt with the strains and clashes between church and synagogue between the years 65-100 C.E.

[16]Paul M. van Buren, *Discerning the Way: A Theology of the Jewish Christian Reality* (New York: Seabury Press, Crossroad Book, 1980) 53, italics in original. Van Buren stresses his indebtedness to Franz Rosenzweig's monumental *Star of Redemption,* trans. from the 2d ed. of 1930 by William W. Hallo (New York: Holt, Rinehart & Winston, 1971), easily the most impressive and moving effort by a modern Jew to provide theological space for Christianity.

old shibboleths about Judaism as a religion of law and Christianity as a religion of grace. An ironic and bold approach that few Jews or Christians will adopt, it is one of a number of possible perspectives on the covenant theme. The main difficulty with this approach is like that we have just considered, namely, the tendency to downplay differences between the two religions, differences that very quickly undermined whatever common ground first-century Christians and Jews initially shared.

A fourth approach is to affirm both the Jewishness and the distinctiveness of Jesus. Overwhelmingly, even those modern Christian theologians most sensitive to the Jewish-Christian dialogue want to go further than simply acknowledge the Jewish context of Jesus' life. They also want to describe ways in which Jesus distinguished himself from his contemporaries. Thus Clark Williamson, a Protestant, begins by stating, "We usually err in interpreting Jesus in ways not in continuity with the Judaism of his time." But he goes on to note, "Creative transformations may indeed have occurred in Jesus," even though they did not occur in a vacuum.[17] Alan Ecclestone, a priest of the Church of England, believes that one cannot avoid investigating what Jesus taught that led Christians to ascribe to him such titles as Christ, Son of God, Son of Man, Lord, and Savior. "The first thing that stands out is the preaching of the coming of the Kingdom of God."[18] Clemens Thoma, a German Catholic, writes, "In his relationship to the God and Father, Jesus gathered together Old Testament Jewish traditions of piety in an original way and endowed them with new beauty. Yet it would be a radical mistake to represent Jesus, on principle and in any way at all, as being in opposition to the God of the Torah. However, he did experience this God in a uniquely close and intimate way."[19]

Whether one describes Jesus as unique in his creativity, kingdom teaching, experience of God, authority, or self-awareness or as special in any other way, Christians and Jews should not—because in the end they cannot—discount the role of Jesus in sparking yet another religious revolution, one which that had a more far-reaching impact than that generated by Pharisaic Judaism. "But who do you say that I am?" Jesus asked his closest friends (Mark 8:29 and parallels). In faith we Christians may affirm with Peter, "You are the Christ." We ignore at great cost both Jewish

---

[17]Williamson, *Has God Rejected His People,* 29.

[18]Alan Ecclestone, *The Night Sky of the Lord* (London: Darton, Longman & Todd, 1980) 83.

[19]Thoma, *Christian Theology of Judaism,* 115. See also Aldwinckle, *Jesus,* 43; Pawlikowski, *Christ in Christian-Jewish Dialogue,* 103; Joachim Jeremias, *New Testament Theology,* trans. John Bowden (London: SCM Press, 1971) esp. 1:31ff.

teaching regarding Messiah (Christ) and Jesus' admonition to Peter to tell no one about him. Jesus may have accepted, as applying to himself, the designation *Christ*. Any acceptance certainly did not carry the weight of modern Christian understanding of what the word means, and at any rate, the text is enigmatic. We cannot know with certainty, or rather, we must balance what we know with what is obscure and cannot be known.[20] Certainly Jesus did not there at Caesarea Philippi claim to be God. Nor did he there or anywhere else speak of himself as one person of the Trinity, or as God-man. Such language came later. But there and elsewhere he did express a unique awareness of his relationship with God and concerning his role in mediating the divine-human encounter. Thus Matthew 11:25-30 records that he addressed God as (not un-Jewishly) "Father, Lord of Heaven" and went on to declare (perhaps unJewishly) that no one knows the Father except the Son and anyone to whom the Son chooses to reveal him. He concluded by inviting his hearers to find rest in him. Mark 14:62 records that Jesus accepted the designation "Christ, the Son of the Blessed." And John 20:28 records Thomas's affirmation of faith, "My Lord and my God."

Any attempt by the Christian to grapple with Jesus' question "Who do you say that I am?" brings the believer face to face, in faith, with the person of Jesus. Jesus the Jew penetrated more deeply than anyone ever before to the heart of Israel, thus opening people to knowledge of God. Even, and perhaps especially, in the light of the Jewishness of Jesus, the absolutely distinctive element in Jesus' relationship to first-century Judaism, and the root cause of Jewish-Christian separation, is the person, Jesus himself. The following passage by the Jewish Oxford scholar, Geza Vermes, warrants attention:

> Second to none in profundity of insight and grandeur of character, he is in particular an unsurpassed master of the art of laying bare the inmost core of spiritual truth and of bringing every issue back to the essence of religion, the existential relationship of man and man, and man and God. . . .
> The uncovering of Jesus' real background and true Jewishness is meant to

---

[20]I am *not* saying that the Gospel of Mark, in this instance, or the New Testament generally is unreliable. Provided that one is prepared to accept a good deal more from the background to the New Testament witness than has often been the case, one may accept much of the New Testament as historically trustworthy. On this, see David Flusser, *Jesus*, trans. Ronald Walls (New York: Herder & Herder, 1969) 8. At the same time, one must tread carefully. The wounds of Jewish-Christian enmity are deep. Whatever one says about such difficult issues as the search for the historical Jesus or for the authentic words of Jesus, or about the meaning of the Christological titles in the Bible, one must see not to deepen the wounds or exacerbate the enmity.

be no more than an endeavour to clear away misunderstandings which for so long have been responsible for an unreal image of Jesus, a first step in what appears to be the direction of the real man. . . . The positive and constant testimony of the earliest Gospel tradition, considered against its natural background of first-century Galilean charismatic religion, leads not to a Jesus as unrecognizable within the framework of Judaism as by the standard of his own verifiable words and intentions, but to another figure: Jesus the just man, the *zaddik,* Jesus the helper and healer, Jesus the teacher and leader, venerated by his intimates and less committed admirers alike as prophet, lord and *Son of God.*[21]

Most Jews have not and will not admit to so positive an evaluation of Jesus. Rather they will affirm, with the American Jewish scholar Samuel Sandmel, "When we Jews have understood Christian explanations, and when we have not, we have consistently rejected the Christian claims about Jesus. We have not believed that Jesus was the Messiah; we have not been willing to call him Lord; we have not believed that the *Logos* became incarnate as Jesus; we have not believed that Jesus was, or is, the very Godness of God."[22] Christians may legitimately continue to articulate their understandings of the person and work of Jesus knowing that Jews, even when they understand Christian explanations, may continue to reject the Christian claims. Reflection upon the Jewishness of Jesus does not preclude identification of distinctive elements in Jesus' teaching and self-awareness. But such reflection may—as this chapter has already suggested—preclude some traditional affirmations. Thus Christians must do their homework and investigate possible implications for Christology and theological education that derive from affirmation that Jesus was a Jew. Especially pertinent is the warning by the Jewish writer Hyam Maccoby, "The real issue in recent study is whether traditional Christian theological views of the life of Jesus—that he created a new religious outlook; that he thereby incurred the enmity of the religious establishment, the pharisees; that his death was voluntary sacrifice, not the failure of his hopes—can be maintained in the face of the 'Jewish' interpretation of Jesus's Life."[23]

Christology

Among traditional Christian affirmations concerning Jesus, whom we call the Christ, which do we scrap? Which do we retain? Which do we add?

---

[21]Geza Vermes, *Jesus the Jew: A Historian's Reading of the Gospels* (London: St. James Place, 1973) 224-25, italics in original.

[22]Samuel Sandmel, *We Jews and Jesus* (New York: Oxford University Press, 1965) 44.

[23]Maccoby, "Is the Political Jesus Dead?" 86.

Let us begin with some statements from one recent book on Christology, Jon Sobrino's *Christology at the Crossroads: A Latin American Approach*,[24] and inquire how the author portrays Jews and Judaism. While there are dangers in such a procedure, it has the advantage of illustrating the need for, and difficulties in, rethinking a central Christian doctrine such as Christology in the light of the Jewish-Christian dialogue and general interfaith relations.

Sobrino begins by arguing that "the historical Jesus" is the starting point for Christology. This historical Jesus—scarcely understood as a Jewish Jesus—"enlightens us with regard to the basic meaning of liberation as well as his personal way of carrying it out" (p. 37). He comes proclaiming the kingdom of God and seeks the liberation of those "in total discontinuity with," and "the 'poor' or 'lowly' persons" marginal to, Jewish society (pp. 47, 57). "Jesus' pardoning activity" is available only "to sinners . . . willing to accept the idea that God is really approaching in grace. . . . The other kind of sinner, the Pharisees, who put their trust in the works prescribed by the Mosaic law, are not pardoned by Jesus" (p. 49). Jesus teaches his followers to believe "that God is infinitely greater than the God preached by priests and rabbis" (p. 57) and calls them to make an "epistemological break. . . . It is no longer a matter of co-operating in a project that stands in continuity with their own legitimate aspirations as human beings and Jews. Rather than following something pretty much in line with Jewish orthodoxy, they must follow something which will call that very orthodoxy into question" (p. 58). The crux of the matter "centers on Jesus' conception of God. "His God is distinct from, and greater than, the God of the Pharisees" (p. 207).

Although Sobrino nowhere identifies the teachings Jesus rejects with those held by *all* Jews, over and over he does present Jesus as in conflict with Jews and their religious teaching. Thus, although Jesus "participated in the prayer life of his people," he opposed those "who thought they had God neatly boxed in their traditions" (pp. 152, 165). Jesus died on grounds of blasphemy (p. 204). The Resurrection established a basic tension between "the historical Jesus and the Christ of faith in Christian living" (p. 381). Making this leap from the historical Jesus to the Christ of faith, Sobrino fails to refer positively at any point to such Jewish motifs as election, exodus, the prophets' understanding of the kingdom of God, cov-

---

[24]Translated by John Drury (Maryknoll NY: Orbis Books, 1978). For critical reviews, see Pawlikowski, *Christ in Christian-Jewish Dialogue*, 69-72; and Clark M. Williamson, "Christ against the Jews: A Review of Jon Sobrino's Christology," *Encounter* 40:4 (Autumn 1979): 403-12.

enantal ethics, or messiahship. He thereby misses an opportunity to correct the anti-Judaic dimension of his Christology.

While Sobrino does not intend his book to be anti-Judaic, it provides an example of Ruether's point that Christology has traditionally been tied to deprecating Jews. Of course, Sobrino's book may simply be a bad example, but I think not. A number of surveys of Christian theology and Christian education curricular materials reveals that many long-standing stereotypes, pernicious doctrines and assumptions that cannot be sustained in the face of modern scholarship, remain in force.[25] In one such survey, Charlotte Klein, a Jewish convert to Christianity, identifies the following six theses, or presuppositions, that inform German scholarship concerning "the nature of Judaism":

1. Judaism has been superseded and replaced by Christianity.
2. Consequently—this is rarely expressed so brutally today—Judaism has scarcely any right to continue to exist.
3. In any case, its teaching and ethical values are inferior to those of Christianity.
4. The Christian theologian continues to assume that he has the right to pass judgement on Judaism, its destiny, and its task in the world—or even to be permitted to dictate this task.
5. Only some few real specialists in the departments of Jewish studies make a fresh examination of authentically Jewish sources. In most cases the material collected in certain works about the turn of the century is taken over as a matter of course and quoted, without bothering about the Jewish interpretation of the sources or considering how the Jews see themselves.
6. We often find that the same author when he expressly speaks of Judaism in an ecumenical context has a strikingly different approach from that which he adopts when he is dealing mainly with the Christian religion and mentions Judaism more or less incidentally.[26]

---

[25]So Pawlikowski, *Christ in Christian-Jewish Dialogue,* 74-75, concludes his survey of modern theology. One survey of official church documents notes the stark contrast between the persistence of long-standing views contained in them and the more positive Christological claims by Christians actively engaged in Jewish and Christian affairs. See Michael B. McGarry, *Christology after Auschwitz* (New York: Paulist Press, 1977). Borowitz, *Contemporary Christologies,* notes with appreciation efforts by some Christian thinkers to overturn the destructive teachings of former days.

[26]Klein, *Anti-Judaism in Christian Theology,* 7. Klein intends her study as an updating of George Foot Moore, "Christian Writers on Judaism," *Harvard Theological Review* 14 (1921): 197-254. See also Eva Fleischner, *Judaism in German Christian Theology since 1945: Christianity and Israel Considered in Terms of Mission* (Metuchen NJ: Scarecrow Press, 1975).

What is distressing is that Klein's study focuses on books currently used by Christian seminarians. She thereby begins to establish a link in the chain by which serious scholarly distortions of Judaism continue to manifest themselves in pulpit and pew as popular anti-Judaism or anti-Semitism. Even though Klein concludes with a brief examination of the Anglo-American scene, where she finds that the situation is better, Christians on the whole have not yet found a language by which they may speak simultaneously both of Jesus as the Christ and of Jews or followers of other religions in a positive manner.

One helpful step would be to shift the focus of Christology away from titles such as Son of God and Son of Man, language that when used can misrepresent the first-century meaning of the phrases and become absolutist and triumphalist.[27] Another helpful step would be to focus Christological reflection less on the *who* question and more on the *content* of Jesus' teaching and work that prompted his earliest disciples—all Jews—to respond as they did.[28] In doing so, Christians will necessarily grapple with such Jewish motifs as covenant, election, exodus, kingdom of God, knowledge of God, and messiahship. They will also, one hopes, grapple with scholarship that has called into question traditional Christian views of the life of Jesus that have divorced Jesus from his Jewish context and begin to reformulate their understanding of first-century Judaism, the deicide charge, and the continued life of Jews as God's people.

The challenge to rethink Christology in the light of contemporary Jewish-Christian relations should not be taken as a call to abandon everything that Christians hold to be true concerning Jesus. One may develop a Christology that is sensitive both to Jews and Judaism and to what is uniquely Christian. A Christian conviction that lends itself to such an approach is the Incarnation.[29] At the heart of the reality of the New Testament Christological titles is an attempt by the early church to articulate its understanding of the intimate divine-human relationship enfleshed in Jesus. Already during the ministry of the great Hebrew prophets (Amos, Hosea, Micah, first and second Isaiah, Jeremiah, Ezekiel), in some of the wisdom literature, and during late second-temple Judaism, one may discern a movement away from the external of religion toward a more personal understanding of how God relates to humankind. Ellis Rivkin, of Hebrew

---

[27]See Raymond E. Brown, "Does the New Testament Call Jesus God?" *Theological Studies* 26:4 (December 1965): 545-73, esp. 546.

[28]Ecclestone, *Night Sky of the Lord,* 82.

[29]Pawlikowski, *Christ in Christian-Jewish Dialogue,* chap. 5.

Union College in Cincinnati, believes that at the bedrock of emergent Christianity lay the following ideas characteristic of Pharisaic teaching: "(1) God the Just and Caring Father so loved each and every individual that (2) He revealed to Israel His twofold law—written and oral—which, when *internalized* and faithfully obeyed, (3) promises to the Law-abiding individual eternal life for his soul and resurrection for his body."[30] Elsewhere Rivkin explains that Pharisaism was strikingly congruent with Pauline Christology.

> Each [of the pharisaic and Pauline systems] was believed by its devotees to be the creation of God the Father. Each promises to deliver from sin and each offers eternal life and resurrection for the believing individual. Each preaches that Reality is within, not without. . . . Each acknowledges that the Messiah will come—or come again—but, until the unknown and perhaps unknowable day, salvation is at hand: for the Pharisees in the twofold law; for Paul in the ever-redeeming Christ.[31]

Similarly, Jacob Neusner, leading North American Jewish scholar of Pharisaic Judaism, affirms that the three constants on Judaic thinking about God—creation, revelation, and redemption—form a framework of confessing and blessing the one unique God.[32] These modalities are paralleled in the Christian understanding of the one God known in three persons.

Articulation of Christian convictions concerning the cross and resurrection may similarly express sensitivity to Jews and Judaism. Some recent (although in fact quite old) approaches to the atonement emphasize God's loving participation in human life to the point of death as a paradigm of divine self-disclosure and human response. Jesus' resurrection becomes a symbol of redemptive love and hope, experienced proleptically, that one day "all may call on the name of the Lord and serve him with one accord" (Zeph. 3:9).[33] In the context of Jewish-Christian relations, such an under-

---

[30]Ellis Rivkin, *A Hidden Revolution: The Pharisees' Search for the Kingdom Within* (Nashville: Abingdon Press, 1978) 302-303, italics in original.

[31]Ellis Rivkin, "The Meaning of Messiah in Jewish Thought," *Union Seminary Quarterly Review* 26:4 (Summer 1971): 401.

[32]Jacob Neusner, *The Life of Torah: Readings in the Jewish Religious Experience* (Encino CA: Dickenson, 1974) 17-18. He mentions Orthodoxy in particular. For example, Orthodoxy elaborates the idea of deification expressed in the phrase "God became man that we might become as God is."

[33]This text is cited among the documents of Vatican II *Nostra Aetate,* The Declaration on the Relationship of the Church to Non-Christian Religions, in which the Roman Catholic Church makes a significant effort to search into the mystery of the bond that spiritually unites Christians and Jews. A subsequent guideline clarifies that "reflection on the mystery

standing of cross and resurrection enables the Christian to reconnect Christianity with such Jewish motifs as exodus and Sinai; to overturn characteristic Christian behavior toward Jews; and to share a common hope that one day God will reign, his purposes being fulfilled on earth and in heaven.

Thus far we have touched on some areas of Christology that must be abandoned, reformulated, or emphasized in new ways. We may also need to move in entirely new directions for which we have few reliable biblical or theological guideposts. One such area is to develop a Christology that expresses what Christians believe unique concerning Jesus while providing positive theological space for other religions, including Judaism. Judaism did not die after Jesus Christ, although very early Christians began to think of themselves and the church as "new Israel," and as having replaced old Israel.[34] Only very recently have Christians begun to grasp what problems this development entailed. One pioneer in this regard is Karl Barth, who insisted that we must reread the Bible in such way as to understand the continued existence of postbiblical Judaism. "The Jews can be despised and hated and oppressed and persecuted and even assimilated, but they cannot really be touched; they cannot be exterminated; they cannot be destroyed. They are the only people that necessarily continue to exist, with the same certainty [that Christians share] that God is God."[35]

Increasingly, theologians have followed Barth's lead in formulating new covenantal understandings free of implied negation of Jewish existence. Of course, one reason why the whole area of interfaith dialogue is so troubling to many Christians is that it appears to contradict their deepest understandings of Jesus as Savior, Lord, and true God by relativizing Christianity, weakening the believer's missionary mandate, and stripping Christianity of Christ. This result is not necessary for, without relativizing or dogmatizing Christian claims, we may affirm *both* the absolute and uni-

---

of Israel is indispensable for Christianity to define itself, both as to its origins, and in its nature as people of God." This is a significant step forward toward a Christian theology of Judaism that understands Judaism not simply as preparing the way for Christianity but as having ongoing validity in witnessing to God's faithful love. See Helga Croner, comp., *Stepping Stones to Further Jewish-Christian Relations: An Unabridged Collection of Christian Documents* (London: Stimulus Books, 1977) 1, 7.

[34]Peter Richardson, *Israel in the Apostolic Church* (Cambridge: Cambridge University Press, 1969).

[35]Barth, *Church Dogmatics,* vol. 3, pt. 3, p. 218.

versal significance of Jesus *and* the positive place of Judaism and the other religions in God's purpose.[36]

However troubling such a direction may be to many Christians, it is the direction in which the Christian community must move, even in the face of internal criticism and doubt. Is Jesus, then, only *a* savior and not *the* savior? Are we no longer to call upon Jews to recognize Jesus as Messiah? Who is at the center of faith? It is possible to call Jesus *the* Savior and acknowledge, in humility, that not all people will come to God through Jesus. It is possible to share among Jews what we believe while at the same time seeking to learn what they know of God. And we may place Jesus at the center of our discipleship while accepting that God has entered into the lives of our non-Christian friends in ways that are holy, precious, and even worthy of our own devotion. The statement of an American Baptist task force on evangelism expresses well the spirit with which we may enter into relationship with our Jewish brothers and sisters. ''We should use our freedom to make known, to all who will listen, those mercies we have received from God through Christ in keeping with his loving spirit. In our witness we invite others to look with us to Him who has brought us to faith in God. We stand ready to listen in love to their witness to the truth that has claimed them.''[37] While not all will adopt this viewpoint, openness to it may lead to new answers to questions arising from biblical and historical scholarship on the Jewish-Christian relations.

Implications for Theological Education

Even though the place of Jews and Judaism in the Christian seminary curriculum has received little explicit attention,[38] this chapter and the theme

---

[36]The work of two colleagues points in this direction. Russell Aldwinckle concludes his book *Jesus—a Savior or the Savior?* by affirming that "the claim for the unique saviorhood of Jesus is not inconsistent with a genuine openness in regard to the destiny of those, whether in the past or the present, who have not yet confessed him as Lord." (p. 214). See Clark Pinnock, "Can the Unevangelized Be Saved?" *Canadian Baptist,* November 1981, 5-9. Also, see the unpublished paper by the Canadian Baptist missionary Ronald K. Ward, "Sorrowful Yet Always Rejoicing: A Canadian Baptist's Reflexion on Modern Christian/ Muslim Sharing," available from McMaster Divinity College.

[37]"A Statement by a Task Force of the American Baptist Churches, Convened by Dr. Jitsuo Morikawa, Secretary for Evangelism," 1973.

[38]One exception is a 1965 study conference supported by the Anti-Defamation League of B'nai B'rith, the Bellarmine School of Theology, Loyola University, and the Divinity School of the University of Chicago. The papers are presented in J. Bruce Long, ed. *Judaism and the Christian Seminary Curriculum* (Chicago: Loyola University Press, 1965). A survey of nineteen volumes of *Theological Education,* published quarterly (now sem-

generally suggest important areas to be examined in the context of theological education. Biblical scholarship could take Jewish commentary and interpretation more fully into account. Theological work could seek to eliminate anti-Judaism from traditional Christian doctrines. Historians of Christianity could seek to make explicit the responsibility of Christians for the translation of theological anti-Judaism into social anti-Semitism. Courses on preaching, worship, and Christian education could seek to rid sermons, liturgies, and Christian-education materials of anti-Judaism. Missilogical courses could confront students with the challenge of proclaiming Christ in the context of religious pluralism. And seminaries could encourage contacts with Jews and Judaism, including use of supervised field education, as a means of enabling students to meet rabbinic leadership and Jewish community agencies.[39]

In terms of my own seminary teaching context, I know how impossible such an agenda will appear. We strain to incorporate a few essentials in an already crowded curriculum. How can we possibly adjust our program of study to take yet one more theological concern into account? In my own courses, I am able to pay attention to the issues raised in this paper only peripherally, except in my required course on the world mission of the church. In that concept I treat the whole area of interfaith dialogue and invite discussion, at the very least, of Jewish-Christian relations. I have encouraged students to attend a Shabbat service and sought other strategies to enhance awareness of Jews and Judaism.

But something more is required. Most Christians live in a predialogic world. Before they will be able to move with any sense of responsibility and vision into the world as known by Jews or adherents of other religions, they must develop some fundamental tools and claim mastery of basic information. For pastors-to-be, theological education in most accredited institutions in North America has proved adequate in certain areas. However it is woefully inadequate in others, including Jewish-Christian relations. One curricular starting point should be the introduction of special courses on interfaith dialogue and on Judaism, Jewish history, and Jewish-Chris-

---

iannually) by the Association of Theological Schools since 1965, reveals the shocking fact that not one article has ever dealt with the question. One issue refers to the admission of Jewish schools (see 4:4 [Summer 1970]: 289). Apart from liberation theology, missiology generally receives scant attention in the journal. A related issue is the dearth of programs or courses for those in theological education. Seton Hall's Institute of Judeao-Christian Studies remains a solitary, pioneering venture.

[39]Ruether, *Faith and Fratricide,* 259-60. The work of the International Council of Christians and Jews (address: Martin Buber House, Werlerstrasse 2, Postfach 305, 6148 Heppenheim, Federal Republic of Germany) is important in this regard.

tian relations. In the case of the second course, it would be an advantage that it be taught by a Jew or include Jewish lecturers. Faculty and students would then be exposed to a world quite different than that in which they live. Such a course would enable students to hear Jews bear witness to the same God our own Lord worshiped, and faculty would derive other benefits including the opportunity to reflect on their teachings as it bears on the Jewish-Christian reality.

Attention should also be given to continuing education and relations with denominational boards and officers. The leadership of our churches must be challenged to examine the language with which we speak of Jews and other peoples in our sermons and liturgies. We need to explore new approaches by which to reclaim a vital sense of connectedness to the Jews as God's people. Rather than the anathemas and misrepresentations of myriad centuries, a new world of mutuality and love may yet unfold. Biblical scholar Frederick C. Grant writes compellingly of one possible benefit from renewed connectedness with our Jewish roots.

> I wish that Christians would occasionally say the Shema with its accompanying prayers, or the use of ancient Jewish grace at meals, or offer the sublime prayer of the Jewish wife and mother as she lights the Sabbath lamp. I myself have conducted Christian services which included the Shemoneh Esre, and have found that it was full of meaning to the congragation. Such practices would be only a beginning, but they might lead much further—not to the conversion of Jews to Christianity, which I am not urging—I wish we might give up all "mission to Jews" and begin to understand one another; or the conversion of Christian to Judaism, though I would gladly see far more men and women converted to the imperishable heart of the Jewish faith, its utter trust in God, its utter devotion to his revealed will. It might even lead to a revival of religious faith and a deepening of moral conviction, by which our world could be led out of its present chaos. . . . It would not necessarily lead to the Kingdom of God, but at least our faces might be turned in that direction.[40]

Some congregations already have found ways meeting Jews. Study groups with members of neighboring synagogues have been formed. Congregations have invited Jews to participate in worship and have responded to reciprocal invitations. Jewish congregations are willing to organize events, for example, preparation of a special Passover sedar, which combines teaching and worship. Christian might consider sharing in Jewish observances, including *Yom Ha Shoah* (Holocaust Day). Reflection on the

---

[40]Frederick C. Grant: *Ancient Judaism and the New Testament* (New York: Macmillan, 1959) 155.

meaning of the State of Israel for Jews is also important. Such a list can be expanded many times over. The role of the seminary in this regard is to encourage the process both in its courses and through continuing education, and through the church involvements of the faculty.

A word of caution is in order. It is important to recognize that barriers erected through many centuries will not come down readily.[41] Jews are especially sensitive to overtures from Christians if they sense that proselytism is intended in any way. In their relationships with Christians, Jews are not motivated—as are many Christians—by guilt or missioary zeal. They seek only recognition. As Rabbi Solomon Bernards of the Anti-Defamation League summarized at one conference,

> The Jewish people must feel free to live out their destiny in complete acceptance by their Jewish and Christian neighbours, and to do so without feeling that they are theologically and socially objectionable to their fellow men. The real problem confronting this Conference is that if there is to be an extension of the interchange of ideas, values, and interpretations at the lay level of the Jewish and Christian communities, a deep sense of mutual trust and respect must first develop among the thoughtful leaders of both communities.[42]

No lasting healing of the deep enmity that has often characterized Jewish-Christian relations will be possible before Christians and Jews develop this sort of mutual trust and respect through person-to-person contacts and the introductory studies suggested above. From these initial steps will grow reformulation, by Christians in conversation with adherents of other religions, of Christology and the broad outlines of Christian missiological thought. Beyond these areas are the realms of interfaith dialogue and the shaping of an interplanetary society in which the reconciliation achieved among people of religion is paradigmatic of the drawing together of all things in heaven and on earth by God. The following story summarizes my own conviction about the urgency of the task. When the great French military figure Marshall Lyautey was in his late eighties and retired on his farm, he approached his gardener about planting an orchard.

"But," protested the gardener, "the trees will not bear fruit for twenty years."

"Then we must begin planting at once."

---

[41]See my *Crossing Barriers in World Mission* (Toronto: CBOMB, 1983).

[42]Long, *Judaism and Curriculum*, 150-51.

Chapter Eleven

What Future for a Unique Christ?

John A. T. Robinson†

What future for a unique Christ? It is a surprisingly modern question. It is safe to say that, even when I was an undergraduate, it would not have rated in the top ten. It was something that, if one was a Christian, one simply tended to take for granted. We were not still quite with Fielding's Pastor Thwackum and his splendid simplicities. "When I speak of religion," he said, "I mean the Christian religion. And when I speak of the Christian religion, I mean the Protestant religion. And when I speak of the Protestant religion, I mean the Church of England." But in practice one got away with talking about "our incomparable religion" (or liturgy or whatever) because in ignorance it never received comparison or in insolence was placed beyond it.

But now the situation is very different. In fact, even to claim that Jesus Christ is unique or final sounds arrogant, and most young people I suppose would begin by assuming the opposite. Indeed many Christians seriously wonder in what sense if any they should even try to defend it.

There has been a challenge on at least two fronts. First, and most obviously, from other religions. Unlike our fathers, we now actually live in a multifaith society, and in many cities in Britain we have to take this fact into account in our educational syllabus. Hindus and Buddhists, Sikhs and Moslems, are our neighbors, and every variety of Eastern wisdom is on offer in the subway. Gurus come and gurus go, and even our divinity faculties were not confined to Christian theology. We cannot go on talking about Christ as in the days when Christians and humanists had it to themselves.

The other challenge is more subtle but, if anything, more profound. Jungian psychology, for instance, which is the most sympathetic to religion, speaks very positively of the Christ figure as an archetypal image of the self. Yet why confine this to Jesus or tie it to that particular bit of history? If I were born in India or China, I would image it very differently.

Humankind has developed a rich store of symbols. That of the Christ crucified and risen may, as Jung says, be a very profound one. But why make it exclusive? For many, other images—of the mandala or the lotus—will speak more compellingly.

In what sense, if any, should a thoughtful Christian want to maintain that Jesus was unique? I think we can rule out two senses. One is the weak sense in which each and every one of us is unique, an unrepeatable individual. That truth is very mysterious but not very significant, though *it is* important to say this of Jesus against some forms of traditional Christian doctrine that have stressed that he was man at the expense of his being genuinely and in every sense a man. Second, the opposite extreme is to say that he was absolutely unique *in kind*. He, after all, was the Son of God. He may have lived like a man, he may have been like us in every respect (except sin), but he entered our human scene from without, like a cuckoo born into a human nest. He was an anomalous exception—a heavenly being *becoming* a man rather than a regular product of the evolutionary process like every other member of the species Homo sapiens.

Now one can dress up this second claim in all sorts of ways, and it is at the heart of what many Christians would say was of the essence of the Christian faith, but I do not think one can get round the conclusion that this approach is presenting a Christ who was unique because he was abnormal. And the corollary of this position, if one presses it, is that he is of very doubtful relevance for the rest of us. He did not start where we start, and I believe in fact that it undermines the gospel rather than defends it. If this view is what is meant by the uniqueness of Jesus as the Christ, then I think it is rightly under question, and it is healthy that, both from inside and outside the church, traditional presentations of the doctrine of the Incarnation and the person of Christ should have come under examination. To cite the titles of two recent English symposia, if *The Myth of God Incarnate* had done it better and if its answer *The Truth of God Incarnate* had even heard the question (and not assumed that truth was simply the opposite of myth), some useful clearing of the ground might have been effected; instead, I fear both sides have queered the pitch. (Though a third volume has since put some constructive things together out of the rubble.)

Let me state the only sense in which I would want to defend the uniqueness of Christ: Jesus is unique because he alone of all humankind of whom we have any external evidence or internal experience was truly normal. He was *the* son of man, *the* son of God, the Proper Man, who lived in a relation to God and his fellow human beings in which we are all called to live but fail to live. I do not mean that he had everything or was everything, but here was a man who uniquely embodied the relationship with God for which men and women were created. In this man, God was reflected—as John puts it, in a simile from family life—as in an only son of his father— he who had seen him had seen the Father. Or as Paul puts it, he was the image of the invisible God, the perfect reproduction (as opposed to the distorting mirror) of his fullness, his glory. Unlike the contributors to *The Myth* volume, I would want strongly to retain and insist upon the category of incarnation. For in this man, the Christian gospel dares to assert, we see the Word, the Logos, the self-expressive *activity* of God in all nature and history, what God was and is, enmanned as far as human nature can contain it in an actual historical individual who is bone of our bone, flesh of our flesh—the only truly normal son of man and son of God.

And I would equally want to insist, strongly, with the New Testament witness, that "God was in Christ reconciling the world to himself." In Christ God was doing something for us that we could never do for ourselves. That is the emphasis that those on the inside of Christian theological discourse want to hold to who would cling to substitutionary language, though I would prefer with the great weight of the New Testament witness to stress the *hyper,* on behalf of, rather than the *anti,* instead of; for Christ died not in order that we should not have to die but precisely so that we could die, to sin rather than *because of* sin. He died as our representative rather than as our replacement. And he could do so only as a man who was totally and utterly one of us. Yet his act was God's act. To adapt a distinction of Austin Farrer's, he was not a man doing human things divinely but a man doing divine things humanly. He was *doing* something distinctive in kind, which is what the older apologetic sought to safeguard (falsely, I believe) by saying that he *was* different in kind from us, thus cutting the ground from his solidarity with us. And this is what, again, it sought to express by insisting that, in order to save us, he must be God, and not (just) man. But the New Testament does not say that God was Christ, or that Christ was God, *simpliciter*. It says that God was *in* Christ, acting redemptively and conclusively, doing (as we might put it) his "own thing," in one who prefectly embodied who he was and what he was about.

That is, in all conscience, a tremendous claim. But before going on to say how I would defend it, let me refine it further against misunderstanding.

To believe that God is best defined in Jesus is not to believe that God is confined to Jesus. On the contrary as John makes clear in his Prologue, the life and the light focused in this man are the life with which everything is alive and the light that enlightens every person coming into the world. Jesus is not the exclusive revelation or act of God. The Bible itself insists that he has not left himself without witness everywhere, that at sundry times and in divers manners he has been speaking to his world. As a Jewish writer so beautifully put it, well before the birth of Jesus, "Age after age she enters into holy souls and makes them God's friends and prophets." The many-faceted splendour and the strange and often dark shapes under which God has been apprehended and worshiped are becoming more familiar to us, the more we know both of comparative religion and depth psychology. The Christ image is infinitely bigger and richer—and more disturbing—then what Christians under the influence both of Catholic triumphalism and of Protestant particularism have made of it by drawing a tight little circle round the historical Jesus (or rather, their image of him) and calling it the whole of God. Being honest to Christ today, which means being honest to what the whole Bible and the whole church and the whole person, under the continuing revelation of the Spirit, see in him, means being honest to the fact that Christ is bigger than Jesus and God is bigger than Christ. And the fact that most laypeople—and let us face it, most ministers and most of us—find that idea, initially at any rate, threatening is an indication of how blinkered and one-eyed our education has been.

The very term *Christ* is in the first instance, of course, not Christian but Jewish. It soon became the proper name for Jesus, but it remains a title like *the Buddha*. The Christ figure, like the Logos, is much wider than Jesus. It stands for whatever reveals, mediates, embodies the invisible, timeless mystery of *theos* in the finite, temporal, and human. The Christ is God with us, or God in us, the manifestation of the divine in the human, or, as Jung put it, the God image in us, the archetype of the self, consubstantial with God and man. The Christ in this sense covers a concern as wide as humanity, though the actual word *Christ* may appear to exclude the Hindu or Moslem, just as the actual word *God* may appear to exclude the Buddhist.

The New Testament message is that the Christ has appeared in Jesus, that in him the universal light of the Logos has been focused as in the burning glass of a single historical human being. But even as a proper name, *Christ* includes more than Jesus or anything limited to thirty years of this man's historical existence. It embraces the cosmic Christ, the heavenly Christ, the Christ incognito in the least of these, the Christ that is to be. Indeed, half the New Testament message of the Christ is of the Parousia, which in effect says, "You ain't seen nothing yet." Moreover, this Logos, decisively disclosed in Jesus, is seen by the New Testament writers as the light and life of *every* person. In his light we are enabled to see the light of God everywhere. It is not that outside him there is no light.

The New Testament message is that Jesus is the Christ, that the Christ you have been looking for, or, as Jung might have put it, the Christ of the collective unconscious, is to be recognized in this man. But I believe that today we are being forced to state more carefully what we mean by this *is*.

Let me give an analogy I have used before. According to traditional Roman Catholic teaching, the Roman Catholic church was quite simply the Holy Catholic Church and vice versa. The rest of us were out, our orders null and void. Vatican II rephrased it more carefully. The two are to be conjoined not by a simple *est*. It is not that the Holy Catholic Church *consists of* the Roman Catholic Church but that it *subsists in* the Roman Catholic Church—the true church is in but also beyond it. Similarly, I believe we must say that the Christ subsists in Jesus, not that the Christ consists of Jesus. To believe that God is best defined in Christ is not to believe that God is confined to Christ. Or, to use a distinction familiar to theologians, Jesus is *totus Christus*—he is the Christ through and through; his whole being is an open window into God. But he is not *totum Christi*, all of Christ, the entire manifestation of the Christ figure. Similarly, Christ is *totus Deus*. As Michael Ramsay has put it, "God is Christlike and in him there is no unChristlikeness at all." But he is not *totum Dei*, all there is of God is to be seen in the world. This distinction leaves me free to say as a Christian that he is for me the focus, the definitive revelation of all the scattered light of God reflected and refracted in many other images; that, as Paul put it, he is *the* image of the invisible God, in whom all my experience is given coherence and integration as in no other. But it does not require or indeed allow me to say that he is exclusively this, that there are no other faces or foci of the Christ except that which I have seen in Jesus nor other faces of God except the human face of God in Christ.

No other task I believe is more urgent for the church than to learn how to restate its conviction of the centrality of Christ both in relation to other faiths and in relation to insights of modern psychology without either being imperialistic and triumphalist (which, let us face it, we were when in the period of Christendom we had it to ourselves) or lapsing into a helpless syncretism, in which all religions and all insights are as good as each other or can be regarded ultimately as saying the same thing (which they are not). This is one of the points at which we must be both humble and honest and at which a true theology must give us the tools of discrimination. And we shall not find them without engaging in the risk of genuine interfaith and, what Raymond Panikkar in his latest title calls, intra-religious dialogue. But I need not pursue this further because I have tried to spell it out in my *Truth is Two-Eyed*, in particular in the chapter on the uniqueness of Christ.

As Paul puts it again, in the magnificent words that form the motto of this divinity college, *ta panta*, not just all things, but the whole sum and structure of the universe, everything within and without, *en auto(i) synesteken*, in him coheres and hangs together. In the title of a book on Indian Christian theology, which has to face this question more urgently than most, he is "unique and universal."

I would call myself a Christian because I would in all humility dare to make the same claim. It is not because I do not see any light or anything of God in all these other figures or images: on the contrary, I am more aware especially as a result of my visit to the East of how one-eyed and blinkered we have allowed ourselves to become. I need these other figures and images to complete, clarify, and correct (to use Reinhold Niebuhr's formula) what comes to me through my own tradition. It is rather that what I see in Jesus as the Christ, and not only in the thirty years of his earthly life but in what Augustine called the *totus Christus,* filling and reconciling the entire cosmos incorporates and integrates more of my experience than any of the other focal figures or archetypal images.

Since I have mentioned Jung, let me use a category of his that I think provides a crucial test of this claim—the shadow. This concept stands for all those elements in experience that are not in themselves evil but that we would rather not have to live with or acknowledge, the things about ourselves or our world that we repress or project on to others—all the dark aspects of life we would rather reject than integrate. Maturity, wholeness, and, individuation, he said, comes from being able to incorporate and integrate the shadow. But we are tempted to disown it and to project images of God or the Christ figure as archetypes of the self from which these aspects of reality, without us or within, are hived off on to some antibody, like the Devil or AntiChrist. And Christians, said Jung, have been as guilty of this separation as anyone, leaving themselves with a God or a Christ figure that rejects so much in experience—the suffering, the absurd, the impersonal, and, in the case of chauvinist males, the feminine—instead of taking it up and creatively dealing with it. For this reason "the unacceptable face of Christianity," to be seen so often in church history, constantly stands in need of completing, clarifying, and correcting by the truth that can come through the dialogue with other religious and indeed with psychology and humanism and Marxism and light from any other source.

Indeed, I become more and more convinced that the Christ in the broad sense of the image of the invisible unconditional reality of *theos,* in the visible and conditional, is far bigger than what E. M. Forster called "poor little talkative Christianity." He can and must be seen to wear other clothes, just as the first council of Jerusalem was stretched to see that he could not be confined to Jewish clothes. Indeed we may even have to be prepared to sit light to the name Christ or to the word *God* if they have overidentified the unconditional with the conditional and equated rather than located the Beyond in the midst.

But when all has been said that has to be said—and even Jesus himself, as the author to the Hebrews boldly says, had to be perfected, made whole by the things that he suffered—I am still persuaded, or I would not call myself a Christian, that this particular model of the Christ incorporates the shadow, enables the antinomies of experience to cohere and hang together, more creatively than any other. Thus in its central and distinctive mystery of the cross and the Resurrection, Christianity integrates and transfigures the light and the dark sides, I believe, more profoundly than in the coexistence, for instance, within Hinduism of Krishna and Kali, the figures of dalliance and destruction; it deals with the problems of suffering, and above all of sin, more radically and dynamically than the impassive serenity of the Buddha, however moving; and for all its sanctioning, especially in Protestantism, of the great white male upon the throne and its current rejection in Catholicism of women priests, it incorporates the female more fully than the patriarchal religions of either Judaism or (especially) Islam.

I make this claim with great humility and open-endedness—without presuming to say that it *must* look like this to others. Yet, for all I receive and still more need to receive from elsewhere, I would not be honest to my apprehension of the truth if I did not also want to insist that for me the revelation of God as Father in the cross of Jesus and the disclosure of man's destiny, as one of the early Christian fathers put it, "as in a son," represents the interpretation of the less than personal in experience by the personal in a manner and to a degree that I do not see anywhere else. And I would echo the testimony of a Christian theologian who has reflected on these questions as deeply and as long as any of our generation, now a neighbor of mine in Cambridge, Norman Pittenger. "For myself I believe that the finality of Christ is nothing other than his decisive disclosure that God is suffering, saving and ecstatic love. Surely you cannot get anything more final than that. But there may be many different approaches to this, many different intimations, adumbrations and preparations."

Yet, for the New Testament itself, Jesus, and his resurrection, is but the firstfruits of the harvest to come, the "leading shoot," in Teilhard de Chardin's term, of the new humanity. Indeed, in the words of an Indian Christian theologian, which echo the church father Irenaeus, "the Incarnation is as much about what man is to become as what God has become." The finality of Christ is not a misleading phrase only if we remember that, for Paul, "the perfect man," like "the last Adam," is a description not of the historical Jesus but of that new spiritual humanity into which humankind has but begun to be built. If for Christians Jesus is of unique and definite significance (a less misleading expression than *final*), it is not because he is the last word, beyond which it is impossible to say anything, or some static norm, like the standard meter, against which every other has forever to be lined up, but because they believe as I believe that he offers the best clue we inhabitants of planet earth have been given to what Blake called "the human form divine" or Tennyson "the Christ that is to be."

Contributors

Russell F. Aldwinckle, B.A. (Honours, London University), B.A., M.A. (Oxford University), Docteur en Theologie (Université de Strasbourg); Emeritus Professor of Systematic Theology, Divinity College, McMaster University

Joseph D. Ban, B.Sc. (University of Pittsburgh), B.D. (Colgate Rochester Divinity School), Ph.D. (University of Oregon); Professor of Christian Ministry and Director, Master of Religious Education Program, Divinity College, McMaster University

Paul R. Dekar, B.A. (University of California, Berkeley), M.Div. (Colgate Rochester Divinity School), M.A., Ph.D. (University of Chicago); Professor of Christian History, Divinity College, McMaster University, and Professor, Faculty of Theology, McMaster University

Patrick T. R. Gray, B.A. (University of Toronto), S.T.B. (Trinity College, Toronto), S.T.M. (Yale University), Th.D. (Trinity College, Toronto); Associate Professor, Department of Humanities, Atkinson College, York University

Melvyn R. Hillmer, B.A. (University of Alberta), B.D. (McMaster Divinity College), Th.D. (Harvard University); Principal of McMaster Divinity College, Professor of New Testament Interpretation, and Professor, Faculty of Theology, McMaster University

T. Raymond Hobbs, B.D. (University of London), Th.M. (Baptist Theological Seminary, Ruschlikon), Ph.D. (University of London); Professor of Hebrew and Old Testament Interpretation, McMaster Divinity College, and Professor, Faculty of Theology, McMaster University

Jean-Marc Laporte, M.A. (University of Montreal), L.Ph. (Gonzaga University), S.T.L. (L'Immaculée-Conception, Montreal), Doct. Es Sc. Religion (Strasbourg); Associate Professor of Systematic Theology, Regis College, Toronto School of Theology

Joanne McWilliam, B.A., M.A. Philosophy (University of Toronto), M.A. Theology, Ph.D. (University of St. Michael's College); Associate Professor, Religious Studies and Theology, Trinity College, University of Toronto

Iain G. Nicol, M.A., B.D., Ph.D. (University of Glasgow); Professor of Systematic Theology, Knox College, Toronto; formerly Director, Toronto School of Theology

Clark H. Pinnock, B.A. (University of Toronto), Ph.D. (University of Manchester); Professor of Systematic Theology, Divinity College, McMaster University

John A. T. Robinson†, B.A., M.A., B.D., Ph.D. (Cambridge University); formerly Bishop of Woolwich, England, and Dean of Trinity College, Cambridge University

Index of Authors

Index of Subjects

Index of Bible References*

Acts, 56, 58-59, 73
Adam/Eve, 59, 92, 98, 115, 125, 129-30, 139, 145, 153, 162, 168, 190, 223
Amos, 210

Colossians, 1, 8, 20, 36

David, 53, 59
Deuteronomy, 34, 201

Ecclesiastes, 33
Exodus, 34
Ezekiel, 35, 210

Genesis, 48, 84, 90, 92-93, 165

Haggai, 28
Hebrews, 12, 60, 73, 126
Hosea, 210

Isaiah, 20, 28, 30, 33-35, 43, 49, 57-58, 126, 210

Jacob, 84
James, 16
Jeremiah, 36, 210
Job, 36
John, 8, 15-16, 20, 39, 40, 46-51, 58, 61, 63-64, 76, 80, 88, 91, 96, 112, 122, 132, 148, 159, 185, 204, 206

1 Kings, 35

2 Kings, 31, 34-35

Leviticus, 34, 201
Luke, 16, 20, 39, 42, 46, 55-59, 61

Malachi, 28
Mark, 16, 20, 32, 39, 42-49, 53, 56, 205-206
Mary, 57, 129-30, 134
Matthew, 16, 20, 28, 42, 46, 52-56, 59, 70, 201, 204, 206
Micah, 35, 210

Paul, 8, 12, 15-16, 40, 60-61, 180, 203-204, 219, 223
Peter, 44-45, 47, 53, 58-59, 205-206
Philippians, 180
Prophets, 31
Proverbs, 31, 33-34, 73
Psalms, 31, 33-34, 36, 43, 52-53, 73

Revelation, 60
Romans, 12, 15-16, 150

1 Samuel, 35
2 Samuel, 34
Sirach, 34

1 Thessalonians, 204

Zechariah, 28, 54
Zephaniah, 211

---

*Index prepared by Maureen Hamilton Isnor.